Th
You m

N

The Knight of the Two Swords

THE KNIGHT OF

University Press of Florida

GAINESVILLE TALLAHASSEE TAMPA BOCA RATON

PENSACOLA ORLANDO MIAMI JACKSONVILLE

THE TWO SWORDS

A Thirteenth-Century Arthurian Romance

Translated, with
notes and commentary, by

Ross G. Arthur and Noel L. Corbett

Copyright 1996 by the Board of Regents of the State of Florida
Printed in the United States of America on acid-free paper
All rights reserved

01 00 99 98 97 96   6 5 4 3 2 1

Library of Congress Cataloging-in-Publication Data
Chevaliers as deus espees. English
The knight of the two swords: a thirteenth-century Arthurian
romance/translated, with notes and commentary, by Ross G. Arthur
and Noel L. Corbett.
   p. cm.
ISBN 0-8130-1439-5 (alk. paper)
I. Arthur, Ross Gilbert, 1946- . II. Corbett, Noël Lynn, 1938- . III. Title.
PQ1441.C63313 1996
841'.1—dc20   95-25880

The University Press of Florida is the scholarly publishing agency for
the State University System of Florida, comprised of Florida A & M
University, Florida Atlantic University, Florida International
University, Florida State University, University of Central Florida,
University of Florida, University of North Florida, University of
South Florida, and University of West Florida.

University Press of Florida
15 Northwest 15th Street
Gainesville, FL 32611

Contents

Introduction

By the middle of the thirteenth century, European poets could confidently expect that stories of King Arthur and his knights would find a knowledgeable and receptive audience. Such tales, which circulated orally in Welsh, Breton, and French for many years before being committed to writing, entered the world of literature in the twelfth century, first via Latin prose with Geoffrey of Monmouth's *History of the Kings of Britain,* then through Wace's French adaptation of Geoffrey's work, the *Roman de Brut.* These sweeping historical narratives, which begin with the fall of Troy and proceed generation by generation down to the eventual defeat of the Celtic peoples by the Saxons, soon inspired a new poetic genre, the adventure romance. Beginning with Chrétien de Troyes and his twelfth-century contemporaries, poets selected either one knight or a single episode from the vast inventory of Arthuriana as their focus for an independent work of art. These individual works quickly became part of the broader European cultural tradition, and Arthur, Guinevere, Lancelot, and Gawain soon became familiar names all across Western Europe.

The Knight of the Two Swords occupies a special place in the vast corpus of medieval stories about the Knights of the Round Table. Working in the mid-thirteenth century, when most Arthurian tales were written in prose and were increasingly dominated by religious concerns, our anonymous poet composed a decidedly secular work in traditional octosyllabic couplets. Modern critics routinely subdivide the genre into "biographical romances," which relate the full life story of a single knight, and "episodic romances," which focus on a short period of the career of a major character such as Gawain. Our poet combines the two approaches, offering the young noblemen in his audience a double perspective on how to establish a reputation for themselves. His work is not governed by the abstract spiritual values and divine interventions so typical of Grail legends; rather, his pair of protagonists—Sir Gawain and the initially nameless hero—achieve their goals through acts of personal valor and individual prowess. In the end, land, wealth, and preeminence at court all come to them as tangible rewards for knightly courage and accomplishment.

The primary social function of medieval romance is to celebrate the class in power. In *The Knight of the Two Swords,* celebration of the nobility is most striking at the beginning and the end of the narrative. The chivalric adventures are framed by elaborate descriptions of court feasts at which noble men and women take delight in the privileges conferred by their rank. Only the "finest people" are allowed to attend, and a medieval audience would have immediately recognized them as noble by their physical appearance, the quality of their dress, and the obvious deference with which they are treated. Their names and titles further emphasize their social distinction, for Yvain, Lancelot, Kay, Caradoc, and Bademagu, to name but a few, were known to the audience from their frequent appearances in earlier romances. Everyone is wearing the finest clothes and adornments imaginable—sparkling gems, costly furs and fabrics imported from distant lands—and they are treated to incredibly sumptuous feasts. All of them are unquestionably noble and beautiful: indeed, consistent with the rhetoric of the genre, it is possible for each and every one present to be "the best and most beautiful person imaginable." These scenes of pomp and circumstance are the signs of a normally functioning society, in which the places of honor are properly occupied by people entitled to them by birth and by virtue of their personal merit.

The explicit exclusion of lesser beings from these banquets introduces a note of uncertainty into the text: what is it that entitles these noble creatures to lead such a life of ease, wealth, and luxury? Within King Arthur's court, knights enjoy differing levels of power and varying degrees of honor: what is the basis for these fine distinctions? In other times and places, such questions might never be raised, and the characteristic form of literary expression might be purely lyrical. In medieval France, however, the recognition of underlying social tensions between the class of warrior knights and an emerging bureaucratic monarchy triggered a shift from pure celebration to vigorous class justification and inspired the creation of narratives that actively argued the case that those who enjoyed high status deserved it fully.

This particular poet anticipates and seeks to forestall counterarguments in as many ways as he possibly can. To produce dramatic tension, the social equilibrium must be temporarily disrupted so that when it is eventually restored, it will appear to be the product of righteous social endeavor. Renegades who oppose the established order must first be disciplined, then either eliminated or else integrated into its structure, and those brave men who steadfastly support the social order must be properly rewarded for their efforts. The people who benefit most from the social system are shown not only to welcome periodic challenges to their rank but even to long for them; in this way the privileges they enjoy come to be linked to an ideal of what constitutes "real" worth. In these poems, at least, the truly noble never rely on past achievements or undeserved entitlements; rather, nobility and individual accomplishment are treated as essentially the same thing.

Each medieval romance accomplishes its literary goals in its own fashion, and each poet makes a selection from standard motifs in ways that highlight the particular social and ethical concerns of his intended audience. The interest of *The Knight of the Two Swords* lies in the wide range of social questions it addresses and the broad selection it makes from a familiar set of episodes and motifs. Every medieval romance has unique features, and this one is no exception; but if a topic is raised or a motif utilized in three or four other narratives of the period, then the chances are good that it will also appear in this one, presented in a way that not only deepens the reader's grasp of the poet's concerns but also contributes to an understanding of the genre as a whole.

Arthurian knights may display their courage either in a series of single combats or as the leaders of massed armies, and their amorous adventures tend to be either physically pure or purely physical. Our author draws freely on all of these possibilities. Other poets may present challenges to the established order in the form of a disinherited damsel in distress, as an impending military threat, or as a direct challenge to property rights; in this text we find all three. Romance protagonists typically acquire control of a realm through inheritance or marriage; here, however, it is made to appear that the Knight of the Two Swords becomes a king as the direct result of his personal accomplishments, for which his subsequent marriage and inheritance are earned rewards.

Stories of an enchanted sword that can be worn only by one deserving knight, of maidens who love Sir Gawain but have never met him, of heroes who discover their names only when they have proven their worth, of protagonists who temporarily lose their names (and their reputations)—all these are developed separately in *Beaudous, Hunbaut, The Avenging of Raguidel, Perceval, The Fair Unknown, Lanzelet, The Perilous Graveyard,* and *Lancelot.* In *The Knight of the Two Swords,* by contrast, these elements are intimately interwoven. Other recurrent motifs include a spurned lover who threatens to "win" his sweetheart by force, a mysterious chapel lost in the perilous forest, a horde of imprisoned knights awaiting liberation, an island realm controlled by a self-reliant queen, and a mortal conflict between two valiant knights who have pledged to remain boon companions forever.

Romances insist, repeatedly and obsessively, that knights must accept responsibilities along with the privileges of their rank. Romance knights toil endlessly, from dawn till dusk and often beyond, responding individually to countless challenges to authority, seeking out wrongs to redress and crimes to punish wherever they can find them. The social imperative to prove one's worth becomes clear from the sheer number and variety of tribulations the best knights must confront and from the battles they must win. They give up the comforts of the court to penetrate the hostile wilderness, following trails through menacing forests. They cannot expect to find good food or fine lodgings, and often they are forced to settle for such modest fare as some peasant or hermit may chance to offer.

Outsiders who might otherwise perceive nothing more than a life of ease and luxury could easily be reminded of the many occasions when a knight turned his back on the chance for comfort, especially when it did not seem to him that his reward had yet been properly earned. For example, this poem might have been brought to a prompt conclusion soon after the Knight of the Two Swords appears on the scene. At line 1645, this protagonist wins the chance to marry the Lady of Cardigan and settle down as lord of all her lands. Instead he sets out immediately on an adventure-packed journey that is prolonged until the poem's closing lines. But the author does not need to explain the knight's sudden departure, either by establishing psychological motivation or by inventing some external challenge; the medieval audience understood that it was totally unacceptable for a new knight to accept a lady or her domain without first proving his worth.

The Knight of the Two Swords is a "double romance," nearly twice the length of a standard adventure romance and composed of two interlocking narratives. The "Gawain portion" of the text traces a path not unlike those of other Gawain romances, such as *The Avenging of Raguidel* and *The Perilous Graveyard*. Gawain's first actions are motivated by an overwhelming desire for revenge, but at a later stage he is seen to be fighting selflessly to rescue imprisoned knights. Early in the story he undertakes the defense of a castle, partly because of his keen desire to win the castellan's beautiful daughter; later in the narrative, however, he fights without expectation of personal reward. For members of the audience who identified with Gawain, such a progression would lead—little by little—toward a more altruistic vision of knighthood.

Though the poet's depiction of Gawain's amorous character—and the not-so-subtle antifeminism it implies—is entirely consistent with medieval literary tradition, the Gawain of this poem differs from other romance Gawains in at least two significant ways. First, his defeat at the hands of Brien des Iles is all but unique in the Arthurian corpus. Gawain has a good excuse for seeking revenge—Brien attacked him when he was not properly armed—but this does not account for the poet's decision to have Gawain lose his battle. In an earlier romance entitled *The Knight of the Sword*, for example, a lightly armed Gawain encounters an equally unscrupulous opponent and nonetheless manages to defeat him and take his life. Second, this particular Gawain has committed a serious offense. Despite his oft-repeated assertion that he never conceals his name, Gawain has allowed himself to be disguised as another man, Brien de la Gastine, and has participated in a deliberate act of treachery. This deception results in the death of Bleheri, who is none other than the father of Gawain's faithful companion, the Knight of the Two Swords. Given these complex circumstances, our poet arranges to have Gawain atone for his fault, demonstrating that while even the best of knights occasionally make a mistake, they always set things right.

The progress of the poem's second hero is signaled by the many names he bears. At various points in the narrative he is called the "Handsome Young Man," the "Knight of the Two Swords," "the Knight of the Swords," "the Knight of the Ladies," and "Meriadeuc." These names, along with the several swords he carries, invite us to consider the wide range of qualities that constitute knighthood and various ideas about how it may be achieved. Medieval handbooks on the dubbing ritual go to great lengths to explain that swords have *meaning*, that they imply both responsibilities and power, and that a knight has obligations to the person who grants him a sword. In this poem, the Knight receives one sword from King Arthur, another from the Lady of Cardigan, and a third from a mysterious knight of the spirit world. The sword given by King Arthur empowers the young knight and makes him a defender of King Arthur's realm, yet it implies that he is merely Arthur's vassal; the second sword takes him away from the security of the court and obliges him to prove his worth as an adult, but it also implies that he is the Lady's vassal. Later, the sword granted by King Arthur is set aside as unnecessary; when the Knight decides not to carry all of his weapons into battle, this is the sword he chooses to leave behind. At that moment, the sword given him by the Lady assumes greater importance.

Commenting on the fact that he carries two swords, the Knight's mother declares that if he had fully understood its powers, the second sword alone would have sufficed. The power of the second sword springs from the fact that it originally belonged to the hero's father; when we learn this fact, the significance of this sword is substantially modified, and the Lady of Cardigan suddenly loses most of her earlier importance, becoming a simple intermediary through whom power and property rights are transmitted from father to son.

The third sword represents a third stage in the poet's definition of his ideas about the nature of knighthood and therefore in his characterization of the Knight's progress from undisciplined youth toward maturity. While the sword conferred by the King and the sword inherited from the father may be routinely passed on from one generation to the next—along with the powers and obligations they carry—the third, supernatural sword must be used for the benefit of others before the Knight's right to possess it is convincingly demonstrated. Although it comes to the Knight in a mysterious way, he has always been entitled to wield it. The proof: "Meriadeuc," his ancestral name, is engraved on its blood-stained shaft. But only after he performs an exceptional act of altruism will he be worthy of assuming this name and of claiming this sword as his own.

Two-thirds of the way through the narrative, the Knight encounters Girflet and identifies himself as "the Knight of the Ladies," because he does not wish to be compelled to return to Arthur's court. "The Knight of the Ladies?" Girflet retorts. "To tell the truth, I've never been in any place where I ever heard any good spoken about such a knight. Knights of your kind are worthless; they have the hearts and souls of women" (8744–47). Girflet clearly believes that any man who associates himself with women becomes weak and effeminate; but he knows nothing of the man he is addressing, so his criticism completely misses its mark. The Knight takes special pride in his role as a defender and protector of women, and in his relationships with women he is far from subservient. Moreover, the poet deals with Girflet's challenge to the Knight's reputation by having the hero surpass all the early exploits of the Lady of Cardigan.

Unlike other romance protagonists, who have only the exploits and reputations of other knights to outdo, this knight must also prove himself more worthy than his future wife. Before the Knight of the Two Swords arrives on the scene, this courageous young lady has played a major role in the narrative, performing an exploit comparable to any ever performed by a valiant knight. She has successfully completed a mission that no man dared to undertake and has thereby remedied an injustice that not even the men of her realm were bold enough to deal with. The Knight must therefore replicate her initial undertaking with variations that distinguish him as worthy of becoming "man of the house and lord of the castle." The Lady has ventured to the Gaste Chapele deep in the menacing forest, so the Knight must go there too; her journey was motivated by self-interest, so his must be inspired by an altruistic concern to assist others. She has freed her land from the arrogant foreigner King Ris, so he must do even more. Not only must he defeat and capture the belligerent king, he must also send him back to Arthur's court to surrender; only in this way can the renegade be disciplined and integrated into civilized society. The Lady of Cardigan may have delivered a pair of shackles to the chapel as evidence of her courage, but the Knight must retrieve them and put them to practical use, returning yet another of Arthur's foes—this time Le Roux, a rebellious vassal, rather than a foreign enemy—to his court, captive, chained, and repentant.

Still, the poet does not offer his audience a ready-made set of ideas about women and their proper roles in chivalric society. Many medieval authors concentrate on only two or three aspects of their female characters: usually women are presented as damsels in distress, as objects of sexual desire, or as beautiful heiresses with lands to bestow on their suitors. By contrast, this poet ranges further afield as he constructs a set of ideal female types to complement his male characters. Curiously enough, the ladies of Arthur's own court—including his nameless queen—are pushed much further into the background than they usually are in romances; here they play little more than a decorative role, and the poet often mentions them as simple afterthoughts. The role of sex object is performed by the equally nameless daughter of the Castellan du Port, who appears in two widely separated bedroom scenes; some may find these humorous, but others will consider them sexist.

In contrast, when the Lady of Cardigan is faced with the need to act on her own behalf because an aggressor has seized her lands, she completes her mission of self-liberation with a resounding success that sets the standard for all ensuing tests of male bravery and endurance. But after a few hundred lines of "masculine heroism," the intrepid heroine becomes a prisoner of her unremovable sword. When the hero finally frees her of this unwanted phallic encumbrance, she lapses into a more traditional female role; the poet transforms her into an heiress impatiently waiting for the King to grant her a husband. The waiting period comprises some eleven thousand lines of knightly escapades and male worth-proving.

Gawain's first scene with the daughter of the Castellan du Port is a good example of a widespread but unstudied romance motif that might be labeled "He could have slept with her but he didn't." Romance poets generally assume that a real man will have sex with any attractive woman no matter what the circumstances. In *The Perilous Graveyard*, when Gawain and a damsel he has met take shelter from a terrible storm beneath a covered cross, the author coyly remarks that he does not know whether they took advantage of their privacy or not. In our poem, in a scene where the Knight of the Two Swords is lying in a bed beside his sister's, the poet feels compelled to reassure us that there was nothing improper in the man's thoughts. Special explanations seem to be in order whenever a hero refuses a lady's advances or whenever he does not have his way with an available maiden. The question of willingness is never raised, and the range of explanations for passing up an opportunity is quite remarkable. A refusal or abstention may be explained by love for another woman (Chrétien's *Lancelot*), by duty to the woman's husband (*Guilhem de la Barra*), or by both (Marie de France's *Lanval*). At the other end of the spectrum, in *The Knight of the Sword*, Gawain lies chastely in bed with a beautiful woman all night long, even though he knows that his comrades will ridicule him for his failure to take action; he also knows that her father's enchanted sword will fly off the wall and kill him if he tries to make a move.

In *The Knight of the Two Swords*, Gawain "wins" the castellan's daughter by killing Gernemant, the family's mortal enemy, and by restoring her father's lands, and he is "given" her by her mother, who is far from subtle as she prompts Gawain to take her daughter's virginity. The consummation of this affair is prevented by an obstacle somewhat more complicated than a magical sword. This maiden had long before fallen in love with Gawain, simply because of what she had heard about him, but she does not realize that the man lying beside her is Gawain; rather, she believes that Gawain is dead. When she tells him this and reveals that her love for Gawain is so great that she will not allow any man to have his way with her, he of course informs her that Gawain is still very much alive and that he is himself the very man she loves. Unlike Gawain's friends and enemies, however, who always believe everything he says and treat him with due respect, this young lady refuses to believe a single word. In effect, she is so in love with Gawain's reputation that she rejects the man himself.

Finally, Gawain is held in check by innate courtesy and good breeding: although his sweetheart is under his complete control, he does not take her by force. Any idea that the poet finds Gawain's self-restraint admirable, however, or that he may be proposing it as a model for the young men in his audience, quickly evaporates when the pair meet in bed for the second time. "So help me God," the damsel declares, "I didn't think that Sir Gawain would ever be so weak or unworthy that a woman could escape from him simply by crying or protesting, especially one he had under his complete control, as you had me on that occasion" (12072–78). Similar sentiments are expressed in other medieval romances, but more often by brutal knights than by innocent young virgins. The lady's assertion that she would have believed his claim to be Gawain if only he had forced sex upon her, and that force would have been the "courtly" way to behave, makes the poet's decision to leave this as his last word on gender relations all the more disquieting.

Li chevaliers as deus espees (ca. 1250) may currently be read in three forms: (1) Bibliothèque nationale MS fr. 12,603, fols. 1–71; (2) *Li chevaliers as deus espees: Altfranzösischer Abenteurroman,* ed. Wendelin Foerster (Halle: Niemeyer, 1877; rpt., Amsterdam: Rodopi, 1966); and (3) *Li chevaliers as deus espees: A Critical Edition,* ed. Robert Toombs Ivey (Ph.D. diss., University of North Carolina, 1973). None of these sources is readily available or easy to read.

Foerster thought that the manuscript had been carelessly copied ("sehr nachlässig überliefert"). Indeed, it contains numerous hypo- and hypermetric lines, a good many single lines appear to have been omitted, and the scribe has left out one rather important episode (between lines 11,703 and 11,704), likely because of visual inattention.

In keeping with the editorial practices of his day, Foerster made numerous emendations to the lines that do not fit the meter or do not make sense; more controversially, he "normalized" the poet's dialect and "improved" the rhymes. Despite such interventions—now generally shunned—his edition is careful and conservative for its time, and it is framed by a substantial introduction and forty pages of notes. His emendations are generally acceptable, and the reasoning behind them is usually transparent. Speculative readings, which Foerster considered preferable but nonessential, are presented in the apparatus. Use of the edition is complicated by the fact that he does not follow modern norms of orthography and punctuation, and his five-page *Wortverzeichnis* offers little or no interpretative guidance.

Ivey's 1973 edition is more conservative than Foerster's, sometimes preserving manuscript readings that require an uncomfortable stretch of the syntactic imagination. His text follows modern spelling conventions, but some of his transcriptions are suspect, not all of his emendations are explicitly noted, and there are some typographical errors, notably the omission of line 4166. In spite of such minor shortcomings, we have often found his edition, his glossary, and his notes to be quite helpful.

It would be unreasonable, however, to delay consideration of this poem as a work of literature until such time as the "perfect edition" had finally appeared. Because life is short and art is long, we have chosen to produce a translation that follows the Foerster edition, carefully checking his readings against Ivey's text. As an imaginative poem filled with scenes of medieval life, as a lively exponent of the Arthurian genre, or as a reflection of the aristocratic mentality of the landed class in thirteenth-century France, *The Knight of the Two Swords* simply deserves to be better known; a reading of it will amply repay the curious student, the literary scholar, and the lover of medieval culture.

No translation can be perfect, and ours is intended as an introduction to the original text, not as a substitute for it. To be sure, we hope that our rendition will stimulate critical study of this work and its place within the romance genre, but such research will necessarily focus on the Old French text. The primary function of any translation is to provide readers with an accurate and accessible version of the original, one that can actually be enjoyed. This critical approach has resulted in a number of large- and small-scale differences between the poet's presentation of his material and ours.

Rather than harness a verse form and select words to fit its meter and rhyme, we have substituted prose for octosyllabic couplets, and we have divided the original 12,352 lines into nineteen coherent episodes. We have tried to keep a stylistic balance, avoiding undue recourse to archaic English yet making no attempt to suppress the medieval flavor of the original. We have followed standard practice concerning English verb tenses rather than replicate the shifting Old French patterns of narrative pasts and "historic" presents. This tense switching is conditioned by the dynamics of backgrounding and foregrounding so typical of Old French literature, most of which was composed for oral performance before a live audience.

Some translators prefer a rigorously literal approach; we have striven for suppleness. Where sentences in the original text are structured in a manner suited to aural rather than visual reception, we have found it helpful to combine, reorder, or subdivide them, so that the end product better conforms to a modern reader's expectations of what constitutes prose. Our approach is similar for the convoluted syntax that often springs from a tight octosyllabic meter conjoined with rhyming couplets. Wherever necessary, we have sought to restore a word order natural for spoken and written language. Where the poet uses synonyms to pad out his line or resorts to fillers like "it seems to me," we have simply decreased the level of re-dundancy. Where the poet's lexicon would seem repetitive to a modern reader, we make appropriate use of synonyms: *declared, remarked, replied,* and *answered* may appear where the original has nothing but a monosyllabic *dit* (= said). For the same reason, when person after person is described as "beautiful," we have introduced a measure of lexical variety, calling upon *attractive, good looking,* and *handsome.* Despite these liberties, we have striven to remain faithful to the meaning and spirit of our text.

Rather than burden the translation with footnotes, we offer a succinct glossary of English words whose meaning may not be fully apparent to the nonspecialist. A short list of textual notes rounds out the volume. In it we cite those passages where our readings differ from those of Foerster or Ivey or where the meaning of the original text may be problematic. From start to finish, our overriding concern has been to produce an accurate yet readable version of this intriguing narrative and to give broader diffusion to a significant chapter in the history of Old French literature.

King Arthur's Court

King Arthur had held his land for a long time without the cost of war and had made all his enemies subject to his will; he was happy, the Queen was happy, and the court was full of good cheer. Then the good and worthy King decided to hold the greatest, most splendid court he had ever held— and he was accustomed to magnificent courts! That was what he most desired, and what he most liked to do, the better to attract and bind to himself the hearts of his knights. He loved and cherished them so much that, if he could have had his way, none of them would have ever left his side. They were forever receiving noble and precious gifts from him, for he wasn't mean or stingy in that respect. He sought riches so as to honor them, and not from any hope of personal gain. His hands were never lacking splendid gifts to bestow, and the more he gave—this fine and generous man— the more he would receive. I can assure you that, far from impoverishing him, largesse brought King Arthur ever-increasing wealth. He was so brave and high minded that nothing he could do for honor's sake seemed to him the least bit onerous or inconvenient. Even the most ordinary days of the week, when his retinue was the smallest, seemed like another king's Easter celebrations. {36}

One day he summoned his bailiffs and his clerics—and he had a great many of them—and when he saw them gathered there before him, he gave his orders at once, telling them to spread the word to everyone under his dominion, to all those who held fiefs or lordships from him, that they should not fail to come to Cardueil at Pentecost to keep him company. Anyone who did not appear could be sure he would forfeit his entire fief, without clemency or pardon, and lose the King's love as well. {50}

When the feast day arrived, the barons assembled from many a land, as they were supposed to, and just as they had been required to do, to join the

King in fellowship. After he had heard Solemn Mass in the great church, along with the Queen and all the other knights, ladies, and damsels—and there were many beautiful ones in attendance—the King returned to his lodgings. When the time was right, he asked that the water be poured for washing, and so it was done without delay; every young lord leapt to his feet and hurried to fetch a basin or a towel. The King washed before all the others did—the noble Queen as well—and then they sat down side by side at the dais in the great hall. They wore their crowns regally, as befitted such a noble occasion. In keeping with the pomp and the ceremony of that high feast day, ten kings wore their crowns. I really must name all ten of them for you. {76}

First, in great splendor and magnificence sat King Lot of Orcany, the father of Sir Gawain. Next to him was King Urien, the father of Sir Yvain. Tor's father, King Arés, was seated next in line, beside King Yder, a wise and judicious man; he was always delighted to appear at court with the other knights, whenever the occasion was right. Then came King Amangon of Greenland; as the whole court knew, he was the father of Lady Guinloïe, Sir Gawain's faithful sweetheart and lover. The father, who knew this very well, loved him with all his might. The handsome Caradoc, King of Vannes, was seated next in rank; then came the worthy and courteous Anguisel, the lord and King of Scotland. Next to him was King Bademagu, from whose land no stranger has ever returned, or ever will. If memory serves me well, King Estrangaré, who held the city of Pelle, was seated next, and King Bruant, who was known as "Four-Beards," Lord of the Lost City, sat and dined beside him. {110}

These ten kings were seated at King Arthur's table, all wearing their crowns, just as I have told you. The three hundred and sixty-six knights sat at the Round Table, all except for three who were out traveling the world, in pursuit of adventures to test and prove themselves; and because of this the King was very pensive. Sir Gawain was one of the three, the second was Tor, and the third was Girflet. The food was all ready and waiting to be served. Kay oversaw the tables on that day, along with Bedevere the constable and Lucan the wine steward; these three men were in charge of the table service. Kay had it announced that no one except knights, high clerics, noble maidens, ladies, and damsels—no matter how valiant they might be—would be allowed to sit and eat within the great hall, and these people were to be left in complete peace. It was estimated that at least ten thousand people dined in the hall that day, not counting the servants. {136}

All the ladies and gentlemen were nobly seated, and they enjoyed themselves immensely, dining in a spirit of good cheer. I don't think that anyone will ever again see so many fine people all gathered together in one place! After Kay had had the first course served to everyone in his usual expert manner, the King bowed his head and fell into deep thought, for he was greatly troubled. From one end of the hall to the other, he saw the tables adorned with so many beautiful people, so many damsels, ladies, and knights, and it seemed to him that they were far more intent on good fellowship than on filling their stomachs. He beheld the ten kings seated near him, all wearing their crowns in his honor; and because of this he thought, all the more apprehensively, that he had never before seen so many beautiful people assembled at any court of his without some adventure arriving. And, as a matter of fact, he had never held such a splendid court and failed to see some adventure present itself. Totally absorbed by these thoughts, he left his meal untouched; and the ten kings took note of this. {165}

Suddenly, a knight mounted on a great palfrey came riding up at a gallop. He was quite without armor and clad in a crimson scarlet that suited him marvelously well; he was wearing a finely tailored coat and mantle, fully lined with supple fur, and trimmed around the edges with precious black zibeline. {174}

He did not come into the hall on horseback, but stopped and dismounted outside. A boy ran up to steady his stirrup, and the knight told him to wait there a little while and look after his horse. He looked all around the hall and thought to himself that any man who had all these followers must be quite a remarkable person indeed. Then he directed his gaze to the head of the hall and saw the dais where the King, the Queen, and the ten crowned kings were sitting. He recognized King Arthur immediately. And even though he had never seen him before, he could tell exactly who he was because it seemed that far greater honor was being paid to him than to any of the others. He looked so much like the lord and master that there was no doubt about it in his mind. {198}

The knight made his way into the hall, where he was closely scrutinized by one and all; he was tall, handsome, bright, and well dressed. He walked right up to the King and stated his business impudently: "King," he said, "I am a messenger from King Ris of Outre-Ombre, and I offer you no greetings." {207}

Pensive though he was, the King looked up—never losing his composure—and told him to deliver his message, leaving out nothing of what he had been instructed to say, for he wanted to hear every last word of it. {213}

The messenger was unperturbed when he heard the King's command.

"My lord," he said, "King Ris, a man of great wealth and power, sends you word that nine years have elapsed since he first set out from his country. In those nine years he has defeated nine kings by sheer force and acts of prowess; they have all done homage to him, and he has enlarged each of their fiefdoms. None of them has left his company; rather, they are now serving him with all their households. He has cut off every one of their beards to make the lining of a mantle for his sweetheart. In addition to the lining, she has also asked him to make the trim out of your beard, and he has promised her everything she wants, down to the very last detail. {234}

"And so he sends you word through me, because he considers you to be the greatest and the noblest king in the world—after himself, that is—that as a mark of his esteem for you he will make the mantle's tassel from your beard. He wants you to come and meet with him, and he wants you to hold your land from him; he will increase it for you. If you do not agree to this proposal, he will come into your land with such a mighty army, and with such overwhelming force, that he will never leave until he has totally dispossessed you and appropriated your entire realm as his own. He will not depart until he has taken your Queen and given her to the King of Northumberland, who has asked to have her. In addition to all this—as befits a man at war with you—he sends word that he has already entered your land with ten thousand of his finest knights, not counting the pillagers, to do battle in any way they please. Be further advised that he has the Queen of Cardigan under siege; he will not soon leave that place, not for the power of any man alive, and not until he has taken all of her land." {264}

The King heard the messenger out; he was angered in his heart and greatly humiliated by the man's words. He wondered how anyone could possibly send him such an insulting message. He felt great shame on account of the barons who were gathered there in his company. The messenger kept on prompting him for his answer, and in due course the King replied: "Knight, I understand the outrageous words you have spoken here today, in the presence of all my noble subjects. You may advise your lord to try his hand at some other scheme. He will have to wait a long time before he gets my beard to put into some mantle! And if indeed he has the castle of Cardigan under siege, I am greatly troubled by that. Tell him that before he departs I will treat him to the sight of such a company, and to so many banners and ensigns flying, that nothing will avert fierce strife between us—unless he manages to find some way out—and he will learn just how powerful I am. Truly, I will never be happy again until I have remedied the shame and offense he has done me through this message, and corrected his insolent behavior." {293}

The messenger went back to mount his horse and departed, going on his way in haste. You may be sure that no one there provided him with an escort; instead, everyone agreed that no one had ever sent such an arrogant and insulting message to such a noble king, or committed an outrage in more urgent need of redress. The King asked that all of his men be summoned without delay. It was to be proclaimed everywhere he had even the slightest power that no man able to defend himself should dare remain behind; everyone was to be in readiness at Cardueil within forty days. The outraged seneschal sent the word out far and wide, in keeping with the good King's orders. {312}

King Ris and the Lady of Cardigan

We will leave the King now, for we must say a few words about the messenger. He made his way back in great haste, like a man on an important mission, riding at high speed, feeling quite insecure, and keeping a sharp lookout for his personal safety. He kept on going until he emerged from a great forest right before Cardigan; he had left King Ris there a few days earlier, but now he couldn't find him. He stopped dead in his tracks, quite dumbfounded, wondering where he could have gone, the King who had been laying siege to the city. He didn't know if King Ris had captured it or not, and he was quite perplexed. And then, not far away, he saw a monk riding along on a mule. He approached him and asked if he knew anything about the King who had been besieging the city. The monk replied that the King and his men had taken the town by force, along with the lady inside, and that he had imprisoned her knights and all the inhabitants. "And because of that, my friend, you will understand that they've all left here and taken up residence inside the city. That's everything I know about it." {343}

"May you have good fortune, dear lord!" the messenger said; then he left, riding off smartly toward the city. He got there before long but didn't speak to a soul, and no one said a word to him. It was well past the hour of nones when he reached the great hall. He dismounted—there were plenty of men waiting there to take his horse—and went inside, passing through many halls and galleries thronged with knights. The meal was already prepared and King Ris most nobly [. . .], and they were all dining together. The King was seated at the dais eating his meal, and the messenger greeted him with these words: "My lord, God bless both you and your companions!" {362}

When the King heard this, he replied at once: "Knight, did you meet with King Arthur? Do you know if he will hold his land from me and pay me homage? And did you deliver the message about my wanting his beard?" {368}

"Yes, indeed, my lord, I told him everything. And I can tell you right now, just as he told me, that you will have to wait a long time for it, and you will be greatly discomfited before you get a single hair from his beard, or secure his homage, or acquire his land. Indeed, you will be ravaged by war before he ever holds land from you! He will not fail to come and confront you with his army, wherever he may find you. He will never be happy until he redresses this offense. And I can tell you that he is very confident of getting satisfaction." {382}

"He is not a very wise man," said King Ris, whereupon the messenger fell silent and departed. The King was infuriated and pondered the matter for a long while, for he hadn't gotten exactly what he wanted. {388}

As the King was considering this situation, an unbelievably small dwarf burst into the hall. He had come in haste from far away, riding at great speed on a mule whiter than the new-fallen snow. In his hand he held a silk whip with an ivory handle engraved with a trefoil emblem; the craftsman had obviously taken great pains with it. He was wearing a coat and a mantle of silk, dyed bright crimson like a summer flower and trimmed with green sendal. Right away he dismounted and went to take out a pair of shackles that had been carefully wrapped in a fur mantle; their links were made of gold and the cuffs were all of crystal. Trundling along the ground, the dwarf approached the King, carrying the shackles in his hands. Then he spoke these words: "King, may God save you! I have come to you from the Lady of Iceland, your sweetheart. Through me, she sends you her greetings and commands you to take these shackles and with them to keep your covenants with her as you must, and just as you have promised her. For she intends to keep her agreements with you so that nothing is left wanting." {420}

When the King heard what the dwarf had to say—though he was still deeply engrossed in thought—he replied: "May good fortune come both to my lady and to you!" Then the dwarf took the shackles and placed them beside the King at the head of the table, saying, "My lord and King, what news shall I give my lady from you?" {429}

"Tell her quite frankly," he said, "that never in all my life have I wanted anything so much as to fulfill her every wish. Greet her for me as the lady to whom my heart belongs." And with that the dwarf took his leave and departed. As soon as he saw him disappearing in the distance, King Ris once again returned to his thoughts. {440}

When he had pondered long enough and meditated for quite a while, King Ris looked out across the meadow toward the forest, which, as it happened, was not very far away. He asked if anyone saw what it was he had been gazing at so intently. His companions answered right away, saying: "What is it you see, my lord? Do tell us!" {450}

He replied at once: "Do you see that forest, so close to us, and those lofty walls barely visible over the treetops?" {454}

And they replied: "We do indeed, my lord. What is it you are trying to tell us?" {456}

"What you see out there is the Gaste Chapele," the King observed. "No one has ever gone there and returned to tell about it, so they say. But a few days ago I took leave of my army, just as daylight was failing and it was growing dark. I was armed, so I thought to myself that I would go and see the chapel. I set out on my own, and rode until I got there; then I dismounted and walked right up to the altar, never hesitating. On it I saw an image of Our Lady, Holy Mary. A lamp was burning brightly before it as a sign of veneration, but no man or woman was keeping watch over it. As soon as I saw it, I removed the steel sword from my side and fell to my knees. When I had said my prayers, I took off my coat, and before I left I fashioned an altar cloth from it. Then I mounted my horse and left the chapel, for God had blessed me with His kindness. It would take me a long time to tell you everything that happened to me on the way back. I imagine you would scarcely believe me if I told you about it, so I won't even bother, but there is much in it that you would find disturbing. {489}

"I speak these words as the noblest king alive. I have never gone back on my word, and never would I do so. And so I declare that if any man living person, knight or soldier, lady or damsel, were bold or valiant enough to carry these precious chains to the Gaste Chapele—these shackles that I just now promised to put on King Arthur so that I might send him as a prisoner to the Queen of Iceland, she who desires this and commands this of me . . . , and I am the very man who will do it, for then my lady will truly assure me of her love straightaway—and if that man pledged to go there all alone and return by night, and if he brought me back a piece of the cloth made from my emblazoned coat which I placed on the altar, then when he returned he would receive whatever he might ask me for: anything at all, without an argument." {515}

"We have often heard of the Gaste Chapele, my lord," said the knights, "but we have never heard tell of anyone coming back from there; that is

why no one dares to go near it. And so, despite the fact that there are perhaps some nine hundred knights here, there is not a single one of them—
no matter how bold or hardy he might be—who would ever venture to do
what someone else might do in his place." {525}

"No matter," said King Ris. "You may be sure I didn't tell you the story
hoping to find anyone who would dare to go there; that would be sheer
folly." {530}

Standing before the King was a tall and well-bred maiden. She was
young—not more than twenty years of age—and as beautiful as a young
lady could possibly be; she was also graced with courtesy and good judg-
ment, which like beauty are precious qualities. She was wearing a dark
purple dress adorned with gold trim and embroidery. She was delicate and
marvelously attractive, but quite dejected. She must have been very beautiful when happy because she was so pretty when sad. She had been crying, and for good reason: she was serving before the King against her will,
and she was greatly upset about it. {546}

She had paid close attention to the King's words, that anyone who carried out his instructions concerning the shackles would not be denied anything he might ask for. She thought it over carefully, then said to herself:
"Oh God, what shall I do, when I can neither see nor imagine any deliverance for my land? It will be much too late by the time King Arthur raises
an army on my behalf. I have lost my land for certain, and he will never
manage to defend or restore it. All things considered, there is nothing to
do but to take a chance myself. These knights are not interested in performing such a perilous exploit! In any case, no matter what happens to
me on the return journey, and no matter how things may turn out, I will
venture to undertake this mission. I'm not the least bit concerned for my
personal safety." Then she said: "My lord and king, would you kindly repeat for my benefit what you said just a while ago." {572}

"Gladly," he said, "by my head!" Then he repeated absolutely everything he had said before. And the maiden, who already knew what this
was all about, declared: "My lords, you know perfectly well that the King
does not go back on his word in anything he says, not under any circumstances; indeed, he has never done so in all his life." {580}

"And what do you mean to suggest by that, young lady?" they asked.
{581}

"You will find out soon enough," the beauty answered. Then she turned
to the King and said, "My lord, listen to me: give me back my mule right
away, for I want to set out on the journey this very night, without delay. I
will place the shackles on the altar; of that you may be sure." {589}

"Ah, maiden, hold your tongue!" he said. "You have proposed a reckless escapade. There are many very worthy knights here who dare not undertake this mission, and yet you want to put yourself in mortal danger! Just forget about it; you couldn't find a better way to hasten your own demise, and I would find that a great shame." {597}

"If you had been so concerned for me the other day, my lord, you would not have taken my city and all my people away from me! You would be wrong to doubt my resolve: I am determined to go to the chapel." {603}

"No!" exclaimed the King. "I don't like this proposal one bit, but since I cannot go back on my word, there is really nothing I can do about it. Nevertheless, mark my words and bear this in mind: I greatly fear that some evil may befall you, and that would be a great misfortune. Truly, this is a foolhardy exploit." {610}

All of the knights said, without exception: "Do stay here, young lady, and try some safer undertaking." {613}

"Ah, my lords, please don't be upset," she replied, "but I will not stay here and do nothing!" {615}

At once the King ordered the tables to be cleared, and so it was done. Then he went to relax in his lodgings and summoned his seneschal, ordering him to saddle up the young lady's mule. He did so right away, and before long night began to fall. The King took note of this and had the maiden summoned. "Young lady," he said, "it is time for you to leave now, whenever you are ready." {629}

"My lord," she said, "it is indeed time for me to go." Then she mounted up—it was getting rather late—and the King mounted up too, along with a good hundred knights. They escorted her from there to the main gate, not expecting to see her again as long as they lived—either dead or alive—and everyone said that it was a great loss. {638}

III

The Adventure of the Gaste Chapele

The King left the maiden there, and she rode on toward the forest. She struck the mule with the whip, and it did not hesitate or falter. Covering her head with her mantle, the maiden rode straight into the forest. The night was exceedingly sinister and so murky and black that she could scarcely make out the ears of her mule. She kept on whipping it in earnest and before long she entered a dense thicket, full of brambles and thorns, laden with blackberries and cornel fruit. Her face was all scratched and her dress was torn to shreds; red blood streamed from her body in many places. With the utmost difficulty she kept on riding until finally she reached a meadow. Then she commended herself to Almighty God and called upon Our Savior. Never in all her life had she felt greater dread than at that moment. She was afraid because she heard bears and lions roaring all about her, and other beasts making so many strange and unusual noises that there is not a living soul, man or woman, who would not have gone completely mad before escaping. {673}

Before that terror passed, a mighty noise of thunder arose, and such a blaze of lightning that it seemed the very heavens and earth would collide and shatter. Then she heard a mighty wind blowing so strong that it uprooted huge oak trees in several places and carried them along before her as she rode. The beautiful maiden was so frightened and distressed that she had absolutely no idea how to protect herself. She thought she had been very reckless indeed to have undertaken this journey and would gladly have changed her mind if she could have, for there was no way she could have anticipated anything like this. {691}

Then the wind grew still and she saw an immense fire rising before her, burning so high it seemed to reach the sky and spreading wider than a crossbow's range. She gazed right into the midst of it and saw two black men running about in the roaring inferno, tossing around a dead man's head. She could not avoid them; they came so close to her that she barely escaped getting burned. After this, she was filled with dread; and then she heard a voice so full of anguish that no one could ever describe its sorrow or its lamentation. Thanks to the brilliance of the flames, she could see a knight in full armor approaching, all alone and without a squire. {713}

He was grieving bitterly over a lifeless knight he was carrying across the front of his saddle; the dead man was armed, but wore neither helmet nor shield. The knight lamented at the man's misfortune and fainted repeatedly over the body. The young lady urged her mule to a brisk pace and it carried her so fast that she soon lost sight of the knight; and she kept to her chosen path until she saw the chapel. She did not go past it; instead, she dismounted and led the mule inside as quickly as she could. All of the terrors she had experienced before were nothing compared with those she felt now, and so she made the sign of the cross, confessed her sins, and earnestly called upon Our Lord and His Mother. Then she went and quickly concealed herself and her mule behind the altar, because the knight was not very far behind; in fact, he was now approaching the Gaste Chapele. {740}

You may be sure that he was grieving as much as a man possibly could. He dismounted in front of the chapel, took the dead knight in his arms, and placed the body up against the door. Then he went and tethered his horse to a tree, set his shield against it, and returned to the body, still in tears. He began fainting over and over again; he was so anguished and distraught that he really didn't know what he was doing; even so, he embraced the dead knight sorrowfully and carried him inside the chapel. Right away he removed his gauntlets, drew his sword, and began to dig a grave as best he could in front of the altar. Next he took the knight's body, as was his duty, and laid it to rest. Then he fainted once again, grieving so much that it seemed he truly loved this man more than anyone else in the world and would have liked to end his own life right there and then. {765}

Then he climbed down into the grave with the body so as to complete his task, saying: "My lord, now I must do what you asked me to as you were leaving this mortal life. I must not overlook anything I can do to remedy this evil." He took the knight's good sword, fastened it to his side, and said through his tears: "Dear sweet lord, I envy you your death [. . .] any man or woman who might find you, or disinter you, or ungird your sword. Once he has it girded on, may it never be removed, except by someone as valiant at arms, as handsome and as replete with noble qualities as you have truly been, or unless he is destined to become such a man." Then, securing the sword to the body and covering it with earth, he said: "Dear lord, I leave you here now, the finest man who ever lived, the best man who ever bore a shield or lance. As you were without a doubt the best, the most handsome, the most virtuous, and the most valiant knight in the whole world, I ask God to have mercy on the soul whose mortal remains lie buried here in the earth!" {798}

Then he wept and fainted once again; when he regained consciousness, he put his helmet and his gauntlets back on and departed. From the tree he picked up his shield by the straps and hung it round his neck; then he mounted his horse and set off on his way, weeping constantly. {806}

The knight departed from the chapel. The maiden had overheard everything. Cautiously, listening for any sound, she ventured out from behind the altar and went outside the chapel, to make certain he was gone. She heard a great clamor of people who seemed to be drawing near, lamenting so vigorously that no one had ever heard the likes of it. It was hard for her to keep from weeping out of pity for them, for she could not remember ever having heard any lamentation which stirred even half as much compassion in her heart. She wept most sweetly and wondered who this noble lord could be, this man for whom everyone was grieving so intensely. She would have liked to find out, if she could have, but she just let the matter stand. If they could have had their way, these people—riding along beating their palms together and expressing their profoundest grief—would surely have preferred to die. They met the returning knight and asked him through their tears, "Seneschal, where is our lord?" {835}

The knight could not utter a single word, but fainted right there on his horse; he would have fallen to the ground had they not rushed over to catch him. When he came to, he answered them as best he could, but feebly, like a man crushed by sorrow. He told them he had done everything he possibly could, overlooking nothing of what the knight had commanded him to do while he was still alive; then he declared that there was nothing more anyone could do now. They asked him to take them back so they could visit the grave where the knight lay buried. "No, I will not do that," he answered, "for he said that after I had buried him, I was to find you if I could, and have you all return home. And he also asked me to tell you all to pray Almighty God to release his soul from torment." {856}

"Were those his very words?" they asked. {857}

"Indeed they were," he replied. {858}

"Then we will certainly respect his wishes and not go against any request he made during his lifetime." With that, the company dispersed, overwhelmed by sorrow, and the seneschal went along with them. {864}

The maiden clearly heard them leaving and was much relieved at this, for she had thought she might be taken prisoner. She approached the altar with the shackles in her hands, fell to her knees, and placed them on the altar right in front of the image. But they didn't stay there very long; instead, they drifted up into the air in the very midst of the church. She was astonished and afraid for her life. Praying to God and His Mother to give her courage, she seized the shackles once again and quickly restored them to their place. She was extremely pleased, for this time they didn't budge an inch, and her heart was overjoyed. Then she looked at them sweetly, like one who has seen to every detail. She noticed the cloth that King Ris had put on the altar, fashioned from his coat, and for the first time she could see for herself and know that he had truly been there; everything was exactly as he had described it. Fearlessly, the maiden tore off a piece of the cloth and fastened it to her belt, thinking that now she had successfully accomplished her mission. {895}

She was going to mount up right away, but scarcely had she reached the door when she remembered the sword girded to the knight who lay buried in the chapel. She said to herself that she would never leave it behind out of cowardice, not even if it meant losing her life. She secured her mule once again and began scraping away at the earth with her hands, throwing it aside until she reached the body; then she set about removing the sword, and quickly got it loose. She was very happy once it was hers, for she believed the knight who had fastened it on to be a very worthy gentleman. She covered up the body once again and prayed God to take pity on the knight's soul; then she girded on the sword, untied her mule, and mounted up. She was certain she had forgotten nothing, and then she recalled the words of the man who had attached the sword to the dead knight as securely as he could. So she did her best to take it off, but now she simply couldn't get it loose; then she understood that it would take some worthy man to unfasten it. She thought that if she ever managed to complete her task and return to Cardigan—whatever might happen to her on the way back—she would never have as her master anyone but the man worthy enough to remove the sword from her side. {932}

She genuflected before the church, made the sign of the cross, and set out across the meadow. She rode quickly, going wherever the mule carried her, until she reached the woods. She passed through them with great difficulty, for branches tore at her face and hands—her dress was ripped to shreds—so that red blood gushed out from her wounds; but she paid little heed to any of that. When she had traversed the forest, she went right up to the gate of the city; she did not have to ask for it to be opened, for she found ten knights waiting for her there, on the King's behalf. When they saw her, they made the sign of the cross at least a hundred times. They were truly astounded, and marveled at seeing her again: they had never heard tell of any man who had managed to keep his word, or who had ever returned from the Gaste Chapele. And all of them said to her: "Welcome back, my lady!" {955}

"And may you have good fortune too, my lords," she responded. "Please take me to the King, as is only right and proper." {959}

"We will do so gladly," they replied, and they took her straight to where King Ris lay sleeping. {962}

She appeared before the King with great self-assurance. It was very bright inside because of the many candles burning there, and the King woke up when he heard all the commotion. He was every bit as astonished at the sight of this maiden with a sword girded on as were the men leading her in. The sword was so tightly fastened to her waist that her side was aching from it. When the King saw the young lady, he recognized her right away, even though the flesh of her hands and face had been badly torn by brambles, and her dress as well. He gazed intently at the beauty, because he had never before seen a damsel or a lady wearing a sword. {981}

The maiden stepped forward and declared: "May God save you, my lord and king!" {983}

And he replied as a courteous man should: "May God grant you joy, young lady." {985}

"I have come from the Gaste Chapele, my lord; if you don't believe me, you can examine the proof you asked me to retrieve for you." Then she knelt down and handed him the piece she had taken from the altar cloth. {991}

Then he knew that she had truly been there, for he recognized the evidence. "Alas," he said, "now my pain and suffering will increase for the rest of my days! Now I have lost my sweetheart! I know for certain that this woman will want me as her husband, and I will lose my beautiful sweetheart!" {999}

At that the maiden burst out laughing and said: "Are you really so afraid of that? No," she went on, "have no fear. I will not long for you, nor will I ever have you as my own, so don't ever get yourself upset over that." {1005}

When the King heard her say these words, he was greatly relieved and declared: "Maiden, ask for anything you wish and it will be granted at once." {1009}

"Then get out of bed right now and I'll tell you what it is I want." The King knew that he was obligated to do exactly as she wished. He got up right away, like a man unaccustomed to going back on his word. She said that she wanted him to restore her city to her, to release all her imprisoned men, and to compensate her for all her losses, according to the evidence furnished by all those who had any knowledge of the situation. Then she wanted him to leave her town and swear to her never again to set foot on her land, or to do her any harm. {1026}

King Ris granted her everything she asked—though it must have caused him grief—like a man who could never bring himself to lie. He departed from the town, taking all his knights with him. The sun had already risen and the day was growing bright and clear. King Ris wasted no time, commanding his seneschal to set everything right according to the maiden's instructions: all the people of her realm were to be promptly freed and compensation made for their losses, as set forth in their sworn oaths. The King departed, and everything was done just as he commanded. {1042}

# IV

The Test of the Sword

And so King Ris left Cardigan, the city he had captured, and the Queen remained as its Lady, in full possession and control of everything she could possibly want. She had her damsels and her people summoned before her. Her bailiff, who was far from displeased with the outcome, carried out her orders loyally, and many of her people gathered there in great celebration, as you might expect of captives just liberated from prison. The seneschal greeted her as his Lady and asked her how she had managed to free herself as she had, and who had torn her clothing and injured her hands, her neck, and her face, for her beauty was greatly diminished by it. {1061}

Then she began to tell the whole story from start to finish. But it would be tedious for me to repeat every detail, so I will say no more. The seneschal couldn't stop asking questions: he said he would very much like to know, if she wouldn't mind telling him, why she was wearing a sword. He had seen many a lady and many a damsel traveling abroad, but never had he beheld a lady or a maiden with a sword girded on—and never before had he seen such a fine weapon on a man, however worthy he might be. {1075}

"Just forget about that," she said. "It's really no concern of yours; you will learn more about it in due course." Then she called in a serving maiden named Brangien and said: "Pour some water in basins and bring it to me. I want to wash my hands and face, which are all stained with blood. And bring me my clothes, the best ones you can find." Brangien and some other maidens did so at once, returning almost immediately. They brought the Lady hot water in a gilded silver basin, and she washed off all the grime that stained her face. Then she undressed and put on a white shift and a skirt—which could do little to enhance her beauty—between her body and the harness of the sword, for no matter how hard she tried, she couldn't manage to get it loose. Then she put on a splendid dress of white samite, embroidered in gold thread with many tiny lion cubs and embellished here and there with little stars and flowers. Her apparel was perfect in every way, and her coat and mantle were all of ermine, trimmed with jet-black sable. She found she had to tuck in the folds of her dress between the sword belts and her body, just as she had done with the shift. Then she fastened on a snug waistband with threads of gold over precious golden braid, studded with at least a hundred gems, worth a vast fortune. Then she put on a hat, adorned with precious stones and gold, over her wavy chestnut hair. She had overlooked nothing that might make her more beautiful. {1119}

Then she asked for her palfrey to be harnessed and brought to her, and so it was done. The palfrey was fair, white, and small, and the arching bows of its saddle were decorated with the finest gold and ivory, all engraved with trefoil designs. The bridle was fashioned with gold and gems, as was the harness. The saddle cover was made of a superb white material embroidered with gold. When it was adorned in this fashion, everyone agreed that there had never been a finer or a better outfitted horse. {1133}

When everything was ready, the maiden mounted the palfrey, more splendidly attired and far more beautiful than I could ever describe for you in words. She put her left arm out beneath the drawstrings of her mantle and arranged her skirts between herself and the saddle bow with consummate grace and skill. Then, donning a peacock-feathered hat so that the sun's heat would not bother her, she sat attractively in the saddle. Like a lady of good breeding, she held in her hand a whip, its handle crafted from solid ivory and its lashes made of white silk. {1148}

When the maiden was mounted on her palfrey, so finely and so beautifully adorned, she was the fairest creature that Nature had ever taken pains to create; and indeed Nature had done nothing to conceal her arts. The maiden called for her seneschal and said to him at once: "I entrust you with all my land, my knights, my people and my ladies-in-waiting too, as the man in whom, by my faith, I place my complete trust and confidence; take care of them as you should. I am going to King Arthur's court on my own, as indeed I must." Then, as she departed, like the noble and gracious lady she was, she commended her people to God and they returned her blessing. {1166}

And so outfitted, the Lady of Cardigan, who had endured such pain and misery to liberate her land, set forth all alone, and no one escorted her on her way. She embarked on her journey, riding from dawn to dusk, never sparing herself, and doing her best not to lose her way, until one day she came upon a white monk. She greeted him, but he was so intent on reciting his hours that he didn't even hear her voice. And she spoke to him a second time, saying: "Dear kind lord, listen to me for a moment." He stopped, but when he looked at her he couldn't say a word for the longest time, because he was so taken aback. He thought for sure that she was a phantom or a fairy, for he didn't think that such a beautiful creature could ever have been born. Then he answered her, saying: "May you have good fortune, my lady, if you are one of God's creatures." {1189}

At that she laughed and said: "You may be sure that I am not an evil spirit! For the sake of courtesy, please give me some news of King Arthur; if you know where he is, do not keep it from me." {1194}

The monk replied: "I left him quite early this morning, when I set out from Cardueil. It seems that he had summoned a great many people from all parts of his realm to gather with him there." {1199}

"Could I get there before nightfall?" {1200}

"You certainly could, if you kept on riding as fast as you were doing just now." {1203}

The maiden left the monk as soon as she could and rode on quickly, never sparing the mule. She rode until she arrived at Cardueil, where she saw the people already assembled. Everyone looked at her in amazement, both soldiers and knights, for never before had they seen a woman on horseback wearing a sword. She rode right into the court without pausing; she did not dismount but remained in the saddle, looking all around the hall until she saw where the King was sitting. He had just finished dinner, as had the Queen, and those who had served the meal—the chamberlains who were in attendance—had already cleared the tables. {1224}

She went right up to the King and said: "My lord, may you have a fine day today, you and all your companions!" {1227}

When he heard these words, the King raised his head and saw her there and thought he understood why she had come. He greeted her cordially and said: "I know exactly what you are after, young lady, and you will have help shortly. I have summoned my people from near and far and they are already assembled here. Tomorrow they will undertake the task of confronting King Ris, who has your city under siege. I do not know if he has taken it yet, but I can assure you that they will attack him wherever they may find him, if he has not already fled." {1243}

"My sincere thanks, dear kind lord. But I have not come here for that, since I have already liberated my city and have it once again under my complete control." {1247}

"Now," the King exclaimed, "I want you to tell me just how that came about." {1249}

Without false modesty, she told him everything that had happened: how she had gone to the chapel and back, alone and by night, about all the hardships she had encountered, and how King Ris had restored all her land to her because she had braved such dangers. Indeed, he had given her his solemn word that he would never again return under any circumstances. When she had told the King the whole story, she said: "Now listen for a moment, dear lord, to why I came here. I hold all my land from you and it is your duty to advise me, for no man must have me as his wife except by your consent. And that is why I have come to ask you for a boon, which you must not refuse me." {1269}

"My friend," he replied, "please dismount, and then you may tell me what boon you seek." {1271}

"No, dear lord, you must grant it to me first, before I will dismount." And the King did so right there on the spot. {1274}

Having granted her request, the King stepped forward like a gallant man to assist her. "Young lady," he said, "surely now you will feel free to dismount." At once he went and took her by the waist and helped her down most gently. When he saw the sword she was wearing, he stared at it and said: "Young lady, should we be on our guard because you are wearing a sword?" {1285}

The maiden approached the King and said: "You do not realize, dear lord, what kind of boon you have just granted me, and I would like you to understand what you have agreed to. I would have you give me as my husband a man so worthy that he can ungird this sword from me, without damaging it or slicing through the straps—which are neither rotting nor frayed from use! The man who takes possession of me will be extremely happy, for I want you to know that I am the daughter of a king and a queen. Since both of them are dead and I am their only heir, I hold all the land. One could search far and wide before finding a woman richer or more beautiful than I." {1303}

"There is absolutely no doubt about that, young lady. You will be granted the boon, and gladly. Now it is up to the knights to try and remove the sword, and I do believe that they will bring all their skills and efforts to the task." {1309}

At once he called on Kay, his seneschal, and said: "I want you to have this young lady and her land, provided that you manage to ungird the sword just as she has requested." Kay got up right away and went to kneel at the King's feet. The King made him rise, saying that he did not know of a better way to make use of his service, and that he could not give the Lady to anyone closer to his heart. {1321}

Kay was extremely happy to hear this; he went right up to the maiden and asked if she would accept the King's proposal. {1325}

"Yes, my lord," she said, "I have no objection." With that, Kay promptly took hold of the straps. But no matter how much he toiled and struggled, he failed utterly to loosen them. In fact, the harder he tried, the tighter they got. When he saw that force was of no avail, he finally gave up and said: "Young lady, may the man be cursed who ever sets his hand to this task, whatever the reason might be!" {1335}

"My goodness, Sir Kay, you have spoken like an absolute boor, to say the least! I release you from your offer now and forever: you will never be my lord, that's for certain!" {1339}

Seething with anger, Kay went back to the King and said: "You can promise the Lady of Cardigan to whomever you wish. I don't think that anyone is going remove the sword from her side today. Those straps will only be released with just the right twist. May God never allow any man to take joy of her, or bring his task to a conclusion!" {1349}

The King calmed the seneschal down as best he could, and the maiden too; and right away he called on Sir Yvain, saying: "Step forward, my friend, and take this lady with all her land and fiefs, provided that you ungird the sword—if indeed it can be removed. I can't imagine anyone who would complain about such land or such a lady, if he could possibly have them. Upon my soul, she will be yours, if you succeed!" {1361}

Sir Yvain came and knelt at the King's feet as a sign of his gratitude. Then without further delay he went and said: "My lady, if you don't mind, I will try and see if there is anything I can do to unfasten this sword." {1367}

"My lord," she replied, "I would be very pleased if you did," and he set about his task. But the more effort he put into it, the tighter and more entangled the straps became. He realized that she would never be his, for he simply could not loosen them. "My lady," he declared, "now some other man worthier than I may test his skill, for I believe that I will never be able to remove the sword for you." {1377}

The maiden was left quite upset by the fact that such a fine man had failed at the task. From that moment on, she thought to herself that it didn't matter very much who might try, nor did she think that any man would ever have her, for she knew of no one else quite so fine or so handsome. The King then called on Dodinel le Sauvage and told him exactly what he had told the others. Dodinel approached the maiden and, seeing how attractive she was and thinking the man who would have such a beautiful wife would be very fortunate indeed, put forth his very best efforts. He fully expected to remove the sword, but he was no more successful than all those who had tried before. And afterward he returned to his place, quite crestfallen. {1395}

The King was far from delighted at this predicament; indeed, he wondered how it could possibly be. At once he asked the maiden where she had found such a sword and who had secured it to her side in such a way that no one could manage to get it loose. So she told him the tale of the dead knight from beginning to end: how the man who had laid him in the grave had prayed to God, the words he had spoken, and how she had later taken the sword and girded it on. And with that, no further words were spoken, and the King put a halt to the proceedings. "My beauty, go and get some rest," he said, "for you certainly need it. I will not have any more knights make any further attempts today." {1413}

She realized that it was pointless to go on and agreed to what the King proposed. Graciously, the Queen took the maiden away with her to her chambers and, understanding that she needed rest, did everything she could to make her as comfortable as possible. And so the maiden had something to eat and was well looked after, enjoying good company—which gave her great consolation. When it came time to retire, all the beds were made ready, and though it was very difficult for her, the maiden took off her clothes by force, tugging them out from under the sword harness and pulling them free as best she could. And then she went to bed with the sword still attached. {1430}

In the morning at first light, the King arose and dressed, as did the Queen; and the damsel of the sword got dressed too, taking all the time she needed. The King went to hear Mass and the maiden accompanied him, but she looked very much out of place, for she went inside the church bearing arms. The King heard Mass right away and came out soon after. The beautiful maiden approached him, urging him not to forget her plight and to keep his covenant with her, for the sword was causing her great distress. {1445}

"My beauty, I will keep my promise to you in every respect," he said. "Just be patient a little while longer." Without further ado, King Arthur summoned the three hundred and sixty-six companions, and all of them showed up, I do believe, except for his nephew, who had gone off on an expedition, as had Tor, the son of Arés, and Girflet too. Only these three were missing and not one person more; all the others were present at court and assembled before the King. {1457}

The King said: "My lords, I grant this young lady and her land to the man who can win her by removing the sword, and I don't want anyone left at the end of the day who has not tried his hand at the task." {1463}

Each knight was very confident of succeeding and did not think he could possibly fail. Each one took his turn, struggling and straining, but none was any more successful than those who had already tried. Then the King addressed the twenty thousand men he had assembled there to ride out against King Ris, inviting each one of them to go and test his skill. And so they tried, but none of them was able to do any better. When everyone had tried and failed, the maiden was greatly disheartened, for she thought, when all was said and done, that never in her life would she have a husband. At this point she was absolutely certain that the knight who eventually removed the sword would be a very fine man indeed, a person of great accomplishment. And he would be most welcome to her, if only she could have him, for then she would have the very best man there could ever be, as long as the world might last. Dispirited, she went to the King and bade him once again to keep his covenant with her. "Just wait," he replied, "until Gawain or Tor or Girflet gets back. If this business is not concluded through their efforts, then I really don't know what to say." {1491}

"Dear lord," she answered, "I will be patient, since there is obviously nothing I can do on my own to resolve the problem." Then the King gave orders for the tables to be set and for the knights to be seated right away; and so it was done. Then he went to wash up, as did the Queen, and they both took their seats. The King ate his meal, deeply engrossed in thought. {1500}

When they had dined at leisure, and when the King gave the word, the tables were cleared. After he had washed his hands, he was still very much preoccupied by his thoughts. Then a young man, tall, strong and handsome, capable, and endowed with all the qualities Nature can confer on a man's body—yet he couldn't have been more than twenty-two years old— appeared before the King and said: "My lord, a while ago when your nephew set out from court to seek adventures through the land, he asked you to make me a knight whenever you might hear me ask it of you. And I would like to ask you now to do as he proposed, if you please. And I urge you to keep your covenant with him." {1523}

The King saw that he was tall, elegant, and so handsome that, to his way of thinking, there was no man alive better endowed with noble attributes. The young man pleased and impressed him so much that, to the best of his recollection, he had never seen a human being with more potential than this one. And from this moment on, it would be wrong for him to deny the man knighthood, since age was clearly no impediment. So he said that he would make him a knight whenever he wished, without delay or postponement. And the young man replied: "My lord, I want to be knighted this very day." {1538}

"So it shall be!" the King replied. "Kay, by the faith you owe me, take this young man to lodgings right away, and make sure you provide him with everything he requires to make him a new knight, and let there be no delays." {1545}

"My lord, at your command." {1546}

The seneschal did just as the King had ordered, and the young man went off to wash and bathe, and Kay had him dressed in a robe of fine red samite. When he was fully attired, no man had ever seen a more handsome creature. The robe suited him so well that it looked as if he had been born wearing it. Sir Yvain came in, along with several other knights, and personally fastened on a spur over the young man's finely woven hose. Galés the Bald attached the other spur, and then they all mounted up and went back to the court. Sir Yvain took him by the hand and led him into the King's presence. Everyone gazed at him in amazement, saying that no man alive, or who had ever lived, could compare with him for strength or beauty; nor was there any man alive as likely to demonstrate more prowess or worth—judging by appearances—unless he was somehow lacking in courage. {1571}

The King went to hear vespers, and then they dined. And when they had finished eating, the knights returned to their lodgings, but the young man went to keep vigil in the church. In the morning he heard his Mass and then returned to his lodgings to eat and sleep a little while. He asked them to awaken him as soon as King Arthur got up. And so it was done, and he arose and dressed himself—that didn't trouble him in the least. He put on a coat of arms made of imported material, then he armed himself as handsomely as he could, with everything a knight requires to attack and to defend his person. Then, without further ado, he mounted his horse and rode into the great hall by himself. He dismounted, put down his shield and his sword, walked unaccompanied into the King's presence, and said: "Now I am lacking nothing, Sir, but the girding on of the sword." {1595}

The King immediately had one brought out from his coffers—a sword he greatly loved and treasured—girded it on the young man, and gave him the accolade as was the custom. Then he declared: "May God make you a worthy knight, for I have never seen a man—if you do not have evil as your mentor—in whom prowess might find a better home. May God keep you and protect you, for you are a very handsome man indeed." {1605}

Then the new knight said: "Might it please you, my lord, I would like to try and see if I can unfasten that sword." The King immediately agreed to this. Overjoyed, the knight went right up to the maiden and said: "Young lady, if you please, now that I am a knight I would like to see if I can loosen those silken bands." {1616}

The young beauty replied without conceit: "Dear lord, I should be very much pleased if you would give it a try." {1619}

"Then get up on that table, young lady, for I am on horseback, and would find it very difficult to reach from this height." {1623}

"It was to your great misfortune that you told me to get up on the table! Would it be so shameful for you to dismount in front of me? You are very presumptuous, when so many bold and valiant knights have set their hand to the task and all have failed utterly. You haven't yet accomplished a single feat of arms, and you don't even know if you will ever amount to anything. And yet you have the gall to tell me to get up on the table! But whatever may happen, I will comply with your request, and no one will ever be able to accuse me of haughtiness or unbecoming conduct." {1639}

With that she got up on the table. The knight approached her, still on horseback, took hold of the sword belt, and undid it, just as if he were removing his own. Then he girded it on over his own sword and turned to leave, without saying another word to the King, the young lady, or any of the knights. {1647}

The King called out after him and said: "Come back here, knight! You must have the young lady to whom all Cardigan belongs, where you will have a fair and wide domain." But you may be sure that the knight gave no sign of hearing him; he just kept on going. The King was far from happy at his departure; indeed, he was truly astounded by it. For the young man had been at court for a long time and no one ever had any name for him except "Handsome Young Man." Kay declared: "He was rightly named and properly baptized. But from now on, his name should be the Knight of the Two Swords and nothing else, since he has two of them girded on; he must have no other name." And as the young knight rode off, he thought to himself that that was indeed how he would be known; he would not go by any other name. {1670}

V

The Knight's First Exploits

And so the Knight departed and would not stay at court, despite the King's plea; instead he rode away with determination, passing through towns and fields until he reached the forest, never straying from the straight road. The maiden was left standing there in the middle of the hall, quite dismayed and dumbfounded. Such a noble company of knights, whose renown had spread so far and wide as had the fame of that court—all of the three hundred and sixty-six companions and the twenty thousand men whom the King had assembled there, hardened warriors greatly prized for feats of arms—all had failed utterly to unfasten the sword. And yet this young man who had just been dubbed and hadn't yet accomplished a single feat removed it quite handily, and then just rode off! Then she remembered the words of the knight who had interred his companion in the chapel, and she thought that if there were anyone so worthy, so handsome, and so free of imperfections, this knight must surely be the man. With that she went straight to the King and bade him once again to keep his covenant. {1699}

"Never fear, my friend! I will send after him at once." Without delay he called up four truly exceptional men, Sir Yvain, Ellit, Saigremor, and Dodinel. "My lords," he said, "I want you to bring me back the new knight. Go and equip yourselves in full armor and set out right away. Make sure you don't let him get away, and be sure to find out what name he is using." {1712}

"My lord," they replied, "everything at your command," and at once they had themselves armed. Then they mounted their horses and went on their way, traveling at great speed wherever the most direct route led them, and before long they caught sight of the Knight. Sir Yvain, who had pursued him most vigorously, caught up with him before the others did, so that his horse was all bathed in sweat. "The King sends you his greetings," he said to the Knight, "orders you to return to court, and commands you to tell us your name." {1727}

The Knight, who was sensible and prudent, drew to a halt and said: "May great good fortune come to him, and to you who are addressing me now. I wouldn't want to be known by any other name but the one Sir Kay gave me. In all my life I've never heard myself called anything but 'Handsome Young Man.' I am sorry that the King has ordered me to return to the court, but that cannot be. I have too great a challenge to take up, and I could never turn back. If it were at all possible, I would go back right now for your sake, for you have served me well and shown me much consideration at court. I thank you sincerely for that, and consider myself as honored as I could possibly be." {1745}

"You absolutely must come back," said Sir Yvain. The King made me promise to bring you back and to find out who you are. And indeed, I will take you back if I can. I can offer you no choice but this: either you come back voluntarily or else you will take up arms against me." {1754}

"I would sooner accept your challenge to battle, but surely I do so against my will." {1756}

With that they left the road and rode off into an open field. Each knight was mounted on a great Spanish horse, robust, agile, and swift. Each man readied his shield for combat, each one placed his sturdy lance on the fewter; then the two charged against each other as fast as their horses could carry them. In the joust, Sir Yvain shattered his lance with such force that the splinters flew high up into the air, so high indeed that no one could even see them. The Knight of the Two Swords aimed high and true and struck Yvain, pinning his shield to his arm and his arm to his side. Then Yvain and his horse toppled over backward in a heap, so that their feet were up in the air and they narrowly missed breaking their necks. Sir Yvain was angry and shamed; as he got to his feet, his horse took off. He tried to catch it, but the horse wouldn't wait; it had already left him far behind. And as Yvain was standing there like this, the Knight of the Two Swords rode away. {1785}

When Saigremor saw how the Knight had dealt with Sir Yvain, he went after him at full tilt, expecting to exact proper vengeance for the shame. But why should I make a longer story of it? The Knight of the Two Swords met him head on and knocked both horse and rider to the ground in a heap. The next two went to joust with him as well, but they fared no better. In fact, he knocked all four men to the ground, along with their horses, which then galloped off in different directions, and the knights went running after them. With that, the Knight of the Two Swords left and began to ride away. The four others set out on foot, hiking all the way back to the great hall; this caused a great stir among those who saw them coming, for they didn't believe that such a thing could possibly have happened. {1807}

As soon as the King saw them, he asked: "Where is that knight? Did you leave him behind? Why isn't he with you?" {1811}

"Truly, my lord, it troubles us to say so, but there is nothing we can do about it. You can have him summoned by others, since he will not come back on our account. He has treated us most shamefully, for he knocked all four of us to the ground and almost broke our necks, and our horses' necks too! Never have we seen a knight deliver such blows with a lance." {1821}

When the maiden heard him praised in this manner, she thought in her heart that, if he lived, he would in time become the finest knight in all the world. Then she went to the King and urged him to keep his covenant with her. {1827}

"My dear," he said, "wait until Gawain and his two companions return. Have no fear, for I will send them after him. Almost half a year has passed since I saw them last, and that troubles me greatly. But I have a war to wage against King Ris, who has sent me a most shameful message, and I don't want to dismiss the troops I have assembled here now." {1837}

"My lord, since I must put up with this delay, I will suffer it in patience. But by my faith, I will not leave this court—however long I have to wait—until I am assured that my covenant is kept in every respect." {1843}

"Young lady, I give you my solemn word." {1844}

So the Knight of the Two Swords was successful in his jousts, and he rode off on his way, never stopping to rest. He passed through many a forest, was victorious at all the tournaments, and got out of many predicaments everywhere, however dangerous they were. He performed many feats of arms and proved himself more in two months than any knight had ever done in two years, as far as anyone could recall. And no matter how challenging the adventure, it could not stand against him, and he managed to accomplish more than any knight ever born. His fame spread so far and wide that news of it was reported at the court by people who had heard tell of his exploits. {1861}

The maiden was most joyful in her heart—and rightly so—at the fact that the Knight was making such a name for himself. She frequently reminded the King that he should not fail to keep his covenant, and he gently replied that she should not worry about a thing or be concerned in any way. "My beauty," he said, "I do believe that if we were to leave this place, we could bring your business to speedier conclusion, and therefore we are going to go to Glamorgan." The Lady of Cardigan replied that he should do what he thought best, for she had set her heart on doing whatever the King desired. {1877}

Then they set out at their leisure and headed straight for Glamorgan, taking all the time they needed; not one member of the court remained behind. The King sojourned in that castle and did not leave it for a good week; but no news reached them there and no adventure presented itself. The King was quite vexed at this, and very much surprised. {1886}

VI

King Ris Comes to Glamorgan

One day the King had finished his dinner and was still sitting at the dais, as was his custom. The knights had gone to their lodgings throughout the town to relax and enjoy themselves, and the King's household was somewhat reduced in numbers; there were no more than a hundred and forty knights in the castle, and at the dais there were five men at most, including the King. And he began to meditate. {1897}

All of a sudden, some ten knights came in without saying a word, each one looking extremely sorrowful. They were armed and escorted a litter draped with red samite, borne by two small palfreys harnessed both front and rear. On it lay a knight wounded by the shaft of a lance that had passed through his body, and it was obvious that the other men were greatly distressed at this. Along with the injury to his body there was a great sword wound to the knight's head. It had been bandaged, but he was badly injured and his condition was critical. The knights had their helmets raised, so they quickly recognized King Arthur. Then all ten of them dismounted, took the litter, and placed it at the King's feet right in front of the dais, not saying a word. They all sat down around the litter and began to express such sorrow that no one could possibly describe its like, at least not for a man who was still alive. {1923}

The King was quite mystified by the fact that they had not seen fit to address him. He wondered to himself who they were and who was the knight lying on the litter, causing them such grief. Then he called Sir Yvain before him and said: "Have you seen the contempt these knights have shown me? They are all sitting around right in front of me, and yet not one of them has the courtesy to speak to me! Go and find out whose men they are and where they came from. Find out who this knight is whom they hold so dear and for whose sake they are so stricken with grief. And find out who wounded him like this, in the head and in the body." {1941}

Sir Yvain went down to them, and, just as the King had ordered, he asked the questions word for word, but no one would say a thing. They gave absolutely no hint that any one of them had even seen or heard Yvain. And he persisted with his questions, drawing closer and repeating them over and over again, but they said no more than what they had said before. Sir Yvain was astounded and angry, for it seemed to him that this was a deliberate provocation. The Queen marveled at it, and so did all those who were present. {1955}

Just then they saw another ten knights coming in, the same way as before, bearing a litter covered with finely woven cloth. They all went over to where they saw the first litter had been placed and set theirs down beside it. These men showed their sorrow in a different way than the first knights had done, for on this litter there lay a knight groaning in such agony that they thought for certain he was about to die; he simply could not endure the pain. The wounded knight's shoulder had been pierced by a sword and his hip was broken, and that was why they were displaying such grief; and they refused to speak to any man present in the hall. It was quite useless to ask them anything, for no one gave any sign of willingness to speak, not even under threat. The King was furious at this. {1979}

And as he was in this angry frame of mind, in came a third litter; its occupant was behaving exactly the same way as the others had before, and there were just as many knights with him. {1984}

Why should I make a longer story of it? By my count, nine groups came in this way, all of them acting just like the first one, and the occupant of each litter was in much the same state. And they were all laid out side by side before the King. He went to ask where all these knights were coming from, and all of them kept their heads bowed down, not saying a word. The King grew incensed and couldn't stop asking questions, but they wouldn't even look at him or say a word, not great or small. The King considered this to be a deliberate act of contempt. {1998}

While he was still furious and consumed by anger, the King saw twenty armed knights approaching, and it seemed from their demeanor that they were all men of great worth. These twenty knights were escorting a litter conveyed by two horses and shielded by two imperial drapes, whiter than the new-fallen snow. The litter itself was covered with blue samite and adorned with gold embroidery. On the litter he saw a couch—very noble and costly, and well suited to a gentleman—and lying on it there was a very tall knight. He had been maimed by a sword blow to the ribs and had at least nine wounds to the head. His life was in grave danger from even the least of his injuries, unless he received prompt attention, proper treatment, and expert medical care. These men saw the litters already lying at the King's feet and the knights who were weeping all around them. At this they dismounted, and when the knights at the front of the hall saw them come in, they all got up at once and went to meet them, lamenting all the while. They picked up the litter, carried it to the front, and placed it right at the King's feet; then the lamentations started up all over again, so loud that all the sorrows that had ever been heard were nothing when compared with half of these. On seeing this, the King felt great compassion, and so did the Queen and the knights. {2035}

King Arthur stood up right away and went to ask the men he saw bringing in this last litter where they had come from, what had brought them there, and who all these wounded knights were. But not one of them said a word; instead they gave themselves over to endless tears and lamentation. The King was both amazed and vexed by this, for they would not reply in any way to any question he asked. He swore on the souls of his father, Uther Pendragon, and his mother, Igerne—an oath he would never forswear—that either they would tell him everything he wanted to know or else he would have their heads cut off and slay the wounded men. {2055}

The company heard that the King was enraged and threatening to end their lives, but not even on that account would they say a word; instead they were totally overwhelmed by grief. Then the man lying on the tenth litter commanded them to be silent and raised his head as best he could, quite feebly, as you might expect of a man who had recently lost a great deal of blood. With the greatest difficulty, he began to speak, saying: "If you would promise me, King Arthur, not to do any more harm to me or my men here—we who are now at your mercy—I would tell you anything you wanted to know. That is the only way you will find out, for otherwise we will say nothing, not even on pain of death. We know perfectly well that we are under your power to harm and to destroy." {2075}

The King could see that they didn't need to endure any worse or any greater ills, so he promised them they would have no further harm or suffering at his hands. {2080}

When the King had given the knights and the wounded men this assurance, the man who had arrived on the last litter spoke out with extreme anguish, saying: "You do not understand, my lord King, what men you have here before you. I will tell you who they are, and I will not lie to you or withhold anything I may know or recall about our plight. These knights are all mine and hold me as their king. And I am indeed a king, no matter who has taken me captive like this; truly, I am King Ris of Outre-Ombre, who demanded your beard, who summoned you to come and answer to me, and who ordered you to hold your land from me." {2098}

On hearing this, King Arthur was dumbfounded and said: "Who advised you to come here? You know very well that you have committed a great offense against me." {2102}

"I have indeed, and I regret it deeply." {2103}

"Then," said King Arthur, "I want you to tell me how all this came about." {2105}

King Ris pulled himself up on his elbow, like a man who had nothing more to fear, since the King had guaranteed him the safety of his person. "I left the city of Cardigan a few days ago with all my knights, after I had surrendered it to the maiden who dared to take the shackles to the chapel, where not one of the knights in my retinue would venture to set foot. That is why I abandoned her city and withdrew my troops. And it had already been decided that I should invade your land. I arose very early one day, for it was a warm and sunny morning, and I gave orders to these nine knights, telling them to go to their tents, arm themselves, and then report back to me. I myself was armed, just as you see me now, and I left the army as the leader of ten men, entering the forest of Cardueil as quickly as I could. I had heard tell that this forest was so full of adventures, so enchanted and so marvelous, that it was impossible for a knight to enter it without some adventure befalling him before he left. {2137}

"So I had ridden for a while at a leisurely pace, keeping on course until I left the forest and entered a meadow, which stretched for more than half an Irish league. I looked up to a hillock where I saw a knight standing. He was resting on his sword and he had thrust at least ten others into the ground all around him, and it seemed to me that he was totally lost in contemplation. I thought to myself that this was some knight waiting for adventure, so I sent one of my men at him right away, not delaying for a moment. That was the man who arrived here first. And when the knight saw him coming, he rode down quickly from the hillock and prepared to joust with him. They struck each other so hard that their two lances could not help but shatter. He dealt with my knight so harshly that he soon got the better of him and quickly defeated him by force of arms. He wouldn't hear of taking ransom; instead he made him promise to become a prisoner and surrender to you, wearing all his armor, just as you see him here. {2167}

"When I saw that he had so soundly beaten my man, I sent another knight charging out. But why should I make a longer story of it? I don't know what good it would do to hide the truth. That knight defeated mine in battle, and then he took a pledge of loyalty from him, you may be sure of that, just as he had done with the first one. In the end, all nine fought and were defeated exactly like the first one. This caused me great distress, and I was infuriated that a single knight had defeated nine of my companions. At once I spurred my horse on and charged at him, and the two of us did battle; and he wounded me so badly that I'm sure there's nothing left for me now but death. Truly, he defeated me in battle; that I cannot deny. {2191}

"Then he made me promise, injured though I was—for I had wounds in a good many places—that I would surrender to you as a prisoner. I told him I would not do so, for if you ever laid your hands on me, nothing could possibly stop you from cutting off my head. On hearing this, he stood over me and said he would kill me then. At that moment I felt greater fear than I had ever known, for he really had gotten the best of me. 'My lord,' I told him, 'I will grant you anything you ask, because I think I'm done for. I know that a day of respite is worth a small fortune, as the saying goes, but never will I have mercy from King Arthur.' {2207}

"Dear, gentle lord, I did everything just as he required, like it or not. And then I asked him his name, and he told me he didn't know what it was, but he had heard—when he removed the maiden's sword, whose harness she had fastened on so tightly at the chapel—that Kay the seneschal called him the Knight of the Two Swords. Then he ordered me to come here as his prisoner and submit myself absolutely to your will." {2220}

When the King heard this, he was very pleased and greatly delighted to know that this was King Ris, the man who had behaved so despicably toward him, who had sent him a message of great shame at Cardueil, where he had assembled the noblest men in his land, and who had so deliberately provoked him to war. He declared: "May the man who has gone to such lengths to send me such a noble present enjoy great good fortune, and may God grant me the power to reward him at some future time." {2233}

The maiden who had brought the sword to the court was engrossed in thought. In her pensive state she went to the King and said: "My lord, I would rather not keep you from your land any longer; so I urge you once again to fulfil your covenant with me." {2239}

"Ah, young lady, you know very well that you have granted me a delay until such time as we see my nephew and his companions back at court; we think that they will return before long, and then we will do anything you want." {2245}

She fell silent and went off to one side, quite annoyed by the fact that the matter had been postponed once again. Nothing had been done to advance her cause, that is, to get her the valiant knight whom she so desired and coveted. Nonetheless, she was greatly reassured to know that if she could only have him as her husband, she would be quite certain of having the finest man alive. {2255}

While she was thinking these thoughts, the King summoned his doctors and said: "My lords, go and care for King Ris and his knights, and be just as concerned for their well-being as you would be for mine, and look after all his needs." {2262}

"At your command, my lord." Then they had King Ris borne very gently to a quiet chamber where he would not hear anything that might disturb him, and they had the other knights carried to two somewhat private rooms. They had the injured men's wounds examined, then they washed them thoroughly and bandaged them, carrying out these tasks gladly and to the best of their ability. When they saw that King Ris was improving, they went to King Arthur and informed him that he would survive and that, of the nine others, only two who were mortally wounded were likely to die. {2279}

"Take good care of them," said the King, "and I will be deeply indebted to you. I will be greatly pleased if King Ris recovers, and much distressed if any of his knights should die here." {2284}

Now King Ris was sure that he would recover, and the sort of captivity he found himself in did not trouble him a bit; as far as anyone knew, he was given everything his heart desired, and to his complete satisfaction. He summoned his seneschal to give him his orders and told him to call in his knights—those who had transported the litters—and not a single one of them was to remain behind. They were to leave at once, and the seneschal was to take all his army and safeguard his land no matter what until King Ris returned—assuming that he did indeed recover—and provided that King Arthur agreed to this. And the seneschal accepted these orders and did everything just as Ris had instructed him. He took his leave right away, but King Ris remained at court convalescing, and no one neglected to give him all the care and attention he required. So effective were the doctors' efforts that within a month King Ris and his knights were recovering quite nicely, as well they should have, all except for the two who had died. {2312}

King Arthur was very pleased with this. King Ris came before him without delay and thanked him for the honor of the fellowship that Arthur and his men had shown him. Then Ris earnestly begged the King to tell him his pleasure, for he was quite ready to do his bidding and carry out his every wish. {2321}

And King Arthur replied: "Have no fear, lord king, I would not do you any harm for any reason. I would be showing little honor to the man who sent you here if any outrage were committed against you now, in any way, great or small. I am freeing you and your men wholly because of the love I bear for that knight." {2329}

Then King Ris began to marvel at these words. For the first time he saw and understood that Arthur was the finest king in the world and that everything he had heard about him from others was true. And when he fully realized the King's great integrity, he thanked him most sincerely for it, saying: "I used to think there was no king more powerful, more wealthy, more valiant, or a better knight than I; but now I know of no king finer, worthier, or more courageous than you. And so I wish to become your liege man right away and hold my fief from you; I want you to be my protector. When King Arthur heard this, he was very pleased, and he took him as his man. And King Ris said: "My lord, if you thought it right, I would gladly go and see my knights and my land once again." {2353}

"You may ask for that with complete confidence," said King Arthur. "I would never want anything else, for I will be assured that your will is [. . .] without any interference or contradiction." {2358}

And waiting no longer, King Ris took his leave of the Queen and all the other women gathered there in the chambers. Then he mounted his horse; King Arthur and a good five hundred knights who were in readiness escorted him on his way. And so, I do believe, they accompanied him until they reached the forest, conversing all the way, much to King Ris's delight. Then they all took their leave of him, and King Ris rode away. {2372}

VII

The Return of Gawain

With that, the two kings went their separate ways, as indeed they had to, with good will on both sides; and as King Arthur was leaving King Ris, he fell behind his men and grew extremely pensive. And as he was thinking, it seemed to him that he heard the sound of a horse whinnying down by the sea; he looked in that direction and saw a knight in full armor approaching him at great speed, so he made a halt. The knight's shield was so badly defaced and damaged that he couldn't even make out its colors, for it had been badly battered by many blows of sword and lance. The knight kept on coming until the King got a better look at the horse; he recognized it right away. He knew for certain that this horse belonged to his nephew, Sir Gawain. Then his heart began to fill with apprehension, as he feared that this might be some knight who by his prowess had slain his nephew and, to compound the outrage, was now coming to the court to boast about his feat and show off Gawain's horse as the proof. And as the King was in this troubled state of mind, Sir Gawain drew near, and on seeing the people gathered there, he recognized them as his uncle's men. {2408}

Sir Gawain kept on riding until he made out his uncle, then he raced on ahead as fast as his horse could carry him, like a man brimming with joy. He headed straight for him at top speed, and King Arthur was greatly relieved when he recognized his nephew; he too was overcome with joy. And then the kissing and embracing began, and the joy between those two men was immense. I don't know how many years had passed since the King last felt such elation. When the knights saw this outpouring of emotion, they were astonished and headed in that direction right away, to find out who the newcomer was. And when Sir Yvain saw him, he too was ecstatic, and so were Kay and all the others; as soon as they recognized him, they began to rejoice and celebrate, and one and all they bowed their heads to him. Gawain and the King went on talking freely. The King asked him where he had been and where he had stayed so long, and Gawain set about telling him everything that had happened to him since his departure. {2435}

"Then," said the King, "would you recall a young lad you left in my keeping, asking me to make him a knight whenever I might hear him make the request? Indeed, he asked me, and I acceded right away, as well I should have. For never had I seen or known a young man handsomer in every respect." Then he told his nephew how the new knight had removed the sword, how he had departed abruptly, how he had sent King Ris back to his court, and everything about his travels. {2449}

"My lord," said Gawain, "this knight you are talking about is becoming more and more renowned; his reputation and his fame have already spread to many a land. A great many people have told me about him, people who do not think that a finer man was ever born, or that any knight has ever accomplished so many feats of arms within such a short space of time. I would be delighted to see him again, if I could. And I do believe he would still be at court, if only I had been here at the time!" {2461}

"Dear nephew, that would have made me very happy indeed." {2462}

As they were talking in this way, news reached Glamorgan that Sir Gawain was returning. The Queen was there, and when she heard this news she was simply ecstatic; and the ladies and damsels with her showed as much joy as you could possibly imagine. They mounted their horses as quickly as they could, and the Queen, not waiting for anyone, had already saddled up and gone to meet Sir Gawain, her heart bursting with joy on account of his return. Those who saw her riding all alone asked why she had undertaken such a trip, for they had heard of nothing that would explain why she was out riding all by herself. {2481}

"Haven't you heard the news from anyone? Sir Gawain is coming back!" {2483}

And when they heard this, everyone joined her who possibly could; the whole town set out at once, on horseback or on foot. Each and every one of them felt happiness such as they had never known before. They left the town following the Queen, making such a display of joy that the King couldn't understand who all these people were, pouring out of the castle. And they told him they had heard the news of his nephew's return; and indeed there was not a young man or woman left who hadn't heard of it. {2497}

"Dear nephew," he said, "you may certainly be flattered, for everyone loves you sincerely, calls you 'Lord' and cherishes you, God be praised. And look, the Queen is riding out to meet you with her noble entourage;

they show you no less honor than if you were related to each one of them—as a brother or a favorite cousin—and not a soul is left inside the town." {2507}

Once he saw the Queen, Sir Gawain did not wait a moment; he hurried forward to greet her, exclaiming: "How marvelous to see you again, my lady!" {2511}

"And may you enjoy good fortune, dear nephew; you are a most welcome sight!" Then their mutual delight was as great as you could possibly imagine: they kissed each other on the eyes and lips, and embraced each other over and over again. And all the common people bowed to Gawain and welcomed him back. Anyone who couldn't get close pushed forward anyway, and there was such a throng milling about him that he could scarcely move. Only with great difficulty did he manage to break free; then he rode away from the crowd, and he and the Queen talked all the way back to Glamorgan. {2526}

Once they were inside the castle, they saw Tor, the son of Arés, returning from another direction, and soon they saw Girflet, the son of Do de Cardueil, coming back. This brought great joy to the King's heart, for now all three of them had returned. He declared that he would not stir from the castle until the three men were well rested. Indeed, he would stay a week or more, if need be; and the knights were immensely pleased at this. {2538}

While the King was in residence at Glamorgan, the Lady of Cardigan came to him and reminded him of his promise in these words: "My lord and King, it would be fitting for you to keep your covenant with me now, and send for the knight I am supposed to marry." {2545}

"Young lady, you speak the truth," he said, "but just be patient a little longer, on the understanding that I will not seek to prolong this sojourn once those who have returned are well rested, for they are weary and exhausted. I ask for one week's respite, and no more; then I will do whatever you wish." {2553}

"I will grant you that quite willingly," she said. "It would be ungracious of me to do otherwise. But for God's sake, do not put me off any longer than that." {2557}

The King continued his stay at Glamorgan and was very pleased with it; he and his men celebrated joyfully all week long, and they all had everything their hearts desired. King Arthur was relaxing at the table after dinner, as was his custom; no knight but Gawain was in his company, and no one was sitting with them except the Queen. The King began to speak to him in confidence, saying: "Dear nephew, a very grave and serious matter has come up for you, and I cannot postpone it any longer; for I have a covenant according to which you must go and find the Knight of the Two Swords. Indeed, you must do your best to bring him back with you, for I have promised the Lady of Cardigan, who is staying at court right now, that I will give him to her as her husband. And he will have all the honor and the fiefs that belong to her. And she is growing quite impatient: she keeps reminding me about it every day. But for the time being, take it easy and recover your strength before you have to leave." {2587}

"Rest assured, dear uncle, you could not ask me for anything I wouldn't do. Do you know anything about him?" {2590}

The King replied: "Nothing at all; I couldn't even find out his name or where he comes from, but he said that where he was born they called him the 'Handsome Young Man.' Now he has acquired such fame that there is no finer knight alive, and none handsomer or more generously endowed with all the qualities one expects in a man of worth." {2599}

The King said no more, and Sir Gawain went back to his lodgings, taking with him Kay, Sir Yvain, Perceval son of Alain, Le Gros of Vaus de Camelot, and Dodinel, a man of many virtues. And Tor and Girflet were there as well, and Lancelot, Gaheriet, Gal of Galefroi, and Blidoblidas, son of the King of Galway. All these men went back with him, and Taulat de Rougemont too, and together they celebrated in their lodgings, talking about this and that, and Sir Gawain was very happy. All of them washed their hands and then they ate some fruit; everyone sang and made merry until it was time to retire. And beds were made ready for them, and that night they all slept soundly until daybreak. {2622}

# VIII

Gawain and Brien des Iles

And so the knights, who were tired and weary, slumbered in their beds, for they had great need of rest. But it was Sir Gawain's custom to get up at the break of day. He saw the first light coming through the windows, and as quickly as he could he threw over his shoulders a great surcoat with a turned-up collar, all made of silk and lined with petit-gris. He went and opened the door to a balcony overlooking a garden, then he went outside to relax and watch the sun rising bright and clear. Within the garden, so many little birds were singing so many different songs that his heart was filled with gladness. He was so deeply moved that he said to himself no man should ever sleep or lie abed at such a time of day, so invigorating was the experience. Then he returned to his chamber, awakened a young lad he found sleeping there at the foot of his bed, and whispered to him to get up. And the lad did so right away, approached Gawain beside his bed, and asked him what he wanted. And Gawain ordered him to go quickly and quietly and fetch him clean white breeches and a white shirt, and he did so without delay. {2658}

Gawain took them and put them on right away. He also donned a tunic of precious white silk, richly embroidered with gold; he attached his collar with a gold fastener set with gems, quite large and wide and expertly crafted. He spared no effort to make himself look handsome: he girded on a belt made of gold braid and white silk, and then, wasting no time, he put on a mantle of black sendal with a vermilion lining; he wrapped it quickly around his neck so that he would not get burned by the sun. He decided not to wear his surcoat, for he didn't feel at all chilly. He immediately ordered his squire to ready his white hunting steed, and as soon as it was properly outfitted, the young fellow went to get it. Then the lad attached to his feet a pair of golden spurs with a small pair of fasteners made of

41

stout black silk. And then Sir Gawain sent him to fetch his shield, his lance, and his sword. The young man brought them in at once, and Gawain girded on the sword. Then there was nothing left to do but mount his horse; he took up his shield and the lad handed him his lance. With that he departed, ordering the young fellow to make sure no one heard a word about this, if at all possible. If he were compelled to say anything, he was to tell them that Gawain had gone out to enjoy himself in the meadows; and the lad was not to stir from that place. {2699}

Then Gawain left and found the garden gate open; he went out, crossed the moat, and rode into the meadows, which were teeming with grass and flowers and alive with many colors. He saw the forest and headed for it as quickly as he could. There, in the midst of a little clearing, he found the most perfect spot for enjoyment and delight he had ever beheld in all his life, and in the very middle of it stood the most beautiful beech tree he had ever seen; this place was a little further down than the meadows. Nothing could compare with it for beauty, and no one—freeborn or serf—had ever seen such a beech tree before. It was altogether covered with so many different kinds of birds that it was sheer delight to hear their joyous music. For they were singing so beautifully—each one in its own language and its own style—both for the love of springtime and because of the fine morning, that no creature born of a mother had ever given voice to such jubilation. Sir Gawain was so enthralled by the joy he heard that he almost forget himself. When he looked down at his feet, he realized he had put so much weight on his legs that he had stretched the stirrups to their limit and torn them, or very nearly so. He raised his two hands on high and said: "Dear Lord God, I thank Thee for granting me such a noble, gracious, and adventurous life that everyone cherishes me, and holds me in much higher esteem than they have ever done before." {2740}

Sir Gawain was very happy and joyful; the day was fine and the sun rose bright and clear, and he directed his gaze toward the forest. There he noticed a man on horseback, riding toward him at great speed, and it seemed that he was armed as well as he could possibly be, with everything that a knight requires to defend his person against another or to do a man harm; he knew for sure that this was a knight. Then Sir Gawain was happy and in his heart he said: "So help me God! that man is out seeking chivalry; he is going to give me some news, and he will not refuse to tell me anything I want to know. And if I can take him back to the King's court, I will be greatly rewarded for it, so I will try and do just that. King Arthur is always eager to ask for news from knights who travel abroad as this one is doing." {2765}

And as Gawain rode along boasting like this, the other knight approached rapidly on a great Spanish steed, like a man with nothing to fear. Sir Gawain looked at him and admired and praised him greatly in his heart. Then he set his hand to his bridle, pushed his shield aside with his elbow, and rode happily toward the knight with an air of complete self-assurance. He greeted him cordially, saying: "Welcome to you, dear lord!" {2777}

The other man, who did not want to be bothered with formalities and was riding along absorbed in thought, raised his head as he approached. He saw Sir Gawain but did not recognize him, and replied: "I offer you no greetings whatsoever!" {2783}

"You don't? Why not? Have I committed some act of folly for which you should hate me or be annoyed with me? Indeed, if we had some difference to settle, I would be quite ready and willing to resolve it right here and now." {2789}

"As far as I know," said the other knight, "you have not yet done me any wrong." {2791}

"Then why did you fail to return my greeting just now, and why did you answer me as you did, when I believe I have done you no wrong?" {2795}

"I'll tell you why," he said, "and I'll tell you why I've come here. I am a knight of the Kingdom of the Isles, the son of a vavasor. In that land there is no king or lord, only a lady, but upon my soul, she is the most beautiful woman ever born of a mother, the richest, wisest, and noblest woman in this world. Many noble men have asked for her in marriage, men of lower standing than she or of equal rank. I do not know the reason why, but she has rejected every last one of them. Yet I am so bold that I wanted to be her sweetheart. I had my heart so set on her, and I was suffering so much on her account, that I tried to tell her how much I loved her. I implored her, for the sake of common decency, to take pity and have mercy upon me. She asked me why she should, and as I was confessing the whole truth to her, she lowered her eyes and stared at the ground. When she had heard everything I had to say, she was greatly shamed and marveled at how I could ever have thought of proposing anything so outrageous, for I was not of such lineage that I should ever set my sights so high. Then she said: 'If I were not the one who made you a knight, I would have your head cut off. I would never accept any other token of repentance, for you have offered me great shame and profound offense. For I am the fairest and the noblest young lady in this world, except for the Queen of Iceland, my sister; and yet the son of a penniless vavasor dares to ask for me in marriage! I will love no one but the finest and the handsomest man in all the world.' {2837}

"'Truly, my lady, you are quite right to do so, but I am just the man you are describing.' {2839}

"'No,' she replied, 'you are quite wrong. You are indeed one of the best men in this land or anywhere else, and one of the handsomest; I know that perfectly well. But all that means nothing to me, since there is another man handsomer than you, and more worthy.' {2845}

"'That couldn't possibly be, and your saying it doesn't make it so. Neither you nor anyone else knows of such a man, and no one on this earth has ever heard of such a man.' {2849}

"'Then I will tell you who it is,' she said. 'Absolutely everyone says so—and I agree with them—that Sir Gawain, King Arthur's nephew, is much more worthy than you and more flawlessly handsome; indeed he surpasses you by far. And because he outshines every man I've ever met—and all those I haven't met as well—and because I am the most beautiful and the most worthy woman in the world, I will love no other man than him as long as I may live.' {2861}

"'You may say anything you like, my lady,' I replied at that point, 'but I am handsomer, stronger, and better at chivalry than he is.' {2865}

"'I do not believe for a moment that you are such a man,' she replied. {2867}

"'My lady, what would it take for you to believe me?' {2868}

"'Let me tell you what it would take: if you were daring enough to seek him out, all by yourself [. . .]—however dangerous it might be—and if you could prove your worth by finding him and cutting off his head, or by defeating him in battle, then I would believe you without fail, and I would do you the honor of making you lord and king of all my land, and of my person.' {2881}

"'Many thanks, my lady, I will gladly agree to that, and I ask for nothing better from you. I do not think I will stay more than one night in any lodging place, no matter what the effort costs me, as long as I have the strength, until I find him and defeat him in battle, however he may be armed; you may rest assured of that.' {2891}

"Then I took my leave and departed, and I have not stopped traveling since; it has been three months now, and I have still not found the man I am seeking. Some people tell me that Sir Gawain never reveals his name unless he is asked, but neither does he conceal it if anyone asks him, not even for fear of death. And so I do not think I'm wrong or that I'm acting like a boor if I refrain from greeting any knight I meet until I know for certain—without deception or trickery—what his name is. Once I know who he is—that for sure I'm not dealing with Sir Gawain—then I am not a stupid fool to return his greeting freely, for I do not hate any of the knights but Sir Gawain. Now you have heard the whole story of why I do not want to exchange greetings with you. Sir Gawain could rightly accuse me of treason, if he wished, if I returned his greeting and then proceeded to attack him. Now I have explained why I avoid paying my respects to anyone, whether handsome or ugly. And so I ask that you not try to change your name on my account; just tell it to me straight." {2925}

Sir Gawain was not happy about this; indeed he was greatly troubled at the fact that this man was asking him his name. He would have much preferred not to answer, for he had not heard anything in a long time that troubled him quite so much. For he saw the man before him, handsome, self-assured, and extremely well armed, and he considered him a formidable opponent. And for his part Gawain had no armor on, and he realized that this man hated him bitterly; so he was a little afraid of him, and justifiably so. Then he said that he could never do it, not even for fear of death; never could he remain silent about his name, and never before had he done so. "I am Gawain, King Arthur's nephew," he declared, "have no doubt about it. I am the son of King Lot of Orcany and Queen Morcadés." {2945}

When he heard these words, the other knight was suddenly overjoyed to learn that this was Sir Gawain; he lifted up his hands toward Heaven and exclaimed: "I thank you, dear Lord God, for leading me to this place where I have found Sir Gawain! Now I can fight him man to man." After saying these words, he approached Gawain and shouted: "Sir Gawain, I challenge you without respite, take up your position!" {2957}

"Dear lord," he said, "it has never been like this in any land, that a knight who wanted to challenge another man to battle did not wait until both of them were properly armed—if it so happened that one man came upon the other unarmed—unless perhaps there were some life-and-death struggle between the two of them. But even though the Lady of the Isles may say that I am the most handsome of men, I have done you no wrong, for God created me this way. In my opinion, this is most unfair; the match is quite unequal, for you have all the armor that a knight's body requires, and I have nothing but a lance, a sword, and a shield." {2975}

"No matter," the knight answered, "it has already been settled; the covenant was that if I should find you, I would fight you however you might be armed. And if you are defeated by me, I will have kept my word to the letter, and I will get all that was promised me, without any contradiction. So you absolutely must do battle with me, no matter what misfortune may befall you." {2986}

When Sir Gawain realized that there was no way out, that he would have no mercy from this knight, and that he would not get out of this predicament except by doing battle, and when he saw that the other knight was bold and treacherous, he was afraid of him and rightly so, for he could see his great misfortune impending. In spite of this, he exclaimed at once: "Knight, draw back and take up your position. I offer you no quarter!" {2997}

And so the two of them took up their positions in the middle of the field. Sir Gawain knew that he still had a chance to get away for, since the other knight was heavily armed, he wouldn't be able to stop him from escaping. But he repented at once for having allowed the thought to cross his mind. He said that never in all his life, as long as he had the strength, would any tale of cowardice on his part ever be told at court. He did not value his life so highly that, for fear or threat of death, he would do anything that might disgrace him in any way. Thereupon he got a firm grasp on his lance, drew his shield in front of his breast, and charged; his opponent advanced from the other direction. Each man had to look out for himself, for they were converging at a furious pace. Coming on very fast, Sir Gawain scored a direct hit just an inch above the boss of the other man's shield; the lance passed right through to the hauberk and then it shattered. The lance found the hauberk so resistant that it neither tore nor pierced it; instead it simply broke into pieces. {3027}

The other knight struck him back with all the force his horse could provide, for he was after him with a vengeance. He pierced Gawain's sturdy shield and, meeting no resistance, drove the sharpened, tempered steel right through his belly, but the blow missed the vital organs. The knight toppled him from his trusty charger, head over heels and flat on his back. Stricken, pale and ashen, the wounded Sir Gawain lay there, prostrate and unconscious. Because of his great pain, he couldn't even stir but lay sprawled out on the ground. The other knight rode up to him and saw that he wasn't moving—indeed, he looked like a man who would never move again. He was certain he had killed him, for he could see that Gawain had the sharp, glistening steel right through the middle of his belly. And so the knight was delighted and thought that he would be handsomely rewarded for having done what he had promised. {3053}

He went up to Gawain's horse, led it away, and tied it to a tree; then he came back to where he had left Sir Gawain for dead—or so he thought, since he was lying there unconscious, not showing the slightest sign of life. He was overcome with joy and cried aloud: "I praise Thee, Lord, for I have killed the very best and the finest man in all the world! Now I have slain the rose and ruby of the Round Table, for Sir Gawain is lying here lifeless before me. From this moment on, I need not fear losing my sweetheart's love, and I do not doubt that I will be King of the Isles." {3069}

And then he declared: "I would cut off your head, Sir Gawain, but in so doing I would be acting like a churl. I would be greatly reproached if I touched your body after I had killed you, for you have many friends in the world, and you are extremely well known. Nor will I take your horse away from here, for it might encumber me in some tight spot, and then I would be badly paid for my efforts." {3081}

With these words, he tugged at his reins, for he did not want to linger there, and set off for the forest, clapping his hands with the greatest joy that any man had ever felt. And he said that the finest adventure anyone had ever heard tell of—or that had ever befallen any knight—had come to him, just as he had hoped for and exactly as he deserved. Unable to wish for anything more, he went on his way. {3094}

Leaving the gravely wounded Sir Gawain behind, he departed in great joy. Once he was gone, Gawain recovered from his faint, still quite stunned and stricken. He had heard everything the knight said as he was lying there barely conscious, and he tried to see if he could get to his feet; but immediately he fell down again from his pain, for the other knight had done him great harm. Because of all the blood he had lost, most of his strength was gone; and yet he kept on struggling until he managed to sit up. Then, very feebly, using every ounce of strength he had left, he took the shield off his neck and drew the shaft out of his body, suffering extreme agony in the process. Then he bound up his wounds in his mantle, with the greatest difficulty, as you might expect of a man who had been bleeding profusely. He was happy when he saw that the knight had not taken his horse, and that it was still tied to the beech tree. Gawain struggled to his feet, staggered over to his mount, and, wounded though he was, dragged himself painfully into the saddle. He followed the road back to Glamorgan, beseeching God to let him recover all his strength and to allow him to live long enough that he might take vengeance some day on the knight who thought he had killed him. {3133}

Despondent and distressed, he rode along in great pain and anguish, passing through the forest, the meadows, and the streams. He entered the garden through the postern gate and saw the young lad he had left behind with orders to wait for him. When the boy saw him, he ran up at once to steady his stirrup. "Come here and help me dismount," he said, "for I have something of a body wound. But I want you to keep quiet about it, so don't let on to anyone who may ask you that there is anything at all wrong with

me. Stable my horse, then come back quietly and help me get into bed."
{3152}

The lad did as he was told; he went to stable his horse very discreetly,
then came back to Gawain and arranged his bed for him so expertly that
no one in the lodgings was awakened. Sir Gawain lay down to rest, greatly
weakened and in a very bad state. {3160}

The day dawned clear and bright, the morning was pleasant, and the
birds were rejoicing. The King and the Queen had already risen and dressed,
and they wondered what Sir Gawain could be doing. He generally got up
earlier than the other knights and was usually the first one to arrive at
court, unless he was indisposed or had to set out on some new mission. At
once the Queen summoned Lore de Branclant and Faukain de Mont
Esperant, who came in side by side. "Young ladies," she said, "go to Sir
Gawain's quarters and remind him that he is not usually the last man to
arrive at court. Tell him to get up and get dressed, for a knight who aspires
to joy or wants to win his sweetheart's love should not lie abed so late. Tell
him not to stay there any longer, for the King and I both request his company. We have been up for a long time now and we want to go to church."
{3189}

Without delay, the young ladies went off. They asked the chamberlains
where Gawain was sleeping, and they were promptly told. They went
straight to his chamber, knelt before his bed, and said: "Are you still asleep,
dear lord?" {3195}

"Young lady Lore, I welcome you and your companion," he replied;
"and no, I am not asleep, nor have I slept since daybreak." {3199}

"My lord, you should realize that the King and Queen are already up,
and they send word to you through us to come and join them right away,
along with Sir Yvain. Do not leave him behind for any reason. It has been a
long time, so they tell us, since you were still lying in bed at this hour, or
since you failed to get up before any other knight in the castle. No man
should lie in bed on such a beautiful morning; the King has been waiting
for you at court for more than an hour already." {3213}

When Sir Gawain heard the maiden's words, he paused and uttered a
sigh, then he answered weakly: "Right now it cannot be otherwise, young
lady, so go back to the court and tell my uncle and my lady the Queen not
to be upset, but that I am not feeling well." {3222}

They returned to the court and reported to the King exactly what Gawain
had told them. When the King heard that his nephew was sick and feeling
indisposed, he was greatly concerned, for the love between the two of them
was very strong. And he said to the Queen: "My lady, let us go and pay a

visit to my nephew: it has been a long time since I have seen him so sick that he would stay in bed. If he were not seriously ill, I don't think anything could keep him away from court." {3235}

"That may very well be, my lord," she said. "Let's go and see how he's doing." The King mounted his horse and rode off, along with the Queen and the knights and ladies, for every last member of court loved Gawain dearly. They made no noise or clamor. Sir Yvain had risen, along with a great many other knights who had slept in the lodgings, and they wondered why the King was coming in looking so concerned. Without speaking to anyone, he and the Queen hurried along to the bed where his nephew was lying. He sat down, had a window opened, took a look at his nephew, and, seeing that he was extremely pale, he asked: "How goes it with you, dear nephew? You seem to me quite unwell, and I think you really should tell me what is the matter." {3257}

Gawain replied faintly: "My lord, I have been the victim of great treachery." {3259}

At that, the King drew back the covers and saw that Sir Gawain was wounded; his bed was full of blood, and he was lying there completely soaked in it. The King asked him who had committed such an outrage and who had caused him such great shame. And Sir Gawain told him exactly how it had happened, adding that he didn't know what had become of the knight who had left him for dead. He told him of the knight's great joy, as he left him lying there on the ground, and explained how he had bound up his body with a mantle and how he had returned to Glamorgan. {3273}

The King began to feel faint and started to express his grief; no one could describe the Queen's chagrin, for she tore at her hair and almost died of sorrow. All the knights would have died of anguish if they could have, and the ladies too. Everyone shared in the grief, and I can assure you that no one was left untouched by sorrow or by tears. {3285}

"Ah, dear uncle," said Sir Gawain, "just let it be; you will gain nothing from behaving like this. Send for the doctors and order them to take care of me. I can see no better remedy than rest and repose. Just leave the matter be, until you see what happens." {3295}

The King was far from reassured by this, and continued to lament when he saw that his nephew was trying to comfort him. Like a grieving and disconsolate man, he said: "Dear sweet nephew, what profit and what amends can I have from your efforts, and how will I ever hold land if you die? All the world honors you: you carry the burdens in every undertaking, you calm the angry, you are the world's shield and defender, you have always lived to sustain impoverished ladies, you have always come to the rescue of disinherited maidens, you have always turned your back on evil deeds. From whom will I now have defense or protection for my kingdom? Who will ever wear a shield or helmet for Britain's honor? Oh, God! grant me that the man who committed this outrage may live to regret his act! May no one ever defy you without paying the price for it! The man who did this to you played the coward—that is quite clear—unless he was somehow tricked or deceived into committing this act of treason. May God grant that he yet be repaid for his crime, and soon, without a long delay! The man will get exactly what he deserves, I swear it!" {3331}

When he had lamented over his nephew, like a valiant lord, he summoned those of his doctors whom he trusted most and begged them to devote themselves to caring for his nephew. And they were not to lie or fail to tell him the truth, honestly and loyally, about anything they found wrong with Gawain. They replied that they would do so because, after the King, Gawain was the man to whom they owed their greatest loyalty and their most faithful service. "But now move back a little and give us room to do our work." The doctors did not pause for a moment but removed his clothing, bathed his wounds in warm water, and examined him carefully. After they had checked him over thoroughly, they told him: "Have no fear, dear lord, and rest assured that you will be well again within a month." {3355}

When Sir Gawain heard this, he exclaimed: "May God be praised! For once again I will be able to ride out bearing arms. Now go and reassure the King, who feels such grief in his heart." {3361}

And so they did, and when the news reached the court, everyone was so happy that never before had anyone ever seen sorrow change so quickly into boundless joy. But the doctors insisted that the chamber be kept in peace and quiet, and the entire lodgings as well. They informed the King that it was time for the company to leave, and that only two maidens should stay with Gawain and look after him, for he needed nothing else. {3372}

The King and the Queen left Sir Gawain, and everyone, great and small, went back to their quarters. The doctors returned to Gawain and took great pains with him, putting all their heart into the task. They worked so diligently that within the week the result of their labors was quite evident. By the start of the second week, Gawain was feeling so much better that he got up and began to walk around his lodgings, enjoying himself whenever he pleased; great joy welled up within his heart because of this, for he had feared he was going to die. {3385}

One day, the King came to see how he was doing, and on finding that Gawain was recovering so well, he felt great joy and said to him: "Dear nephew, I would very much like to know who did this to you." {3391}

"I don't know for certain, but when he thought he had killed me, he said that he knew for certain that the best luck had come to him that had ever befallen a knight. Very soon he would be King of the Isles and have his sweetheart—from whom came the lordship of that land—and the most beautiful woman in the world. But of all the things he said, what devastated me was the great joy he expressed when he thought I was dead. That hurts me even more than my wound does." {3407}

"Dear nephew, don't let that bother you; you will yet have your vengeance in full. Don't be concerned about anything but making a complete recovery, and don't give a moment's thought to anything else." {3412}

"Dear uncle," he replied, "I seldom give a thought to vengeance." {3413}

The Queen drew the King aside and said to him: "My lord, your nephew ought to be watched more closely now than before; if he starts thinking he is getting better, he will get up before he has fully recovered and depart in secret. For he is very angry and he will never be happy until he has redressed the offense committed against him. If he should chance to meet his enemy—at any time or place—and if they should fight each other, and if his wounds should open up, or if he should become overheated from exertion, he could easily die, and then you would hear some very sad news indeed." {3431}

"You speak the truth." The King called forth Sir Yvain and Girflet, Garahet and Gaheriet, Tor, Dodinel and Ellit, because he chanced to see them there before him, along with Caradoc Briebras, and he said to them: "My lords, I am making you Gawain's guard and, for the love of God, if it so happens that he should want to go anywhere, don't let him leave until you have informed me of it." {3442}

"Gladly, my lord." The King left the knights and bade farewell to his nephew, entrusting him to their protection. {3446}

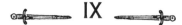# IX

Gawain Sets Out for The Isles

The doctors who had Sir Gawain in their care were so skilled that within a month he was feeling quite well again, for they had done everything they could to speed his recovery. Before the month was out, he realized that his health was fully restored, and because of this his heart was very joyful, and he felt quite robust and energetic. He said to himself that he could easily postpone his departure too long, and that he ought not to have delayed so long taking vengeance on the man who had so heartlessly left him for dead. But he didn't want to drop any hint of what he had in mind. {3463}

One day he had already spent a whole month recuperating, and the knights who were guarding him were no longer paying much attention to their task. It was a fine, warm morning, and there was a great deal of dew on the ground; Gawain got up before daybreak and noticed that no one else in the lodgings was yet up and about. He prodded a young lad who was lying at his feet and whispered to him to go quietly, fetch his arms, and bring them back to the foot of his bed. The lad was not slow to do as he was told. First Gawain put on a shirt made of samite; the lad helped him to lace on greaves of bright mail and then handed him a hauberk. He armed himself extremely well and did it so expertly that he was lacking nothing a knight requires. Then he told the lad to go and ready his white hunter and bring it into the garden. The lad did not fail to carry out his every command. Sir Gawain mounted his horse, put his shield around his neck, and took up his lance; when he was all ready, he told the boy what he planned to do. {3493}

The young lad replied that he would not dare go to the court or even stay behind, for he could not avoid certain death if the King ever found out that, although he was present when Gawain departed, he had failed to inform him of the fact. {3499}

"My lad," said Gawain, "no harm will come to you from this; you must go to a vavasor of my acquaintance and explain that I sent you to him. Tell him to mount up and go and tell my uncle that I am setting out to avenge myself, if I can, on the knight who dared to commit such a grave offense against me. He may have to wait a long time for my return. For never will I come back to court [. . .] until I am avenged, and not until I find the Knight of the Two Swords, whose reputation for chivalry has spread far and wide. He was once my squire, and I will bring him back to court with me if I can find him." {3518}

Sir Gawain then rode off, and the lad did not delay a moment longer than he could help. He went to the vavasor Gawain had told him about and reported everything. At once the vavasor saddled up, went to court, and delivered his message, repeating everything the young lad had said, just as Sir Gawain had ordered. And the King didn't even bother asking when he had left or where he had gone; he simply exclaimed: "May God be with him!" {3530}

Here I will leave off telling you about King Arthur, for now I must report on how Sir Gawain traveled, and never will I have you believe a lie. He journeyed for a good week, passing through many a thicket, many a predicament, and many an adversity. He found plenty of fortified castles, fine towns, and great cities where he often took lodgings. The story tells us nothing about what happened to him there, but he kept on going until he left Britain and entered a forest, traveling all day long without finding a castle or a fortress anywhere. It was already getting rather late, and he did not know which way to turn. That night he had to sleep in the beautiful forest, and his horse ate grass, for there were no oats or hay at hand; and he removed its bridle so that it could graze freely. {3555}

Right at the break of day, Sir Gawain got up, put his horse's bridle on, got into the saddle, and set out, for such lodgings were not much to his liking. He rode off, and having traveled at a leisurely pace until about the hour of tierce, he looked ahead and saw an open field in the distance. He kept on riding in that direction until he left the forest and entered the field; right in the middle of it he spotted a tree and the most beautiful mule you have ever seen. He quickly headed toward it, for he was sure that the mule couldn't possibly be there by itself; it must have been tethered to the tree by some lord or lady or damsel, who might give him some news. He made for it right away, and there he found a tall, silver-haired pilgrim sitting beside a spring. Gawain thought he looked very much like a gentleman, judging by appearances. The pilgrim had a lily-white cloth spread out before him, and on it he had placed a brightly gilded, finely enameled goblet, and he was just about to have dinner. When he saw Sir Gawain approaching, he stood up and exclaimed: "Welcome, dear lord! I have food here, all ready and waiting. Dismount, if you please, for I will be glad to offer you some." {3593}

"And I will gladly accept, with the greatest of thanks. Truly, I have great need of something to eat." {3596}

Then Sir Gawain dismounted, took off his gauntlets and his helmet, washed up, and took his seat. Then, to his great delight, he ate some cold chicken pâté and drank some red wine which the pilgrim had brought along in small casks; it was clear and sweet and beautiful. When they had eaten all they wanted—as you might expect of men dining at leisure—the pilgrim asked Gawain where he was from; and Gawain told him, for he did not want to hide anything from the man. {3609}

When the pilgrim heard that he was from Britain, he promptly inquired: "Please be so kind as to tell me where Sir Gawain is lying." {3612}

"Is lying?" he said. "Just what do you mean by that?" {3613}

And the pilgrim replied, "I mean: is dead and lying in the ground." {3614}

"You must be joking!" said Sir Gawain. "He isn't dead yet." {3616}

"Indeed he is; I know that for a fact." {3617}

"And just how do you know it, my lord? Tell me, how did this happen?" {3619}

"The man who killed him came and told me all about it soon afterward." {3620}

"Then truly he lied to you, for I saw Gawain safe and sound not even a day ago; and never was his health half so good any day in his life." {3625}

When the pilgrim heard the news that Sir Gawain told him, he grew black with anger and said: "And who might you be, you who have brought me this disturbing piece of news?" {3631}

When Sir Gawain heard that the pilgrim wanted to know his name, he told him that he was the very Gawain the man thought was dead. {3635}

On hearing this unsettling news, the pilgrim's face suddenly turned pale, and he fainted and fell over backward. Sir Gawain wondered why this had happened, and when the pilgrim recovered from his faint, he was so enraged and distressed that he could hardly speak. He declared: "Gawain, may God give you misfortune and great torment in your heart, for you have cast my life into sorrow for the rest of my days." {3647}

Sir Gawain had absolutely no idea what this was all about; he was astonished that the pilgrim was so enraged, and wondered why he was cursing him just because he wasn't dead, for he didn't think he had done him any wrong. And so he said: "I would certainly like to know why you are so angry with me." {3655}

"By my faith, I will not tell you!" {3656}

"By my head," he answered, "you will indeed!" {3657}

And the pilgrim, who couldn't and didn't dare move a muscle, answered immediately: "The man who is supposed to have killed you is my son, who is most dear to me. I have every right to be upset, for he was to become King of the Isles on account of his feat. Now the whole thing has turned into a farce, as far as I can see, for you are still quite alive and well. And I, who am a poor vavasor, might have lived with honor forever: but now I have absolutely nothing. In any case, I seriously doubt that you are the real Gawain. But tell me where were you going just now when you came across me?" {3673}

"I was looking for the man who told you he had killed me, and never will I take joy or repose until I avenge myself on him. What troubles me most is all the joy he expressed when he thought he had killed me in the way he did. I will take my vengeance for that if I should live so long, and if strength does not fail me." {3683}

"I'm not much troubled by that," the pilgrim replied, "for the road between here and there is very long, and there are so many dangerous pitfalls and perilous straits that you will never manage to get to your destination, however determined you may be. As for me, I will not put an end to my travels until I reach Britain and learn the truth about Gawain, and whether he is still alive." {3693}

"For the love of God," said Gawain, "tell me now where I might find shelter for the night, for I have great need of it." {3696}

"You are certainly right about that," the old man replied, "for from this moment on I would much rather you had been slain. And yet you ask me where you might find shelter for the night! Truly, if I knew of any place where shame would be done to you, where harm would befall you, or where you might encounter pain or misfortune, I would gladly tell you of it." {3706}

With these words they parted company and kept to the straightest roads they could find, as well they should have. Sir Gawain rode on with such resolve that he soon got out of the woods; he was very happy to come upon a house in a meadow, surrounded by a dilapidated palisade. He approached it, thinking that he might find shelter there, for he saw a bell tower and a chapel inside, and he was sure that people must be living there. {3720}

He went straight to the postern gate, where he saw a great hanging copper plate with a hammer suspended beside it. Sir Gawain took it in his hand, struck three blows on the plate, and a hermit, who had just said his vespers, came to the door. He was tall, robust, and gray haired, with scars on his face, and he appeared to be a gentleman. Gawain approached the gate without hesitation and said: "My lord, for the sake of charity, I ask you for shelter tonight such as God has granted you." {3736}

"If you find my home suitable, then you may certainly have lodgings for our Lord's sake." {3737}

"Dear sir, I am well satisfied with your offer, and I ask for nothing more." {3739}

The hermit saw how courteous he was and led him inside the enclosure. Gawain dismounted, and his host did his best to help him off with his armor. The hermit had a tall, dark-haired, black-skinned churl look after his horse. He led it into the stable, quickly removed its saddle and bridle, and rubbed down its back, first with some grass and then with his coat. The horse began to eat, and the hermit took Sir Gawain into his modest dwelling; Gawain sat down on a sheaf of hay, and then the good man asked him if he had eaten. He replied that he would be happy to eat if the hermit had any food. {3757}

The hermit had been a knight himself and knew just how difficult the life of a knight errant could be, since he had been one of them. He went and fetched a cold chicken pâté he had bought when someone gave him alms for the love of God. Then he took out a white tablecloth and invited Gawain to go and wash up. He washed and then sat down to eat, and the hermit cut the bread for him. And Sir Gawain ate all of the pâté and drank plenty of water with it—he didn't have to worry about getting drunk! {3771}

The good man looked at him and studied him very carefully; as he was staring at him, he pondered long and deep. The hermit thought to himself, from what he had been told, that there was no man who could possibly resemble Sir Gawain more than this one did. So he said: "My lord, do not be upset with me if I ask you who you are. For the man whom you resemble is of such great renown that I would very much like to know your name, and whether you are related to him." {3787}

Gawain replied: "Dear host, since you want me to tell you who I am, I will not hide my name from you. I am Gawain, the nephew of King Arthur." {3791}

And when he heard this astonishing news, the hermit lowered his head in anger. "Oh, God, now the great reward that my nephew was supposed to receive has slipped from his grasp. Not long ago he boasted that he had killed this worthy knight, and yet Gawain is still quite alive and well! My nephew is totally useless and has accomplished absolutely nothing!" Then he got up and strode out of the room, inflamed with anger and rage. {3801}

Then Sir Gawain went and lay down on a mattress stuffed with hay and dozed off. The hermit took note of this and said to his churl, "Come over here, and bring that axe with you!" He picked it up and came closer with it. And the hermit took hold of a stake and crept up on Sir Gawain, full of rage and malicious intent. And the churl was incredibly bristly and hairy and black. "Screw up your courage," the hermit said, "and don't let it fail you if you value your life! For even if there were a hundred men like us, we would not be able to hold out for long against him, because he would kill every one of us on the spot." {3819}

And the churl said: "I am not afraid of losing my nerve." And the two of them went to do evil to Sir Gawain. The hideous fellow got a powerful grip on the axe and lifted it up as high as he could. The hermit, who had provided Gawain with such fine hospitality, did the same with his stake and was just about to drive it home. Then it suddenly dawned on him that he was doing evil and he restrained himself, exclaiming: "No! I can't do it! I will not harm this gentleman sleeping here; I am a recluse and I would be damned for all eternity if I began to do evil once again. This is really none of my business and if my nephew is lying, then he is even more worthless than I thought! Does Sir Gawain deserve to die just because he is alive? I don't think there is a man in the world who does not admire him for his prowess and integrity." {3841}

"Get out of my way and let me at him!" said the churl. "He will be dead before you can move a muscle." {3844}

"No, you stand aside! I've changed my mind; he will not have any more abuse from us, or anything worse than what we've already done to him." {3847}

The churl drew back because his lord had ordered him to. Sir Gawain had heard everything perfectly, and when he realized that they had decided not to do him any further harm, he fell asleep and the two went away. The hermit brought out a mantle and spread it very gently over his guest; he covered him and then departed, and the baron slumbered as long as the night lasted; and even though it was a summer's night, it was not exactly a short one for Gawain. {3862}

In the morning at daybreak Sir Gawain donned his armor, and the churl told him that the saddle and bridle had already been put on his horse. He would have done Gawain great harm the night before, if his master had allowed him to. Sir Gawain mounted up and took leave of his host; he rode all alone through the woods without stopping until the hour of prime. He looked ahead and saw a young lad in a great hurry riding a hunter, the grandest one he had seen in a long time. Sir Gawain called out to him and said: "Welcome, my boy!" {3878}

Ashamed, and wondering why the knight had greeted him first, the young lad replied at once: "My lord, may you have good fortune!" {3883}

"Young man," he said, "where are you going in such haste today?" {3885}

"My lord," he said, "I have been sent with a message for the hermit who lives over there. One of his relatives sent me, a man not doing too badly for himself these days. His name is King Brien of the Isles, and at this very moment he is the most joyful man you can imagine." {3891}

"What's this?" said Sir Gawain. "King Brien? I've never heard of him before." {3893}

"You speak the truth, my lord. I was mistaken; he isn't yet a king. But he has an agreement with his sweetheart according to which he will be king before long, because he killed Sir Gawain—so he tells her—and she believes him without question." {3899}

When Sir Gawain heard that Brien would soon be king, he was greatly upset, angered, and outraged. He declared that if misfortune did not befall him, and if he encountered no obstacles on his way, he would get to the Isles before Brien could marry his sweetheart, and he would put a stop to the wedding. {3907}

The young lad continued: "My lord, every last lady, knight, and beautiful damsel from here to the forest of Moriers who hears this news will do his best to be there. For no one who is not from the Isles could ever hope to see such a spectacle again. And anyone who attends the coronation will have plenty of opportunity to see her there for sure; everything has been arranged. And never before has anyone seen such a beautiful or such a worthy young lady, one so rich and so highly esteemed, or one so well acquainted with the manners and morals befitting a woman. And that is why so many people will be present that no one could ever hope to count them. The Knight of the Two Swords will be there, he who was so successful at the great court of Cardueil, where so many knights tried to unfasten the sword and failed. If you have heard anything at all about this event, and if it pleased you to attend, you couldn't possibly find yourself in better company. Do not consider me presumptuous, but I know the way to the Isles very well, and if you were willing to wait here a while till I return, I would undertake to serve you and be your faithful guide." {3939}

When Sir Gawain learned that the Knight of the Two Swords would be attending the coronation, he wanted to go too, and when he heard that the young lad would act as his guide, he decided to wait for him. He said: "My boy, go and see the hermit then, and do not tarry; I will stay here and wait for you." {3947}

"Thank you, dear lord," the lad replied, and then he set out, for he was eager to return promptly. He went to the hermit's house and delivered his message, carrying out the task he had been assigned. Then he took his leave of the hermit, departed immediately, and returned to find Sir Gawain, who had been waiting for him all alone. {3957}

When Sir Gawain saw him coming back, he was very happy. The boy said to him: "Now give me your shield and your lance and I will carry them and lead you to your destination by a very good and direct route." {3963}

Gawain handed them to him, and the lad, who knew the way, rode ahead steadfastly with Sir Gawain following behind. They rode on until the sun was getting low in the sky; it was past the hour of nones, and they hadn't met a soul anywhere in the forest. Sir Gawain thought it was getting rather late, so he said: "Lad, where in the world is this path leading us? Will it take us to some place of shelter?" {3975}

"Yes, my lord, we have only to cover two more leagues and we will be out of the forest. Then we will see a most beautiful and impressive castle, surrounded by a hedged enclosure. It belongs to a relative of my lord's; he will do you great honor there tonight, for I do believe that the best lady any lord could ever have as a wife dwells in that place." {3985}

And with that the conversation ended. They rode on until they came out of the forest, and then they saw the castle the boy had told him about. "Now, my lord, just keep riding at a leisurely pace," the lad said, "and I will go on ahead and arrange for the lodgings; that is the courteous thing to do, for in that way we won't surprise the lady of the house by our arrival." {3995}

"You are right; it is fitting and courteous that you go on ahead. Now give me my shield, then go and make the arrangements." {3999}

The lad gave him his shield and departed, reaching the castle before long. He found the lady at home, greeted her, and asked where the lord was. She replied that she knew nothing of his whereabouts, for he hadn't told her a thing about his departure or return. {4007}

"My lady, have the lodgings prepared as well as you possibly can," the young lad said, "for I know that you will have a very worthy man as your guest tonight. He is going to attend my lord's coronation; that I can tell you for a fact." {4013}

The lady answered: "He is most welcome, dear friend! I can assure you that he will receive hospitality here and have everything he needs." {4017}

Just then Sir Gawain entered the domain, and when the lady saw him coming, she went out to meet him. As soon as she saw him, she said: "Welcome, dear lord!" and he dismounted. {4022}

"And may you have good fortune, my lady," he replied, striding up quickly to embrace her. The lady helped him remove his armor and gave him a mantle to wear. {4028}

Then they sat down to eat, and they enjoyed more than six different courses, generously served and all quite to their liking; after dinner they washed up and sat down to enjoy themselves until it was time to go to bed. When the beds were made ready, Sir Gawain retired and slept soundly until dawn. {4037}

As soon as he saw the morning light, he got up and put his armor on. The young lad, who strove to serve him to the best of his ability, had brought him his horse fully equipped and harnessed. He mounted it and took his leave of the lady, instructing the lad to ride on ahead. The boy set out briskly, and Gawain rode along behind him at a comfortable and leisurely pace. Just as he was leaving, he encountered the man who was lord of the castle, in the company of ten other knights. As soon as he saw Sir Gawain he greeted him, and Sir Gawain returned the greeting to the castellan and his companions, and then they went on their separate ways. {4058}

The lord reached his residence, and when he arrived he couldn't understand why his wife was up so early. She came out to meet him and exclaimed: "Welcome home, my lord." {4063}

"My lady," he asked, "why is it you are up so early?" {4065}

"Perhaps," she replied, "you encountered a knight not far from here. He slept here last night, and I don't believe I've ever seen a more handsome man. I offered him generous hospitality and showed him honor with everything I was able to provide." {4070}

"And what was his name?" {4071}

"Truly, I do not know, but he certainly seemed to be a worthy gentleman." {4073}

"My lady, never has it happened that any knight ever slept in any lodgings without first being asked his name and his rank." {4077}

"There's not much I can do about it now," she said. "I didn't even think to ask." {4079}

"Then you have acted most imprudently." {4080}

The castellan was quite upset at the fact that a knight had slept in his castle without his knowing the man's identity. At once he had his armor brought in, outfitted himself quickly, and set out on his way. He was eager to meet his guest and find out just who he was. As many as ten valiant knights went along with him, but none of them was carrying more than a lance and shield. The castellan rode on ahead, pursuing Sir Gawain vigorously until he caught up with him. {4095}

When Sir Gawain saw him approaching, he quickly reined in his horse, which wasn't exactly limping along. His pursuer asked him who he was and what his name was. And he replied: "Since you want to know, you will hear the whole truth, for never have I concealed my name. I am Gawain, the nephew of King Arthur." {4106}

When the castellan heard these words, he grew furious and the blood drained from his face. When he realized that this was Sir Gawain—whom Brien, his dear cousin and friend was supposed to have killed, and was for that reason shortly to be crowned king—he was stunned and speechless. At length, he managed to say: "Gawain, may the Lord God who made you bring you shame and misfortune! Your arrogant acts have humbled and disgraced many a gentlemen and many a knight; but as far as I can see, you've gone too far this time! You are a dead man right where you stand, and nothing can possibly save you!" {4123}

When Sir Gawain saw that the castellan hated him more than anyone in the world, he replied in a courteous tone: "My lord, if I knew what wrong I had done you, I would quickly make amends." {4129}

"I will take care of that myself. You are a dead man! I challenge you to battle!" {4131}

"And as for me, I won't offer you any assurances, for I see that you are no friend of mine." {4133}

They drew back and took up their positions, spurred their horses, and with their long, stout lances struck each other mighty blows to the shields. But both lances did not shatter, only the castellan's did. And so it happened that Sir Gawain did not fail in his jousting; he struck the castellan square on the boss of his shield, knocking the man and his horse down in a heap on the ground, breaking his arm and his collarbone. Gawain turned aside and left him lying there, for he did not want to waste any more time. The men who were following their lord continued spurring on their steeds, but when they saw that he had fallen to the ground they dismounted and raised a great lament; they thought for certain they had lost their lord and that he had been slain. He had indeed been badly hurt, and he said to them: "My lords, I am severely injured; I know for sure that my arm is broken, and my collarbone as well." {4159}

When they heard these words, they were somewhat relieved and went for their horses, swearing that this harm would soon return to strike the man who had dealt so harshly with their lord. But before they could leave, the castellan called out after them, saying: "My lords, do not trouble yourselves to pursue him; it's no use. For no matter how many of you there were, you would all be killed before long. I don't think there is a better man in the world than he, and he is well armed. You could not prevail against him, so just forget it. Instead, make me a litter and carry me home." They did so right away, and carried him off, all of them weeping profusely. {4180}

The Adventure at Chastel du Port

So that is what happened to the castellan, and Sir Gawain went back to the lad, who was riding on ahead, just as he had ordered him to. When Gawain handed him his shield and his lance, the boy saw the newly made dent. The leather straps and the wooden slats of the shield were also broken, and he thought to himself that he had not seen those holes the day before, but he pretended not to notice anything. So they rode along without stopping until they left the forest. It was already past the hour of prime when Sir Gawain came upon a very deep river, which was at least a bowshot wide. On the opposite bank stood a beautiful, strategically situated castle with lofty walls and towers made of hard stones and mortar; all around it there were great moats full of water, very wide and deep, and it was just as solid as you could imagine because of its walls and its massive foundations. Sir Gawain asked what the name of this fair castle was and who it belonged to. The lad told him that it was called Chastel du Port and that its master was known as the Lord of Chastel du Port. He had endured such a ruinous war that of his four castles, all that remained to him was the one they saw before them. If they could only pass through his domain, they would shorten their journey by a good four days. {4221}

"We will go and ask the lord what he has to say," said Sir Gawain. "God willing, he will not be so churlish as to deny us his permission." {4225}

With that they rode off at top speed toward the castle. They found it very fair and imposing, but the surrounding lands were devastated, and all the houses thereabouts were burned out and lying in ruins. They came to a great tower where they found a gate, and through that gate they entered the town. They found the streets most attractive and lined with noble mansions; every roof was covered with tile or lead; no one had ever seen such beautiful dwellings within such a fine fortress from here to Sicily. You may be sure that there were many different kinds of people inside the town. The two men followed the road until they reached the main entrance in the palisaded stone walls that surrounded the palace, and they saw broad moats full of water and sharp, pointed stakes. They crossed the drawbridge and entered the courtyard; inside they found many dwellings. There was a small garden in the courtyard, and inside it stood a young elm tree. The garden was enclosed by a low wall, and the lord of the castle was sitting inside it. There was no one with him but his daughter and his wife, who was of a beauty greatly to be admired in a woman of her age; she was very gracious and well bred and about fifty years old. The lord was tall and handsome, and he must have been at least sixty years of age. He was nobly dressed in precious vermilion scarlet, of that you may be sure. {4265}

Their daughter, who was incredibly beautiful, just as Nature had created her, was sitting in front of her parents. She was no more than seventeen years old—tall, innocent, charming, and modest—and she was reading from a romance of Troy. She was wearing a delicate linen dress and a fine white shift, and she was very attractively put together, as if Nature had brought all her arts to the task. She was tiny and elegant at the waist; her thighs were shapely, her hips slim and attractive, and her breasts nicely filled out. It was a delight to see those little breasts jutting out, so firm and pointy as they pressed up against her dress; her throat and her body were whiter than new-fallen snow. There wasn't a wrinkle or a blemish on her long, slender neck. She had long, curly hair; so fine was its color that the purest gold with which silver goblets are gilded would seem pale by comparison. She was wearing a most becoming garland of flowers which kept her hair in place. Her forehead was full and broad, without a single line. Her laughing blue-gray eyes were wide and bright and attractive enough to please even the most discriminating. She had a long, straight, turned-up nose that was very attractive; her mouth was small, her lips dark red and full; and she was absolutely stunning when she smiled a little, for her lips greatly enhanced her beauty. Her complexion was so fresh that both rose and lily suffered by comparison. Her white teeth were like polished ivory, and evenly spaced, just as Nature had intended. {4311}

Never before had Sir Gawain laid eyes on such a beautiful creature! He was already burning with the fire of love; as he gazed at her, he thought to himself that he had never seen three women so beautiful since the day he was born. And if anyone could have taken all of their beauties and combined them in one woman, still she would not have been quite so beautiful as that young lady was. Gawain had already set his whole heart on having her; as a matter of fact, he drew closer, for it seemed like the right thing to do, and said: "May God protect you one and all, and grant you your every wish." {4327}

The lord, the lady, and the damsel were quite astonished, for it had been a long time since they had heard of any young lord courageous enough to pass their way. However, the lord was not so surprised, rude, or ill mannered as not to return the greeting courteously. Rather, he exclaimed: "Welcome to you, dear lord! Should it please you to stay with us, you may be sure that lodgings are ready and waiting, both clean and comfortable. For we will offer you hospitality so good and so fine—the very best we possibly can—and indeed you will have a great deal more than that." {4343}

Sir Gawain replied: "Dear kind lord, my hearty thanks. I would not be averse to taking lodgings here, but please understand that I cannot pause or remain for long. I have undertaken a mission of great importance. I am a knight from a foreign land, the Kingdom of Logres. I have traveled here seeking to redress an offense, and I pray you—should you be so kind—to grant me passage through your land, for I am absolutely determined to reach my destination. I know that I may not cross except at your command." {4357}

And when the castellan understood that Gawain was asking for permission to travel through his domain, he began to ponder the matter seriously, his head bowed in thought. Then he started to cry and tears fell from his eyes. When his wife and daughter saw him weeping, they too were deeply moved and began to sob uncontrollably. Sir Gawain was quite bewildered when he saw them crying simply because he had asked the lord's permission to pass through his land. He thought about it for a moment, but couldn't see what the problem was. He was troubled for the young lady's sake; he was already so smitten by her that he had set his heart on winning her, absolutely and without reservation. Then he approached the castellan and spoke to him, in a kindly and compassionate voice: "Dear lord, what can be done about this? I asked you for safe passage and I haven't done you any harm that I know of, yet you are weeping and delaying my progress; why is it that you don't even want to give me an answer? May God Almighty confound the man who caused you this distress! If anyone has brought you any harm or shame which I could remedy, I would never ask for respite until I succeeded in avenging you, using whatever strength I might have; indeed, I would do so gladly." {4393}

"Great thanks, sir knight, may God grant you both joy and honor! I will tell you why I am weeping, for I have every reason to do so. I used to be comfortable, rich, and powerful; I lacked for absolutely nothing. I had four rich castles, strong and well fortified with ramparts, located within five or six leagues of here, and I didn't think I had a thing to fear. I know for a fact that I was loved by all my people. From my wife, however, I had no heir except this maiden. In all the world I do not think there is anyone so beautiful or so charming, and her wisdom far exceeds her beauty, which is clearly without equal. Gernemant of Northumberland heard so much talk about my daughter's beauty that he sent me messages over and over again, asking me to give her to him in marriage. I was in complete agreement that he should take her as his wife, but she said she would not have him for anything in the world. {4421}

"When I saw that she was opposed to the idea, I no longer wanted to keep my promise to Gernemant, for I love no one as much as her, so I let the matter be. He took this as a great insult, as an act of contempt and outrage, for he is a man of higher rank than I. And right away he declared war on me, devastating my land and the most beautiful of my manor houses, so that of my four castles only this one now remains to me, and I hold it at his pleasure. For he has given me a truce [. . .] according to which he will allow me one year, during which time he will do me no more harm than he has already done, on the following conditions: if my daughter had some relative or friend who held her so dear that he would dare take up arms against Gernemant and defeat him in battle, then he would return to me everything he has taken away. {4445}

"But if she were unable to find such a man within the year, then I would surrender my castle to him and hand over my daughter, to do with her as he pleases. He is threatening to have all his vilest stable boys sleep with her. My daughter and I have promised to accept these terms. Now there is only a week left before the year is out, and a great many worthy and valiant knights have come here. I feel the greatest sorrow and pity for them because they came here for my daughter's sake and took up the challenge, like the men of great worth they were—but every last one of them was defeated and killed. Now only one week of the truce remains between the two of us." {4464}

When Sir Gawain heard of this outrage, all the blood drained from his face. He felt compassion and turned to look at the young lady on whose account all this had happened, the maiden who had captured his affections. His courage swelled up within his breast, and he declared: "Dear lord, it grieves me immensely to know that such great shame is being done to you. As for me, I can promise you that if your daughter saw fit to grant me her love, I would do battle for you and for her right on the spot. Gernemant has wrongfully dispossessed you, just as you have told me." {4480}

"That is true, dear kind lord, and I thank you sincerely for saying so. But it would be a great pity and a shame if you went ahead—for you seem to be such a worthy man—and if you did battle with him and if it turned out that he slew you." {4487}

"Don't even think about that," he replied. "Gernemant wouldn't be able to hold his own! God is powerful, and justice is on my side, and up till now He has always protected me from harm." {4491}

The maiden looked at her father and then at her mother; she knew that the time was near when they would lose all they had left—little enough, as compared with what they had already lost—and she thought back on everything they used to have. She felt anguish and pity in her heart because her parents had been totally dispossessed on her account and their honor and their lands had been completely ravaged; she thought that now she ought to do something for them. And the matter couldn't come to a worse conclusion, and she couldn't possibly end up worse off than if she had to give her love to Gernemant. For if Gernemant defeated Gawain, she would be left in exactly the same situation as before; but if he killed Gernemant, then she would fare much better and he would have won her heart completely. She could not help but feel love for this knight right then and from that moment on. She gazed at him attentively, for she could not recall ever having seen a knight so well armed or one who looked more worthy, judging by his physical appearance. She said, "My lord, if you are able to defeat Gernemant in combat and cut off his head, I will grant you everything without delay; I will be your sweetheart without reservation, offering you everything you could possibly desire." {4527}

And Gawain, who had just heard exactly what he wanted to hear, could not help but rejoice at these welcome words; for the young lady had said that she would become his sweetheart, if only he could manage to take Gernemant's life. Full of joy, he dismounted and thanked her, saying: "Young lady, now take off my helmet and grant me your love with a kiss. I will be all the more valiant in combat when I think of this." [. . .] {4542}

"That will I do most willingly." Thereupon she removed his helmet, lowered his ventail, and took off his coiffe so that she could get a good look at him. She thought that she had never before seen any man with features so fine; and she thought that he surpassed all men in the world for beauty. He tipped her chin up most gently and kissed her, as a pledge that she was becoming his sweetheart. She did not resist him at all but returned the kiss gladly. Brimming with joy and happiness, Sir Gawain said to her: "Young lady, now lace up my cap for me once again and put my helmet back on my head." {4561}

She did so, and he mounted his horse, asking the lord at once: "Dear lord, how will Gernemant know that I want to fight with him today? For I don't know where to find him." {4567}

"My lord," he replied, "you will soon have him within your grasp. As you are riding through those fields over there, you will see an outcropping of rock where Gernemant built a fortress some time ago, in order to dominate this castle. Before you have gone very far on your way, you will come upon a meadow surrounded by a broad, deep moat. In the middle of it there is a beautiful tree, and under the tree you will find a marble pillar, and by that pillar there is a horn of ivory, ringed with several bands of gold, suspended by a silver chain. As soon as you get there, put the horn to your lips and blow on it, then Gernemant will know for certain that he must do battle with some knight, for that is the horn's only purpose." {4588}

In this way the Lord of Chastel du Port gave Sir Gawain instructions about the path of life or death. Gawain took leave of them all and asked his squire to wait with this noble company until he learned how things turned out. The lad did not try to argue with him, and Sir Gawain departed right away, as you would expect of a man eager to reach the meadow and find the horn. {4599}

He had not gone very far when he came upon the precious horn; then, as quickly as he could, he picked it up and put it to his lips, for the plight of the family touched his heart deeply. He blew on it so hard that he startled everyone for a good two leagues around. Then Gernemant knew that he was being summoned. He had just finished dinner and had sat down to play chess with a knight; never before had he heard the sound of the horn so clear or so forceful. He laughed a vile, contemptuous laugh and exclaimed: "Some knight has challenged me to combat; bring me my arms! He may consider himself a complete idiot for seeking to do battle with me." {4619}

A servant promptly brought him his arms, and he prepared himself for combat. Sir Gawain sounded the horn once again, more clearly than before, causing the castle and all the countryside to tremble. "Listen to how that knight is challenging me to war; hear how he is goading me on!" said Gernemant. "He is a very daring man, but I think I will get there in time." {4629}

Then they all helped him on with his armor, for he did his best to be quick about it; they brought him a great Spanish horse covered with a precious Greek silk, and he mounted without difficulty. Why should I make a longer story of it? He rode until he reached the battlefield and found Sir Gawain waiting for him in the center of the meadow. He went right up to him and said: "You have been calling for me quite a lot with that horn! Vassal, you hardly gave me enough time to put on my helmet. You couldn't have done anything more foolhardy, I do believe!" {4645}

"Do not be surprised," he said, "if I have put you under pressure. For you have wrongfully dispossessed the Lord of Chastel du Port, and without just cause, all on account of his daughter, who would not have you as her husband. I am greatly distressed when a knight, who ought to be a worthy man, commits such an offense. And that is why I should like to ask you to make peace with him, to restore his land, and to renounce all claim to his daughter." {4657}

"You have spoken stupid nonsense, and you will be considered an absolute fool for having come here on such a mission. You have hardly any brain in your head if you want to fight with me. I will do to you just what I've done with all the others who came to do battle with me: all of them met a bitter end. Just look over there and you will see their forty-four heads impaled on those stakes." {4667}

"So help me God, cruel lord, you ought to be burned alive! God can easily protect me from such a fate if He wishes to," said Sir Gawain. "And you may be sure that I have come here for just one reason: to punish you. Be on your guard, for I challenge you to battle!" {4674}

After they had exchanged words in this manner, they drew back and directed their horses at each other. They positioned their shields in front of their chests and charged at one another. They set their lances on the fewters and secured them under their arms; as soon as they collided, both lances broke into splinters. The horses were running full force and they crashed into each other, chest to chest, so they fell to the ground in a heap immediately, all four of them. {4687}

The vassals lay there beneath their horses for quite a while, totally stunned, but then they leapt quickly to their feet, removed their shields from their necks, and bound their left hands with leather straps. Then Sir Gawain went at his opponent with his bare sword, and Gernemant did the same to him. The two of them fought on savagely until the hour of nones had passed. Then Sir Gawain, thinking of his sweetheart, lunged at Gernemant, pressing him as hard as he possibly could. He drove him back, taking ground from him like a man eager to defeat his opponent. Moving in close, Gawain struck him with his fist and the pommel of his sword, so violently that Gernemant staggered; then, taking him by surprise, Gawain brought the man to his knees and knocked the legs out from under him so that he fell flat on the ground. {4709}

Gawain jumped on top of him, seized him by the straps of his helmet, tore it off of his head, ripped off his ventail, and cried: "Knight! You were so arrogant just a while ago; but now you are a dead man unless you beg for mercy. And these are the terms: you will become a prisoner of the beautiful maiden's father, and you will put an end to the quarrel through which you have ravaged his land." {4718}

Gernemant replied: "May God never watch over me if I become that man's prisoner." {4721}

"Then, by my faith, I will cut off your head and impale it on a stake, for I must do with yours exactly what you said you would do with mine just now." {4726}

"Since I have been defeated, I no longer care what happens to me: do whatever you like." {4729}

At once Sir Gawain cut off his head and impaled it on the stake, just as Gernemant had said he would do to him when he was hoping to round out the count of forty-five; then Gawain got back on his horse and slung the horn around his neck. He didn't stay there a moment longer but turned around and headed back to the castle, bursting with joy and happiness. {4738}

And so Gernemant was slain. There was great jubilation at the court, where the lord, his daughter, and his people had watched the battle from start to finish; they had seen absolutely everything. From the courtyard they had watched Sir Gawain as he hastened back to the castle. They felt the greatest joy they had ever known, and rightly so; they could think of nothing else that could have possibly brought them such happiness. For they had been utterly without hope, but now they were on top of the world. {4753}

They went down from the castle at once; not a soul—lord or lady—who had any sense or wisdom remained inside. They went out in a great procession to greet Sir Gawain. He saw the castellan and his daughter coming to meet him, hand in hand. They all put on the greatest display of jubilation that anyone had ever seen or heard. "Welcome back, dear lord," they said; "you have delivered us from affliction, distress, and servitude. Gernemant had dispossessed us all, but now you have slain him. Blessèd be the hour when you were born, my lord, and blessings upon you as well!" {4771}

He removed his helmet, dismounted, and embraced the lord and then his daughter, whom he kissed as well. Do not think that what he did was at all displeasing to the maiden; she was just as eager to let him kiss her as he was to do it. It was most pleasing and welcome to her, and they kept very close to one another until they reached the palace, celebrating as they went. They removed his armor and brought him hot water, and he washed his hands, his face, and neck. The maiden fetched the finest white hose and shirt that anyone could imagine and brought them for him to put on. The lord had him given a robe of blue Tyrian silk decorated with roses fashioned entirely from gold thread, and a coat and a mantle lined with ermine and trimmed with dense black sable, tailored a little short to fit him better. For a finishing touch, the maiden—totally attentive to his needs—gave him a costly belt adorned with gold and gems; he took it, along with a gold clasp with which he fastened his coat. Taking care not to overlook a thing, she put a towel around his shoulders and combed his hair. Although he gave not the slightest hint with his eyes, he was gazing at her constantly, and he kissed her nine or ten times as she combed. Then she straightened his part and put a cap on his head. And when he was finely groomed like this, he was so handsome—as everyone agreed—that never before had they seen anyone quite so attractive; indeed, no one ever had! {4815}

The father said to his daughter: "You have been most attentive to his needs, my beauty. No matter who may envy you or shed tears or suffer pangs of jealousy, now you are the sweetheart of the finest and the fairest knight alive. Truly, God has not forgotten us, for He has delivered us from affliction!" {4823}

"My lord, may God, the source of all things good, be praised for that!" As they were engaged in this conversation, servants went about setting up the tables, since it was almost time to eat. They seated Sir Gawain at the table; the lord placed the maiden directly across from him so that he could see her better and then took his place between his wife and Sir Gawain. The servants served the meal at once, with the greatest of skill. That made him happy, but he could not manage to control his eyes; he just couldn't keep from gazing at the young lady. And as much as he tried to restrain himself, he got so flustered and confused that he all but forgot he was sitting at a table eating dinner. And many a time he took her by the chin and kissed her, no matter who was watching, and everyone was quite delighted at this. {4847}

When they had finished eating, chamberlains cleared the tables and put them away, and then they all washed up. But Sir Gawain and his sweetheart did not linger there. Instead they went off into a chamber where they kissed and cuddled a great deal, you may be sure, and they talked about anything they liked, be it wise or frivolous, until it was time to go to bed. {4858}

The lady, who was a noble and courteous person, had had a bed made up in a chamber. She came in and said to Sir Gawain: "Dear sweet lord, you may retire whenever you wish. You need only give the order and all will be in readiness, for these two lads will stay with you and provide you with everything you need. Meanwhile my daughter and I will go back to the hall, and when all these people have left, we will return." {4871}

"My lady," he said, "I thank you very much; that is indeed a noble promise!" Then the daughter and her mother the hostess left, but the lads stayed behind and both of them took great pains to serve him, helping him to prepare for bed; then they too quickly left the room and went away. It wasn't long before the chatelaine and Sir Gawain's sweetheart emerged from a little chamber and went straight to the bed where Gawain was resting. The maiden was wearing a white shift and nothing else, and around her head she had tied the cord of her mantle, all nice and snug. {4887}

The lady gently nudged Sir Gawain and said: "My lord, I have brought you your sweetheart, and I do not think that you could ever be more grateful to me for any other delight. I am going now and will leave her with you: so do with her as you please. And, I implore you, do not let her get up from bed in the same state as she lies down." {4897}

"Great thanks, my lady. She will have nothing from me that might displease her. May God grant that I be even more deserving in her eyes tonight, and in yours, as much as you could possibly hope for; and may He grant me long life and watch over me." With that, the lady departed without any fuss or bother and pulled the door shut behind her. {4906}

The lovers were left all alone in the room and didn't have a thing on their minds, except for one. For their hearts were perfectly attuned to give each other solace. Gawain took her in his arms and had her remove her shift. Then he took all her clothing and dropped it on the floor. Then he sat up, looked her all up and down, and saw that she was even more beautiful naked than dressed in her finest apparel; he declared that she was the most beautiful creature he had ever laid eyes on. Then he picked up the shift, covered her with it once again, and embraced her. I do not believe that she felt any less joy than he did; he kissed her eyes and her lips, and he simply couldn't get enough of kissing and hugging. {4928}

They carried on with these delights until it was close to midnight, but they never did anything more. He was not in any mood to rest; instead, he was eager to bring the matter to a conclusion. He thought to himself that the time was right to go a little further. With that he drew a bit closer, for he couldn't restrain himself any longer; like a man who simply cannot hold back, he was just about to do it to her. {4939}

But then she began to cry uncontrollably, so that her face was all bathed in tears. Sir Gawain was quite astonished at this, as well he might be. For just a moment ago he thought that he was going to give her joy and solace to her heart's content, and now she was all in tears, and that certainly didn't make her look more appealing. He lay down beside her once again and said: "What is it, my sweet friend? Let me assure you that I've never been so surprised at anything in all my life. I thought that you loved me more than anyone else in the world, and that nothing could possibly come between us. Has all that good will now suddenly vanished?" {4956}

"Ah, my sweet love, I never intended any harm. There is no one I love as much as you, I swear; you need have no doubt about that." {4961}

"Tell me then, sweetheart, why is it you are crying so?" {4963}

"I will be glad to tell you. When you were lying on me just now, I happened to remember some news of King Arthur which reached this land not long ago. There is not now and never has there been a king so valiant in all the world; and he had a nephew so refined that—for courtesy, beauty, and chivalry—he outshone all other knights alive; and all the knights that ever there may be do not have as many fine qualities as he. I heard so much said about him here, young as I was—I wasn't yet fifteen years old—that I fell in love with him. And I vowed that even if I had to keep my virginity forever—no matter how often men might ask for me in marriage, however high their rank—no one would ever have my maidenhood but Sir Gawain; such was his name, I do believe. But now my joy has vanished, for news has spread throughout this land that Brien, who is soon to marry the Lady of the Isles, has slain him. And so my heart languishes in great sorrow, and never again will I know joy. All this came to my mind just now when you wanted to lie with me, and because of that I could not help but cry. It would certainly have been astonishing if my heart did not feel compassion on his account! If I weep because of it, that is my only consolation. Still, since Gawain is dead, I love you more than any man alive." {5001}

When she had finished saying these words, the fire of love flared up in Sir Gawain much more urgently than before. For love of her, he now ached with still more passion, since she had been crying out of love for him. "Then, dear heart," he said, "be grateful to me, for I bring you news that should set your mind at ease: Gawain, the nephew of King Arthur, is still alive and well. I saw him just a short while ago." {5013}

When the young lady heard that Sir Gawain was still alive, she was overjoyed, and it seemed to her that now she had everything she wanted [. . .] and that nothing could ever trouble her heart again. Then she said: "Dear lord, who are you, you who have brought me such news? How do you know he is alive? And tell me your name right away, you who claim all this to be true." {5025}

When he saw that she wanted to know his name, he felt great joy and said: "As God is my witness, I am the very Gawain of whom you speak." {5029}

"Hah!" said the maiden. "You won't get anywhere with that; it won't do you one bit of good. So help me God, no one but Gawain will ever have my virginity, for I have promised it to him in my heart." {5034}

"Please believe me when I tell you that I am really Gawain." {5035}

"There's no use, I won't believe a word you say." {5037}

"My sweet, there's nothing more I can say or do," he replied. "How is it that you won't take me at my word?" {5039}

"I can tell you flatly," she replied, "that I will not believe any man, not until I am at the court of the King who is renowned throughout the world, and not before I have asked him whether you are truly Gawain. I will set out for the court tomorrow; I will wait no longer, because I don't want to delay resolving this matter." {5047}

"Since things can't be any other way," he said, "so be it! But whatever the outcome, I implore you, once you find out for sure that Gawain is still alive, do not set your heart on loving any other man." {5053}

"I would not do so under any circumstances," she said. "I would rather die." {5055}

Gawain was greatly troubled about the bliss that was eluding him, so he said: "Maiden, since that's the way things are, and since it does not please you to do my will, then give me just a single kiss." {5060}

"I most certainly will not! I intend to save both my maidenhood and my lips for the man who has touched my heart. God willing, I will never allow a knight even to touch my lips until I find the man for whom I am suffering such agony and whom I so desire to see. He will have both my body and my mind, to do with as he pleases. Still, to tell the truth, I want you to know that I love no man more than you—except for the King's nephew—for you have rescued me and delivered me from great shame." {5077}

"Since the matter is that important to you," said Sir Gawain, "I will not mistreat you or offend you in any way." Then the maiden donned her shift, took her mantle, and left, waiting not a moment longer; so he had no more delight from her, and she went away to lie in her own bed. {5086}

XI

Gawain, Brien, and the Knight

Sir Gawain was left all alone in the room, pensive, distraught, and exasperated; he tossed and turned all night long, bothered and agitated. And he was entitled to be upset, considering the joy he had lost. He tossed and turned and could not get to sleep, although he finally managed to, with the greatest of difficulty. When morning came, before the sun was fully up, he awoke, for that had always been his custom. He looked around the room and saw two young lads sleeping there; he called out to them, and they came over to help him get up, and he arose without wasting any time about it. The lord and lady came in and asked him: "My lord, why is it you are up so early? Is there some reason for this?" {5108}

"May God grant you a blessèd day! I cannot stay here with you any longer, that is certain, and I cannot postpone my departure; rather, I have the most pressing need to travel that I have ever felt. But if I were able to remain here, I would be extremely happy to do so." {5115}

"Ah, dear lord, I would never have thought that you could so easily abandon my daughter and your sweetheart," said the lord, "and us whom you have so recently rescued and delivered from ruin and servitude and restored to our rightful heritage; you have given us back absolutely everything. And now we are losing you irretrievably, and all our prayers are to no avail." {5125}

"I cannot stay here for any reason, but must make haste to leave; have my arms brought in at once." And then the lads did as they were told. He put on his armor without wasting any time, and when he was ready he mounted up, gave his shield to his squire, and took his leave. Then he departed, waiting no longer, and the two of them rode away. {5135}

The young lady went to her father and declared: "Dear sweet lord, do not contradict me, but I must do my best to go to King Arthur's court, even if it causes me grief. For the longer I stay here, the greater will be my distress." {5143}

Not wanting to do anything which might displease her in any way, he replied at once: "My sweet daughter, I only want things to turn out as you would wish." {5147}

She put on a dress with a purple and black train highlighted with delicate gold embroidery, very finely fashioned and trimmed with fur. And she was wearing a mantle of thick sable, as black as coal, with ermine trim of the same kind. She was riding a small Breton palfrey, as white as the new-fallen snow, and it wore a saddle cover of flowered gold silk and a brand new saddle adorned with ivory and gold; the bridle was embellished with gold and gems, and the harness was decorated in the same way. The palfrey was of the long-haired kind, from head to toe, and one could search far and wide before finding a finer or more beautiful horse. She mounted it, donned a hat, and took a silken whip in hand; and so outfitted she took her leave and set off for the court. {5169}

She did not stop for lodgings until she reached Carahaix, where the King was holding his court. As she entered the city, most of the people stopped to gaze at her, and everyone exclaimed that they had never heard tell of such a beautiful maiden or of one so finely dressed. She kept on riding until she reached the court; she did not stop and look around but headed straight into the hall, where she found the King, who had just finished dinner and was still sitting at the dais. She went up to him and declared: "My lord, may God save you, the most valiant man there is or ever was and the finest man who ever wore a crown." {5189}

King Arthur took note of the maiden who was addressing him and replied: "May God grant good fortune to the most beautiful of all young ladies." {5193}

"King Arthur," she said, "give me some news of your nephew, the handsome, bold, and courteous Sir Gawain. I came here to learn the latest word of him and that is the sole purpose of my visit." {5198}

"Of course, I will gladly give you news of him. It hasn't yet been two weeks since he left my side." {5201}

When the maiden heard the King say that his nephew was alive and well, the blood suddenly rushed to her cheeks. She grew even more beautiful and was quite ecstatic. But she thought herself a fool for now she realized that it was Gawain—no doubt about it—who had almost taken her virginity. Then, in a ladylike way, she began to tell the King the whole story: how his nephew had cut off Gernemant's head in an act of knightly courage, how she had become his sweetheart, and how he had restored to her father all the land he had lost, land which Gernemant had seized from him, and how she had doubted Gawain's word because she thought he was dead. She declared that she would not stir from the court until Gawain came back. {5221}

The King took her in his arms at once and helped her gently down from her palfrey; then he personally escorted her to the chambers where the Queen had gone and was lying on a bed. She got up at once, and the King said to her: "Look here, my lady! I have brought you Sir Gawain's sweetheart." The Queen was very happy at this; she embraced the maiden and kissed her, saying that she was most welcome there and that she would cherish her friendship, both because of her good breeding and on account of the love she bore for the young lady's sweetheart. {5236}

The daughter of the Lord of Chastel du Port remained at court under these favorable circumstances, loved and cherished by one and all. Gawain, who did not take kindly to the offense Brien had committed against him, took pains to ride on steadfastly, both he and his squire. One day they had been traveling for a long time without stopping for food or drink, and day was quickly turning into night. Sir Gawain, who was not yet sure of finding shelter, called out to his squire and asked him where they might stay for the night. {5251}

"My lord," he answered, "I expect to find you very good lodgings at Nevois, for they have everything there of one kind and another to do proper honor to a gentleman. There is no lord in that dwelling, only a lady, and she is my mother. Tomorrow, when we are ready, we will attend the coronation. For truly, Brien is to be crowned king on the Feast of Saint John; and tomorrow the bans will be proclaimed everywhere that the Queen of the Isles has dominion." {5263}

"I do believe you are telling the truth," he said, "and I'm very glad to hear it." It was not much longer before they reached the abode. That night they fared very well indeed, with everything that each of them required. In the morning, as soon as he saw the light of day, Sir Gawain arose, made ready, and mounted his horse. The young man took his shield and lance and rode on ahead until they left the forest. And right away they saw the city of Rades, which looked quite impressive, for there were many fair churches within its walls, their tall spires all covered with lead. It was not situated in a wasteland; rather, it stood amidst fair and fertile fields. There was a forest and a river and vineyards where they produced wine; there were cultivated fields, meadows, and gardens. The city was enclosed by solid walls with plenty of lofty towers, and it was surrounded by extensive moats. As for the main castle, you may be sure that in all the world—

in any land—there was none finer, better located, or better fortified against attack. {5292}

Sir Gawain gazed at the city in amazement, and shortly after that they reached a meadow, where he beheld so many tents and pavilions, both high and wide, that the field was completely covered with them. Then he asked the young man to tell him what city this was, who all these people were, and who was the lord of the castle. {5302}

And the young lad replied: "This is the city of Rades you see before you. So many people have gathered within its walls that, of necessity, some have had to leave the city itself and take up residence outside. They have all come seeking lodgings here, and all of them will be attending the coronation." {5309}

When Sir Gawain heard that, he said at once: "Tell me, my friend, where are the Isles located?" {5312}

The lad began to laugh and replied with a chuckle: "My lord, you entered the Isles four days ago without even realizing it. I will tell you no lies: you should know that the Isles is what they call the surrounding country, and the city itself is named Rades; it is the chief city of the kingdom and a powerful archbishopric as well. You should also know that the archbishop has four great bishops under his sway. The Queen holds the cities, and my lord will be soon recognized as King." {5326}

When Sir Gawain heard all this, he was exceedingly pleased because before him he saw the town and the very place where he expected to find Brien. Then he approached the lad and said to him: "Brother, now give me my shield, for I will stay here and wait a while until all the people have assembled and the lady and Brien arrive for the ceremony at the church." The young man went over and handed it to him, saying that he would go inside and deliver the message to his lord, who was to become king. {5341}

"Young man," he said, "you know me very well, and you have served me faithfully. To tell the truth, I have never known a squire who served me better. If it should so happen that you come to the land of Logres some day, and if you wanted to become a knight, it would give me great pleasure to dub you personally." {5349}

"May God grant that I meet you once again," he replied, "under more favorable circumstances." The young man departed right away, bidding Gawain farewell, leaving him there all alone. {5354}

With that, the young lad set out on his way across the meadow, riding at full speed, while Sir Gawain stayed behind all by himself. He dismounted and waited around for quite a while, until the hour of prime had passed. And then he thought to himself that he might well be lingering there too long, so without wasting any more time, he mounted his horse and set off at a brisk pace. He rode through the throngs of people and right past the tents and pavilions; it took him quite a while because there were so many tents pitched there. When he finally reached the city, he went inside and surveyed the streets, high and wide and beautifully decorated with hangings, noble coats of arms, and ornaments of every kind, all quite lavish and opulent. The streets were packed with knights and ladies, young maidens and people from many places and of many different ranks, all mingling with one another. He admired the city greatly, so much indeed that he said to himself he had never seen one quite as beautiful—as far as he could recall—or quite as rich, or one where there were such vast throngs of people. He continued on his way, not stopping until he reached the Queen's mansion. He made a halt in front of it, where he found a grassy square; it was a good bowshot in length and just as wide. The Cathedral of Saint Moissant, the archbishop's seat, stood at the very head of the square. Gawain stationed himself to one side so that everyone who was going to the church would have to pass right before his eyes, and there he remained, holding his lance at rest. {5399}

It wasn't very long before he saw a great many knights approaching, carrying candles. They were all on foot, finely dressed and outfitted in costly and becoming attire, with many kinds of colored silk, and there was an endless procession of them. After them came dukes and counts: some were castellans and some were lords and others still were noblemen of great distinction, a good five hundred of them. Then came the Queen dressed in a gown of black samite, which suited her marvelously well. No one had ever seen samite so finely embroidered or so beautifully decorated with animals and birds of every kind. She looked most elegant and finely coiffed with a headband of gold braid; over her curly auburn hair she wore a hat adorned with gold and rubies. And it was sheer delight to gaze upon her, for her beauty was unmatched in all the world, and all the beauties that ever there may be were nothing as compared with her loveliness. She was tall, pretty, and innocent and not yet eighteen years of age. The archbishop walked on her right and a duke on her left, leading her horse by the bridle. {5431}

Then Gawain saw Brien coming; he looked very noble and daring, and there were a good two hundred knights with him as he rode down the street. He was wearing a robe of blue samite adorned with golden birds, and his chaplet was trimmed with gold and shimmering gems. He was handsome, elegant, and as genteel and good looking as you could possibly imagine. The Queen was seated there on a throne of ivory, newly decorated with precious enamel work. The archbishop sat next to her on another throne, and he arranged the four bishops side by side. Each one was wearing his miter and was just as well attired as you could wish in vestments of the Holy Church. Each of them was seated on a bishop's throne. {5451}

At that moment Sir Gawain thought to himself that never in all his life had he seen people more lordly in appearance, and that never before had he gazed upon such noble beings in any place he had ever been; he also thought that those who were paying Brien so much honor had no right to do so, for if they only knew the truth, this affair would be proceeding quite differently. {5461}

Hardly had he said this when a knight came riding up, armed as a knight must be to attack another man or to defend his person, and he had two swords girded on. He passed through the throng and came to a halt right beside Sir Gawain. Gawain looked at him and recognized him instantly, but he didn't let on; the knight didn't recognize Gawain at all. And so the two men stood there, side by side. {5474}

Everyone who had heard about the coronation had gathered there from many different places. Some who owed service came because of the bans and the summons, for they held their fiefs from the lady. But others came because they had heard that the Queen was the most beautiful creature in whom beauty then made its home; and so people had been summoned from far and wide. The Queen commanded the Archbishop, who was sitting beside her on a throne, to rise and explain publicly the covenant she and Brien had agreed to and the circumstances giving rise to it. {5491}

Then the Archbishop stood up and spoke these words: "My lords, hear the understanding, just as it has been agreed to by Brien and the Queen. She made it known—and this is the absolute truth—that she would take Brien as her lord because he assured her that there was no better knight in the world. And she replied that she knew of a man far more handsome, well bred, and accomplished: Sir Gawain, the nephew of King Arthur. Brien maintained that Gawain was no more handsome or valiant than he was. And so the two of them finally reached an agreement: she instructed him to go and seek out Gawain and defeat him man-to-man on the battlefield and to bring her back his head; then she would take him as her husband and make him king. And he told her that he had searched until he found Gawain, defeated him in combat, and killed him. Granted that there is more knightly prowess in Brien than in any other man alive, it pleases my lady that he become her lord and husband. We have explained this situation in detail because she wants you to know all of the facts." {5519}

When the Archbishop had spoken these words, Brien got to his feet and declared, so that everyone could hear: "Gawain has truly been slain. I am the man who killed him, make no mistake about it, and there is not a single knight in all the world, wise man or fool, who is as worthy as I am." {5525}

When the Knight of the Two Swords heard that Brien had committed such an offense as to kill the worthy Gawain, and that he was going around bragging about it like this, he immediately spurred his horse, never letting up until he reached the Queen. He asked: "Who is this outrageous, arrogant knight who claims to have justly slain the finest knight that ever lived? And who is this knight who dares to congratulate himself so for his virtues and his beauty?" {5538}

"I am the man," said Brien.

"You are?" said the Knight.

"Indeed I am." {5539}

"Indeed you are not, you are quite mistaken. If Sir Gawain is dead, as you maintain, then I declare that, after him, I am the finest and handsomest knight in all the world, the one who has sought and found the most adventures, and the man who has defeated the most opponents since being dubbed a knight. If you wish to deny this, here I stand, ready to prove my worth against yours without the slightest delay, right here before all these people." {5551}

When Sir Gawain heard this man boasting about his prowess—as he stood there lance in hand—he grew furious. He rode up to him right away and exclaimed: "What is that you just said?" {5556}

"Sir knight, I said that since I heard the news of Sir Gawain's death, there is no better or more handsome knight in all the world than I." {5561}

Sir Gawain retorted: "Indeed there is a man just as good or better." {5563}

"No, there isn't," he replied, "and never will there be such a man! If you wish to defend your claim, I am quite ready to do battle with you here and now and to prove that I am just as worthy as I say." {5568}

There was a great uproar in the crowd because of these two knights who were challenging each other so aggressively in the presence of the entire assembly. Each of them was claiming to be better than Brien, both in prowess and in beauty. The lady called a halt to the ceremony, saying that she would proceed no further until she had seen the battle—from start to finish—between these two men who were challenging one another. {5581}

The two knights scarcely waited a moment; they took their distances, one from the other, turned their horses around, pricked them with their spurs, and thrust their shields forward with their elbows, bringing them into combat position. They charged, with lances lowered, as fast as their horses could carry them, and when they collided the impact was so great that both their lances shattered and the fragments went flying through the air. Then they drew their swords and struck each other fierce blows. Each man attacked the other with such force that everyone agreed there had never been such a brutal skirmish between two knights, or one so evenly matched. {5599}

And because the battle was so violent, Sir Gawain pulled back and stalled for time. He thought to himself that he was doing wrong to fight with this man; for if it turned out that he did him harm, this was his friend. And if he had somehow offended him, or if he could find some way to set things right, he would gladly make amends. And as he was standing back thinking about this, the Knight of the Two Swords called out to him: "My lord," he said, "so help me God, since the day King Arthur dubbed me and allowed me to go and ungird the sword from the Lady of Cardigan— a task I heard many people grumbling about—and ever since the day I left Glamorgan, where the King made me a knight, I have not encountered anyone who gave me such a fierce and violent battle. And if you were so inclined, dear lord, would you be kind enough to tell me your name?" {5625}

Sir Gawain was very happy when he heard that the Knight wanted to know his name, and he replied: "I am none other than Gawain, the nephew of King Arthur." When the Knight heard the truth, he was delighted and overcome with joy. Paying no heed to those who might see what he did or tell tales about it, he dismounted, sword in hand, walked up to Sir Gawain, and said to him: "Forgive me, my lord, for doing battle against you here; it was foolish of me to do so, for I am your squire, the young man you left behind at court, the one you asked King Arthur to make a knight. I would never have fought with you, dear lord, not for anything in the world, if only I had known your true identity. I beg your forgiveness, and I recognize that I have acted wrongly toward you." {5647}

Sir Gawain dismounted too, and they embraced each other and made peace. It wasn't long before the Knight of the Two Swords fell at his feet, asking him not to refuse a request he was about to make of him. Sir Gawain said that he would do absolutely anything he wanted, provided that he did not ask to fight the battle against Brien. {5657}

"Please, my lord, I know of nothing else I could possibly ask of you." {5659}

"It is not right for me to grant you such a gift," he said, "for the quarrel is mine and, as far as I can tell, no man holds this matter closer to his heart than I do. Under no circumstances would I allow anyone but myself to take on this battle." {5665}

And the Knight answered: "Dear lord, since it does not please you, I will say no more and keep my peace with good grace." {5668}

Without saying another word they walked toward the Queen, who was in the square. Brien did not know what to do when he saw the knights approaching. He knew for certain they were not coming to offer him their fellowship, for they hated no man more than him, and with good reason! When they were standing before the Queen, Sir Gawain said: "Lady, please listen to me for a moment. So help me God, our Almighty King, Brien is a sly and dishonest man, no matter what he may have led you to believe. These noble men gathered here waiting for you to marry him are wasting their time. I do believe he will pay dearly for his actions, unless he regains a sense of reason and justice. He has committed a great misdeed, and he compounded his offense when he told you he had killed and slain Sir Gawain and when he claimed to surpass him in prowess and beauty. And no matter what he has said or recounted, I tell you that Gawain, the nephew of King Arthur, is still alive and well, and I am ready to prove it to you here and now." {5697}

"Brien," said the beautiful maiden, "did you hear what this man just said? So help me God, it is a great shame that you have deceived me with a falsehood and made me agree to something from which I will never draw honor. I was supposed to take you as my husband, but you were misleading me all along!" {5705}

Then Brien stepped forward and said: "My lady, it is true beyond a doubt that I defeated Sir Gawain at arms and slew him in battle." {5709}

"My lady," Sir Gawain retorted, "since he makes this claim, ask him to tell you the whole truth, by God our Sovereign, and you will find out what kind of chivalry he used in this combat. Then you will understand what he has been boasting about so much, and what kind of honor you stand to gain from it." {5717}

The Queen looked at Brien and asked him to recount the whole business so that her knights and lords could hear all about it. "My lady," he said, "you must not think that I am lying. I have proved my worth in so many places and I am so well known everywhere, that I ought to be believed without question. For what I have told you is indeed the truth, and I stand by my word." {5727}

"Truly, I say that you are lying, and I want the Queen to know the whole truth right now about how you went after him. It is a fact that you found him without armor, that you would not give him any quarter, and that he was compelled to fight with you before he could leave the field. He could have escaped easily, but he was unwilling even to entertain the thought; instead, he jousted and was wounded because he had no armor on. You performed no great act of prowess! And though you saw him all bloodied and lying on the ground, he was far from dead, but you did him no further harm. By that God from whom all bounty flows, know for a fact that Gawain, the nephew of King Arthur, is still very much alive and well. And here I stand, ready to back up my words against your person, right here in the presence of this noble company, without delay or postponement. My lady, I offer you my guarantee of that." {5752}

Brien was shamed and humiliated before the Queen and her people, and he wondered who this knight could be and where he had come from, this man who was challenging him so boldly, claiming that Sir Gawain was still alive. His confidence was badly shaken, and his face lost all its color. He stepped forward and declared: "My lady, so that no shame may arise from this matter in the future, I am ready to defend myself against this man, for never did I commit such a vile deed as to kill Gawain by treachery." He gave her his pledge at once, wasting no time about it. Then he went away and armed and outfitted himself, returning promptly to the square on horseback, equipped with everything a knight needs to defend himself and to attack another. {5773}

Sir Gawain saw him coming and mounted his horse. Why should I make a longer story of it? The square was immense and the field was level, and they turned their horses around to face each other. The steeds were pawing at the ground, and the knights positioned their shields with their elbows, setting them in front of their chests. As fast as their horses could carry them, with lances lowered, they collided so hard that both weapons shattered on impact, flying up in splinters. Then they drew their swords, removed their shields from their necks, and wrapped the straps around their hands to protect them from injury, for both of them knew how to skirmish. Like men who had no love for one another, they held nothing back. As long as they had breath, they struck merciless blows at each other. {5795}

Then Sir Gawain suggested to Brien that they dismount, for they would fight a good deal better on foot and much more nobly than they could on horseback. Brien said not a word but charged directly at Sir Gawain. Gawain reached out and grabbed the reins of his bridle, pulling so hard on them that no force in the world could have prevented the horse from falling over backward, taking Brien with him. After they had fallen to the ground in a heap, Sir Gawain dismounted, giving his opponent plenty of time to get to his feet. But as he saw him lying there, he remembered Brien's villainy, how he had been unwilling to spare him when he found him without armor. And, recalling how joyful Brien had been when he thought he was leaving him for dead, Gawain took the offensive without another moment's hesitation. Brien was ready and waiting for him and put up a stout defense, for he was a bold and hardy knight, worthy and confident of his ability. And you may be sure that he was no less exhausted than Sir Gawain, and both of them were severely injured. Sir Gawain, who had taken the offensive more often than his opponent, came rushing at Brien, took ground from him, and drove him this way and that until, in a fit of rage and sheer brute force, he struck him such a mighty blow to the shield and body that the man fell to his knees; then he hit him one more time and Brien collapsed on the ground. Then Gawain pounced on him and quickly tore off his helmet. {5832}

Brien begged him for mercy so that all could hear, asking him to show compassion and take pity on him for the sake of common decency. Sir Gawain, who understood this man's distress and shame, realized that if Brien lived he would suffer a good deal more torment than if he killed him, for he would always remember the honor he had lost in this way and the fact that his sweetheart had witnessed his downfall. He granted him mercy and guaranteed him safe-conduct, provided that he promise to go as quickly as he could and deliver himself into custody at the court of the good King Arthur, without seeking a delay or making excuses. {5849}

"Ah, noble knight, now you have done to me the worst thing you could possibly think of. Even if you were the King himself, you could not protect me now, not for anything anyone could ever imagine! For if I am hated, it is not without reason. They know full well that the man in whom all prowess flourished was slain by me. If they find out at the court that I am Brien, the one who caused such great distress, everyone will become my enemy and everyone will want to take vengeance on his account." {5861}

"You must not delay because of that," said Gawain. "But have no fear, for I want you to travel under my safe-conduct. As a token, say that you come as a prisoner, and tell them you were sent there by the man who set out to pursue the knight who succeeded in removing the sword from the maiden, where all the courtiers strove valiantly but to no avail, for they were quite unable to complete the task. Since then he has encountered much of good and evil and undertaken many a perilous journey; let them know that he has found the Knight, and that the two of them are now traveling together as companions." {5877}

With that he rose from Brien's body, having promised him his personal safety. And then Sir Gawain mounted his horse right away; the Knight of the Two Swords did not hesitate but mounted up as well. The Queen sent over a count to find out who they were. They did not wait for an instant but rode off without speaking to anyone, leaving everyone quite astonished. The Queen was vexed; she kept on asking about these men and trying to find out who they were, but no one knew a thing about them. Finally, she ordered all her men to make haste and give chase and to catch up with the two knights as quickly as they could, for they were not yet far away. {5895}

As many as ten men, all of them knights, leapt into the saddle and rode in earnest until they had left the city behind. When they saw the two knights they had undertaken to pursue riding on ahead, they quickened their pace until they drew abreast of them. And when the pair heard the sound of the horses approaching, they came to a halt; the ten knights advanced and offered their greetings, and one of them—who seemed to be a worthy gentleman of mature years—spoke up and said: "My lords, if it pleased you to come back, the Queen would gladly show you joy and honor; that is why she sent us after you, should you be kind enough to return." {5915}

"Dear lord, I'm afraid that cannot be," replied Sir Gawain, "but tell her in the future not to believe quite so much of what she is told." {5919}

"Dear sweet lord, how will my lady know the truth about you, you who have defeated Brien, who was supposed to have killed Gawain? She has been asking to know more about you, but no one can tell her anything; so she sends you word through us, dear lord, requesting that you tell us your name." {5927}

"I am quite happy for you to know my name. Truly, dear lord, I am Gawain, the nephew of King Arthur." {5929}

"Who do you say you are? Gawain?" {5930}

"I am indeed, that is exactly what they call me, and I am the very Gawain whom Brien boasted so much about killing today—and now he is properly rewarded for his conduct! And the man you see here with me is the Knight of the Two Swords." {5937}

"Ah, dear lord, then do return with us, for the sake of honor and courtesy." {5939}

"No, we will never go back, dear lord, not for anything anyone might say, so don't bother to say another word about it." {5942}

The two companions rode off without further ado, and the gentlemen and knights who had come after them were unable to accomplish anything more with their entreaties. They quickly returned to where they found the

Queen—to whom much land belonged—and right away she asked them if the two knights were going to come back. {5951}

"Truly, my lady, they will never heed our advice now," said the worthy knight, "and they were unwilling even to consider returning." {5955}

"And who are these knights, departing like this, against my will?" {5957}

"My lady, I will tell you: one is Sir Gawain, about whom Brien spoke so disdainfully and went around boasting about killing." {5961}

No sooner had he said this than the Queen fell down in a faint, for she loved Gawain with pure devotion, more than any man who had ever lived. They splashed water on her face, and she quickly regained consciousness. She considered herself greatly humiliated on account of her people who were assembled there. They soon dispersed and went away, and with that the court came to an end. The lady asked to be ushered out, and so it was done. Then she summoned before her those men from whom she customarily took advice and counsel and said to them: "My lords, if I may be so bold as to say so—please do not hold it against me—I would like to send word to King Arthur's court to find out if these knights were telling the truth when they said that the worthy Gawain is still alive. If that were so, I would never have any other man as my husband. For there is no one better or more handsome in the whole world, and he is the son of a king and a queen. And I understand that he has not yet taken a wife. I'm very happy about that! If you don't mind, tell me what you think, and don't worry about whether your counsel pleases or offends me." {5990}

And so the Queen explained what she wanted them to advise her about, holding nothing back, whether they saw things her way or not, and they all went off to one side to deliberate. Some of them were Brien's relatives, and it became clear from their discussions that they would never hear of the lady doing anything of the kind she had proposed, and they gave their reasons, all of them quite plausible: it would be most unseemly and it would look like lechery if she asked for Gawain just like that, and perhaps he would reject her. And it was impossible for a knight who was so well traveled, so handsome, so worthy, and so valiant not to have a sweetheart already. Furthermore, he might hate her because he knew very well that she had sent out a highly trusted knight to kill him, and one who was supposed to be worthier than he. If he were not inclined to marry her and therefore refused her proposal, that would be quite a humiliation; it would be much better to tell her not to send any message at all. {6019}

With that they broke off their deliberations; and all of them were in complete agreement. They came back and one of them reported what had been said, telling the lady that they advised against her doing what she had proposed, for no one saw any honor in it for her and many people would hold it against her. And so the matter was left at that, and neither she nor her advisors said another word about it. The counselors went away, and she was far from grateful to them, for they had advised her against doing what she wanted to do. She was annoyed and disheartened and no less vexed than before. Yet though she said nothing and gave not a hint of what she had in mind, she had every intention of doing something. But she would never seek counsel from them nor ever waste another word over it; but for the time being I will say no more about her. {6041}

Brien, who had been so greatly humiliated, did not delay his departure. He mounted his horse as soon as he could and set out on his journey. Why should I make a longer story of it? He traveled on day after day until he found King Arthur in residence at Camelot. The King had just finished dinner when, all of a sudden, he saw the young Brien coming into the hall; he was wearing all his armor, as if he had just left the battlefield. He dismounted in the hall, unlaced his helmet, and immediately walked up to the dais, where he saw the King sitting. Right away he greeted him on bended knee, and then he said: "I am your prisoner, my lord. Some time ago, I set out from my country to come here, and I place myself at your mercy. Know that the man who sent me here is the one who set out from your court a long time ago to look for the Knight of the Two Swords, whose fame has spread so far and wide. And when he defeated me in battle, he told me that he had found the Knight, and I can vouch for that, because I saw the two of them together. My lord, do with me whatever you think right and whatever your heart desires; that will be fine with me. But, for the love of God, grant me a boon: let no one ask me my name, and do not try to find out who I am." {6077}

The King, who was happy and joyful at the news Brien gave him, granted him his request readily, saying: "You will have your boon without any problem, provided that you remain at court as part of my household." {6083}

Brien agreed to do the King's bidding although it troubled him greatly; then he got to his feet before the King and thanked him profusely. There were many people attending to him there, and some chamberlains took him away, removed his armor, and helped him make ready. They had him put on fresh clothes, and when he was dressed you couldn't have found a more handsome knight in the palace. The King loved and cherished him and was happy to have him stay at court, but he was quite concerned about not knowing his identity; still, he didn't want to ask him, and Brien did not stir from the court. {6099}

Word spread through the court that Sir Gawain would soon be returning, bringing with him the Knight of the Two Swords, and this news circulated until the Queen of Cardigan learned of it—the beautiful lady who loved him so much, the maiden who had brought the sword to the court— and she was overjoyed at hearing news of the man she had been awaiting so eagerly and for such a long time. When Brien heard this and paid heed to what the knights were saying, he knew that Sir Gawain was still alive. Then he was a little less concerned for his personal safety, and he was right to feel more secure. {6114}

He remained at court in this way, and many people wondered who the handsome knight was, but none of them ventured to ask, for they knew perfectly well of his understanding with the King, and so they kept their peace. Because they did not know his name, they simply called him "The Handsome Prisoner," and he often felt great shame because of this. {6123}

XII

The Knight at the Lac as Jumeles

Now let us return, as indeed we should, to the two companions and how they fared as they went on their way together. They entered the forest and had traveled a great distance without meeting anyone; they talked together of many an adventure and many an exploit. Sir Gawain, who was unafraid to tell his companion anything that touched his heart, had made up his mind what to do: he wanted the Knight to agree to return to court with him, and he wanted the two of them to remain loyal companions. {6137}

And as Gawain was earnestly pleading with him, the two men emerged from the forest and entered a meadow, where they discovered an old nag tethered to a pine tree. It was rather badly injured and had no hide left where the spurs dig in; it was scrawny and emaciated, its shoes were worn right through, and it had every affliction imaginable; truly it was a sad sight to see. [. . .] Its neck was long and its head disproportionately large, and it was so hideous that no one had ever seen such an ugly beast; and all the equipment on its back was not worth so much as a rotten nut. It was champing restlessly at the bit, and as they approached they spotted a squire who had lain down for a nap beside a spring. His clothes were not made of tightly woven scarlet, and indeed he was quite badly attired: he was wearing an old brown cape and hood, all gross, disgusting, and threadbare; the coat on his back had hardly any sleeves, and there wasn't much of it left at the hip, where his sword was fastened on. It was all shredded and torn by brambles and covered with filth. The boy was wearing old hose of frayed and tattered Lincoln cloth, encrusted with the horse's blood right up to top of his thighs. The boots on his feet were badly worn, as were the soles, and the tips of his spurs were missing. {6177}

They drew closer and noticed that he had propped a shield up against the tree. When they saw him they were astonished and approached him right away, not pulling back on the reins, for they wanted to know more about this. When he heard their horses whinnying, he woke up and leapt to his feet, exclaiming: "Welcome, my lords, for the love of God. Please tell me if you know where I might learn news of a man called the Knight of the Two Swords." {6190}

Then the Knight himself replied, asking the lad where he came from and who had sent him. The squire answered: "I would tell no one, my lord, except for that man alone, privately and in confidence." {6195}

And at once the Knight took him aside and said to him: "Now, young fellow, feel free to tell me whatever you like, for I am the very man you are seeking, have no doubt about that; I tell you this on my honor as a knight. On hearing these words, the blood drained from the young man's face, and he began to sob so uncontrollably that it was a long time before he could utter a word. Then, purposefully, he said: "Dear lord, I bring you harsh and disturbing news—news of death—for your dear father has been slain. The man who has brought such shame and affliction upon you has been your lord and faithful friend up till now—of that you may be certain—for Sir Gawain is the man who did it. There you see your father's shield, which your mother has sent you, she who is dying of grief, I do believe. She and all your friends urge you to do everything you can to avenge your father—if ever you held him dear—for otherwise you will be greatly shamed." {6221}

When he heard these words, the Knight grew distressed and didn't know quite what to do. If he fought Gawain right there and then, what would be the result? The whole world would tell tales about it! And if he let Gawain go unchallenged, those who heard about it would rightly call him a coward. On the one hand, the pledge of comradeship binding the two men together ruled out such a battle. On the other, the news that his mother was dying of sorrow and that his father had been slain stirred him to take action. He was torn between the alternatives, not knowing which one to embrace and which one to reject. {6237}

He approached the squire and said, "My boy, you must leave this place; take this shield with you, and I will carry my father's. From this day on, I will never rest until I find Sir Gawain in a place where I can fight him man-to-man in single combat." {6245}

Then the squire departed, going on his way in his seriously weakened state. Sir Gawain came along soon after, totally unaware of what had happened, and the Knight, in an angry state of mind, confronted him at once: "My lord Gawain, you have behaved villainously toward me, and I am distressed by your actions when, in all good faith, I have always been your loyal friend. I have put my best efforts and my great pains to bad use, when I served you in such ways as I thought might please you. You should not have repaid me as you did; I deserved much better. I don't know why I should conceal my rage! If I hate you, I have every reason to do so, for you have killed my father, who didn't deserve to die. From this day on I defy you, be forewarned!" {6266}

With that the Knight took his leave, and Sir Gawain could not get a single word or a glance out of him, despite his earnest pleading. He was filled with sorrow and anguish and vowed that he would never return to court alone—without the Knight—no matter how things might turn out. {6274}

And so the great love and the fellowship between the two knights collapsed and came to a sudden end. The Knight of the Two Swords did not tarry long but entered the forest, turning onto a road that did not lead straight ahead. Sir Gawain rode on relentlessly, pursuing him at great speed. When he came to a fork in the road, he chose the path he thought to be the one most traveled, thinking it was the right way to go, but it wasn't, and he lost track of the Knight; and so he rode on in vain for many a day. The story doesn't tell us just which path he took or what adventure befell him, but he was deeply discouraged, and with good reason. {6293}

The Knight of the Two Swords traveled the road he had chosen and rode on for two full days, unwilling to stop anywhere for any reason. One day he spotted two towers rising from a plain: they were massive, incredibly lofty, and protected by high battlements. There was a very deep lake surrounding them, a good two bowshots wide. He saw no boat at the shore which he might use to cross, and he began to wonder what place this could be, for he saw not a house nor a cottage anywhere around those towers. The waters of the lake lapped right up against the battlements, and he could find neither a boat nor a ford anywhere. He didn't want to leave until he saw if some man or woman might appear or emerge from one of the towers. {6315}

After a while he decided to take a ride through the surrounding countryside just for pleasure, and before he had gone very far, he came upon the loveliest and most appealing meadow he had ever seen, set in a little valley. In the very middle of it, he saw that a very pleasant and attractive spring had its source; it welled up from a beautiful stony bed and flowed straight toward the lake. When the Knight saw this spring, he went over to dismount beside it, for he could better await adventure there than on horseback. At once he loosened the horse's harness and let it hang free; then he took off its bridle and let the horse graze, for there was plenty of grass thereabouts. {6333}

He walked around the meadow and noticed a sword lying beside the fountain, the most nobly crafted sword he had ever seen. He went over, picked it up, and drew it from its scabbard, exclaiming that never before had he seen such a beautiful sword or one so finely fashioned. On either side of the blade there were three tiny crosses and two leopards of enameled gold. But he was astonished to discover that it was all stained with fresh blood, crimson from the tip to halfway up the blade, and he would have liked to know where it came from and whose it was. He was upset and railed at the man who had put it back in the scabbard for not having tried to remove the blood first. He began to wipe it vigorously on his coat of arms, but the harder he rubbed the brighter the crimson sword became. When he saw this, the blood drained from his face and he grew very troubled; he tried over and over again to clean it off, but all to no avail. So he strove no more, realizing that there was something most extraordinary about this sword. Then he returned it to the scabbard and put it back where he had found it. {6365}

He took his helmet off, unlaced his ventail, and sat down. He was quite mystified by the sword, and as he was pondering the matter, he fell asleep, for he was exhausted from his travels and from lack of food. And as he was sleeping, he was startled by some shouting nearby, by a voice coming from farther up the shore. He awoke and leapt to his feet as fast as he could to see who had been shouting so close to him, or so it seemed. Then he looked straight ahead and saw that it was a maiden crying out in a loud, clear voice, over and over again, as if she were in need of assistance. Eager to find out who she was and what she wanted, he approached her, and she immediately came forward to meet him. She advanced and greeted him because she recognized the shield hanging from his neck. {6388}

She said: "Welcome, dear lord. If you were willing to wait for me a little while, I would give you good lodgings for the night and help you cross this lake and reach those towers. But each and every night such a great noise of grief and lamentation arises from within that all other sorrows that ever were or ever will be are nothing by comparison. If ever the people who voice these lamentations were to see you, you may be sure that their grief would be redoubled. Nevertheless, great honor will be paid to you there." {6400}

"Then I will wait for you, maiden, and I am most grateful for everything you have told me." Immediately she headed back toward the forest, much encouraged, and he returned to where he had left the sword. He outfitted himself once again, put his armor back on, and took the sword and hung it round his neck; he didn't dare to gird it on, for he thought it might be enchanted. He mounted his horse, not wasting any time about it. It was well after compline, and night was falling fast. It wasn't very long before he heard a great whinnying of horses; he looked up and saw a crowd of people emerging from the forest, obviously overcome by sorrow and grief, and it looked to him like everyone was weeping. And though they were lamenting in this way, the maiden left their company and came right back to where she had left the Knight. When he saw her returning, he came forward to meet her; but she cried out telling him to stay hidden, so that no one would know of his presence. She was well acquainted with both the safe and the dangerous places thereabouts; she hurried toward him, took him aside, and said: "If I had let these people see you, dear lord, you would have caused such an outburst of sorrow that you would never see the likes of it again. Now let us allow all these people to go on ahead, and we will follow them at a safe distance, very quietly and cautiously; I don't want them to find out that you are here." {6442}

Thereupon they saw a gate open up and a boat come out, in which the people who had been following them were going to cross the lake. They all dismounted from their horses and calmly got on board, not making any noise or commotion. When they had all embarked, the Knight said: "What will happen now, maiden; who will ferry us across? Are we going to stay here then?" {6453}

"Ah, Sir Knight," she said, "be patient just a little, until they cross the lake; you will get there soon enough, and I will go with you." And so she kept him there, and meanwhile the boat advanced until it entered the tower, and the gate closed behind it once again. The knight was very upset and troubled in his heart, and he said: "If only you had wanted to, we could have been across already. Now we could easily mark time here for another two weeks or a full month. There is no easy way to bring the boat back from the other side now." {6469}

When the young lady heard him grumbling like this, she said: "Let us start out, my lord, for we will yet cross over in good time; we certainly aren't going to linger here." {6474}

With that, they emerged from their hiding place. They saw the boat returning from the tower at a good clip, and the Knight felt much better, for he thought someone was coming back to get them. He got off his horse at once and went to help the maiden dismount; then he embarked before anything else could happen, and they made the crossing. As soon as those who were watching them from atop the battlements recognized the shield hanging from his neck, they all hurried down to meet him, looking totally despondent. {6489}

The knight was greatly astonished when he saw all these people; he disembarked and they took him inside. And as soon as they had left the boat behind, they led him into one of the most pleasant, attractive, and delightful courtyards he had ever seen in all his life. Then an old man invited him to sit down, never asking who he was, and ordered the servants to remove his armor. And they, who wouldn't have dreamed of leaving him unattended, removed his armor with the greatest honor you can imagine, and he gladly allowed them to do so. Then the old knight ordered new clothes to be brought to him. The Knight was astonished to find people looking after him so well, so he said: "Noble sir, I should like to know who is the lord of this manor, or the lady, and what the place is called." {6513}

"You will never get a word out of me," he replied, "but you won't have to wait long for an answer, as there are plenty of people here who will tell you anything you want to know." {6516}

With that they let things stand, as he did not want to force the issue and he couldn't get anything out of the man in any case. He didn't want to stir from there but sat around with the other people, waiting patiently. It wasn't long before he saw and heard about six knights come riding through the orchard, carrying huge torches that were burning bright and blazing vigorously, and they were heading straight toward him. At that, the gentleman who had just shown him such honor got up and bid the Knight rise as well. Then the two of them went to meet those who had done their best to make him feel welcome. And though he was not known to any of them, they did so because they found him so tall, so handsome, and so powerful in appearance. They led him off at once, crossing the orchard, and from the orchard they entered the tower, for there was no other place of shelter thereabouts. And yet it was so spacious that it could have housed a hundred knights or more. {6543}

The six knights who were escorting him led him straight to where they found the lady of the manor sitting, but there was no question of her rising to greet him, for she was totally incapable of doing so. And when she saw him standing there so handsome, all her sorrows were suddenly rekindled; first she called him "fair lord" and then "fair son," for she did not know quite which term to use [. . .] on account of her husband who was no longer living, for she spoke like a person deeply depressed and crushed by grief. She saw that he resembled her husband in every respect; never before had she seen a man who looked so much like him. She had him step forward and made him come and sit down beside her, so that she could see him better and examine his features more closely, and he was not the least bit bothered by this. "Who are you, my dear sweet friend," she said, "you who have come here seeking lodgings, where foreign knights are considered mortal enemies? And not without good reason, for they have betrayed and slain the lord of this place. There is no chance at all of your ever leaving here, for the custom is established that all strangers who come this way will lose their lives." {6575}

"Ah, my lady! Please tell my why it is that all who venture here must die? If all strangers died on his account, that would surely be a tremendous loss. But if only the man who killed him were to be slain, and no one else, surely that would be enough." {6581}

"Four days or more have already elapsed since he was killed," she said, "by God the King of Paradise, who made the beautiful Eve from Adam's rib! Since then we have heard nothing from the servant we sent out through the land. We entrusted my husband's shield to him and charged him to search until he might learn some news of a son that I'm supposed to have. King Arthur dubbed him, so they tell me, and gave him Cardigan and all the land belonging to that city, provided that he ungird the sword which the Queen had brought to court; and he did not fail at the task. Now we find ourselves in a desperate situation, for we haven't had any news of him since then. We haven't been able to find out anything about him since he left the court, except—as rumor has it—that there is no knight errant quite so handsome or so ambitious, or one who has resolved so many conflicts successfully; and he is called the Knight of the Two Swords. I don't know why he wears two of them, for the one that the Queen had girded on would be quite sufficient, if he only knew its virtues. Truth to tell, she herself did not understand its powers—the beautiful maiden who acquired it at the Gaste Chapele from the gentleman who had it by his side—the buried knight who knew victory in many a battle on many a field during his lifetime. For in wisdom, beauty, prowess, courtesy, and largesse, he outshone all other knights in the world. Oh Lord, why was he ever slain? May God confound the man who killed him and so brought me down! God has left me sorrowful and disconsolate for the rest of my days. Dear Lord, why does my heart allow me to imagine such a knight, or to behold you, who so resemble the very man I am speaking of? Cursèd be the hour I saw you enter this place. You have only compounded my shame." And as she was lamenting her fate this way, she clasped her palms together and collapsed in a faint, and the grieving broke out anew throughout the castle. {6637}

The Knight was much troubled at this, and he wept without restraint. He quickly took off his mantle and went to help the Lady up. At that moment you could have seen a wave of lamentation sweep through the castle. It wasn't very long before she recovered from her faint, and the knight who was holding her in his arms offered his comfort. The Lady, who would rather have been dead, declared that no living creature could ever console her, so great was her sorrow, and so often rekindled. Nevertheless, he made a covenant with the Lady, as a knight of sincere heart and good faith, that if he could help get redress for her shame, she in turn would strengthen her resolve for his sake, something she had not done since the knight had killed her husband in his outrageous act of arrogance. {6659}

"My lady," he said, "that is my intention, and I offer you my promise: from this day on, I will never come across him in any spot or place without attacking his person, so that either he or I will perish." And that is how he comforted the Lady and succeeded in consoling her. {6667}

Then the Lady began to take heart as well as she could, and yet she could not keep from sighing over and over again, for she could hardly bear to see the Knight in her presence. She almost fainted every time she laid eyes on him, but because she had a covenant with him she managed to control her emotions. She forced herself to cheer up and ordered the tables to be set. Those whose task it was set about their work, and soon everything was in readiness. It wasn't very long before they washed up and took their seats. They enjoyed a five-or six-course meal; I don't want to dwell too long on that, but I can tell you that they were served graciously and lingered a long while over dinner. When it came time to clear the tables, they did so, and then everyone washed up, but neither the Lady nor the Knight left the table. {6691}

Then a squire came in and announced that a young lad was calling out from the shore wanting to cross over, and from his shouts it sounded quite urgent. The Lady ordered someone to go out at once and ferry him across. It wasn't long after that he crossed the lake and entered the castle. He was recognized immediately, for he was one of the servants of the place. This was the man who had carried the shield and who had gone looking for the Knight of the Two Swords throughout the land. He approached the Lady, for no one tried to hold him back, and said: "My lady, your son sends you his greetings and inquires eagerly about you. He is furious about how things have turned out so badly both for you and for him. And he wants you to know—have no doubt about it—that wherever he finds Sir Gawain he will do whatever he can to kill him, or else he will die in the attempt." {6715}

"When did you see him?" {6716}

"Just three days ago, my lady, as he was returning from the Isles in the company of another knight. They were all by themselves, without a squire, and the other man looked like quite a worthy gentleman. I don't know if there was some kind of dispute between the two of them, but I can tell you they were not slow to take leave of each other as soon as your son heard the news I reported to him. I left him there very eager to do everything you wanted—judging from his words and his demeanor—and he undertook to do so quite wholeheartedly." {6731}

As the squire was reporting this news, he was shocked to see the very shield he had given to the Knight hanging on the wall right there before his eyes, and all of a sudden he fell silent. At once the Lady asked him what the matter was. He lowered his head and was reluctant to speak, but at length he replied: "Please forgive me, my lady, but so help me God, in all my life I have never seen a shield that looked so much like my lord's. Truly, it is the same both in size and construction. My only fear was that when you saw that shield you might think I had never met your son. But it would be good to know who brought it back; for if the man who delivered it were willing to tell us the truth, you might learn where your son is, or where he might be found." {6758}

When the Lady heard what the squire said, the blood drained from her face. When she heard him talking about her son, she could scarcely keep from fainting, but she controlled herself because of the Knight's presence. Without delay she summoned all her people, for she wished to hold a conference about the shield the squire was talking about. When they were all assembled, she said: "I would like to know the truth, if possible, about how this shield got back here." {6771}

A knight stepped forward and said: "My lady, you could easily learn the truth and find out how it happened if your guest wanted to tell you." {6775}

She looked at the Knight and said: "Dear lord, tell us honestly if you recognize this shield and if it was you who brought it here; and tell us how you acquired it, who you are, and where you come from. And for the love of God, do not take offense if I ask you your name." {6783}

At once the Knight told her he was indeed the man who had brought it back, but that he had not won it in battle. He had not had it for more than five days, and he had never before seen the squire who asked him to carry it. The squire told him it had been his father's shield and that his mother was sending word through him that his father had been wrongly and shamefully slain. Then the Knight told them all about his travels and how he was known throughout the world as the Knight of the Two Swords. {6797}

The Lady paid close attention to the Knight's every word. She did not wait an instant but leapt up and went to kiss and embrace him. She was happy and very much relieved, for now she had something that she wanted. She rejoiced and she wept; the tears were for her husband, but the joy she felt for her son was greater than anything she had ever known in all her life. Before long this elation eased all her melancholy. She forgot about her grief and said: "Son, I am your mother, and you and your sister are all I have left of your father, for whom my heart suffered many a sorrow before you returned; but you have lessened my grief and my rage immensely. {6818}

"Dear son, you do not yet know what your name is: you are Lord of Vaus de Blanquemore and Lord of the Lac as Jumeles. You have many ladies and maidens, and many noble and accomplished knights who hold rich, powerful, and magnificent fiefs from you. Your father's name was Bleheri, but you cannot yet know what your name ought to be, nor do I myself know what it should be. Before he departed this life, your father implored me not to give you any name until Brien de la Gastine had been slain, he who now holds in his vile hands your sister and ten other maidens, all beautiful and noble women of great worth who were once your sister's companions. Now they all belong to him, and he is sly and deceitful, a wicked, thieving traitor; for he was supposed to take her as his wife [. . .] toward me, toward you, and toward her, for he failed to keep his covenant. And his conduct has truly shamed us in the eyes of our friends. He was unwilling to make amends—not for any count or king—no matter how often he was ordered to do so. To tell the simple truth, Brien could not possibly make amends. His crime and his offense are too enormous, for he is the man who killed your father." {6852}

"He is the man? How can that be? I was told before that Sir Gawain had slain him." {6855}

"That is a fact, but Brien was the real murderer, for he is the one who arranged to have your father killed, and that you must understand." {6858}

With wise words and with many a sigh, the mother talked with her child and said: "Dear son, now hear how your father was wronged: it is true that he had been at war with Brien for a long time and had ravaged his land. He made things so difficult for Brien that in the end he was forced to surrender, because he had no other option. Then your father restored his land to him, as you would expect of a man who held no grudges, provided that Brien promised to marry his daughter and hold his land from him. But no matter what Brien pretended to accept at the time, it later turned out to be a disaster for your father. Listen to what the traitor did next, that vile coward, that wicked scoundrel! He concluded all his arrangements, then he took our daughter away with him. And within a mere three weeks he had refurbished his fortresses and summoned his knights and men, all with the utmost secrecy. Then he entered our land by force, burning and pillaging everywhere. But why should I make a longer story of it? He began waging war on us all over again. {6885}

"My lord, who was incensed by this, was not a coward or a man slow to take action. He quickly assembled everyone who held any land at all from him and everyone who wished to receive great rewards and generous compensation. When both sides had assembled all their men, Brien, who was an evil and cowardly man, lost his nerve and did not dare to attack. Instead, he called upon my lord and made him an offer: there would be no need for war, he argued, if your father would undertake to fight him man to man. And whichever one of them managed to defeat the other would hold both of their lands. He was prepared to set a date for that purpose, if my lord were willing, without postponing the matter any further. {6903}

"When my lord heard this, he showed greater joy than any Christian will ever hear of. He agreed to everything the man requested, since he was sure he would win Brien's land easily. Your father fixed the date without hesitation—the term was set at half a year—for that was how Brien's envoys wanted it. And with that, the men made ready to go home and the army was disbanded. {6915}

"Brien did not overlook a thing, and he did not stay there a moment longer; instead, he mounted his horse and set out all by himself, riding for nine days until he reached Carahaix, where King Arthur was holding court. He went there to request a boon, arguing that the King should not refuse it to him, for he was his liege man and held land from him. On bended knee, but with malice in his heart, he made his request, declaring that he would not depart until the King had agreed to grant him everything he wanted. {6927}

"Not giving the matter too much thought, the King told him he could have the boon he was seeking. Then Brien asked King Arthur to give him his nephew, Sir Gawain—the good and worthy knight who is so highly esteemed throughout the world—to take with him anywhere his council might propose. Furthermore, Sir Gawain was to agree to do anything Brien might tell him to do, without evading his responsibility or refusing to comply; and the King granted him all this. {6939}

"Sir Gawain and Brien set out on their way at once. Brien was full of glee because he now had under his control—to do his bidding without so much as a second thought—the very finest and most worthy knight that ever lived. He led him so far along the way that—to make a long story short—he guided him into captivity and kept him there until the day drew near when he was supposed to keep his covenant. {6949}

"Once again the adversaries summoned their people from near and far in vast numbers. Brien brought his prisoner along with him, armed from head to toe, and no one but these two knew that the other man was Sir Gawain. My lord was full of joy and very anxious to do battle. He arrived at the battlefield and made haste to don his armor, for he was quite eager to fight. Brien came from the other direction, fully armed except for his helmet, and sent word to my lord that he was asking to do battle with him, reminding him of their covenant and suggesting that they renew their pledges. And so they set about that business, so that both sides were sure of what the agreement meant. After they had concluded this ill-fated formality, Brien announced that he would go back to his tent, lace on his helmet, and return on horseback. {6971}

"With that, he went inside his tent; and at once he summoned Sir Gawain to keep his covenant, asking him to fight the battle in his stead. Gawain granted him his request, and Brien quickly handed over all his armor, his horse, and all its trappings, so as to make Gawain unrecognizable, and he mounted up. My lord had no fear of Brien and was quite nonchalant about preparing for battle; he did not even trouble to arm himself with sturdy armor, only what he usually wore when he went seeking adventures throughout the forests and the land; broken metal and tattered mail, that is exactly what they gave him. And he did not want anything else because he had no doubt that Brien was his opponent; and dressed like that he rode out onto the field of battle. {6991}

"And so it happened that they faced their horses off against each other, drew their shields into combat position, and charged at one another to joust. And when my lord struck him, his lance broke into splinters; but Sir Gawain's lance did not shatter; instead it struck full force, high up on the panel of the shield, smashing and destroying it, and the steel tip passed right on through. The hauberk was not sturdy enough to protect him from the steel, and Gawain drove the tip and the shaft of the lance a good way through his body, just as if he were slipping it through soft clay. My lord fell to the ground in agony and the lance broke, but the shaft remained in his body. {7011}

"And then my lord lost consciousness, for he felt the anguish of impending death. Sir Gawain dismounted, jumped on him and unlaced his helmet, and then he stopped, not quite knowing what to do. My dear lord opened his eyes as well as he could in his helpless state and said: 'God, I was born to great misfortune, when I have come to this, for I am dying in great dishonor, at the hands of the worst knight who ever bore arms. I did not think that such a man would ever have the courage to face an armed knight on the field of battle.' {7025}

"'You do not speak the truth!' said Gawain. 'And if you were not in such dire straits, you would lose your head for saying such a foolish thing.' {7029}

"When my lord heard his voice and realized that it was not Brien, he replied at once: 'By God who sustains all living things, sir knight, please tell me where you were born and what you are called. For I would die in far greater peace of mind if I knew for certain that a worthy knight had slain me. I spoke the words I did just now because I believed that Brien was the victor and the man who killed me. If I have done you any wrong, for the love of God, I beg you to forgive me. If you will only acquaint me with your name, I will pardon you for taking my life, as God is my witness, and may He have mercy upon my soul.' {7049}

"When Sir Gawain heard how humbly the man was acting, he knelt down with great courtesy and said: 'You may be certain that I am called Gawain, the eldest son of King Lot of Orcany.' {7055}

"When my lord heard these words, he was much relieved. He said that, if he wished, Gawain could do with him as he pleased, and that he surrendered to him, for in his present state he was quite unable to defend himself. Sir Gawain got up at once and the clamor began; he directed his horse toward Brien's tent, dismounted there, tore off Brien's armor, reclaimed his own, and took his leave. {7067}

"Brien ordered him to wait until he had taken possession of the land. But Gawain, abandoning him without a moment's hesitation, rode off nonetheless. Our knights, for their part, ran up and rescued my lord, displaying the greatest grief that knights had ever shown, until by sheer force they managed to flee the battlefield and return to the defeated camp. But before he would allow anyone to move him—because he knew he was dying—he summoned us all before him and told us he wanted to be laid to rest in the Gaste Chapele, and he asked to be buried there in full armor. {7083}

"He also predicted that he would be found there, that someone would remove his sword, and that his land would never be recovered by any man alive, no matter how powerful, until some knight might gird it on—the kind of man capable of doing his will—one able to gird and ungird it at will. And no man, no matter how accomplished he might be, could ever hope to do that except for one. He instructed us to tell you all this when you returned, and he said that you would not know what name you ought to have, not for anything in the world. And he said that Brien would reap the reward for his treachery at your hands, because he has imprisoned your sister, because he has taken my towns from me and destroyed my houses and demolished my fortresses, and because he has become so swollen up with pride that he goes riding about the country seeking adventures as if he were a newly dubbed knight. And yet he was always a good-for-nothing coward, and never in his entire life had he accomplished any worthwhile feat of arms." {7109}

"He is acting like a scoundrel when he continues to hold my sister captive," the Knight said, "and he committed an act of great treachery when he killed my father the way he did." {7113}

"That is exactly what your father said," she exclaimed, "of that you may be sure." {7115}

"May God grant that he be avenged for this crime before I die," the Knight declared, "and if there is any way I can do him harm, I don't think he will remain on this earth very long." And with that the conversation ended. {7120}

They had talked at great length and, when it pleased the Lady, she ordered that the beds be prepared and asked the servants to set about showing her son the greatest possible honor. Everything was done exactly as she directed, and when the beds were all made ready, they came to get the Knight, for it was well past bedtime; and they led him away to a chamber, taking great pains to show him honor. His mother, who went with him, would not stir from his side. She did not weary of gazing upon him. And if she could have her way she never would have stopped, for she loved him so much, and with good reason. He asked that all his armor be brought to his room, for he was not interested in lingering after sunrise. "Dear son, I would rather you stayed here a month, or two, or three!" {7143}

"Thank you, my lady, but it would be pointless for me to remain here right now, nor is it right or reasonable for me to stay at this time. It would be deemed cowardice on my part and held against me for the rest of my life." And when they saw that he did not want to remain any longer, the man who was looking after his arms promptly went to fetch him all his equipment, returning without delay. When the lady saw the three swords, she was quite taken aback, especially when she noticed the crimson one. It seemed familiar to her, so she examined it carefully, asking him where he had found it and begging him not to evade the question. {7159}

He replied: "I will gladly tell you the whole story." Then he recounted all his travels, how he had gotten there and how he had found the sword lying beside the spring, and how he would like to know more about it, if anyone knew where it had come from and who might have brought it and

left it there. He had found it lying beside the spring, all beautifully orna-
mented and superbly crafted. Never before had he held such a fine scabbard or blade in his hands. {7171}

"We don't know where it came from, dear son, but there is one thing we
do know for certain: no man alive dares to draw it from its sheath or gaze
upon it, nor do I think it very wise of you to have carried it off. It has lain
beside the spring for more than three months now, and no man or woman
has dared to look upon it because they found a letter with the sword explaining that anyone who drew it or carried it into battle would be killed
without fail on that very day, with the exception of one man. Therefore my
heart is sad and troubled that you have taken it. And you will plunge me
into great anguish if perchance you have been so foolish as to withdraw it
from its scabbard." {7192}

"But why consider me foolish? Who then might the man be, the one
who could draw the sword safely?" {7194}

"You will soon find out because the letter explained everything: 'To the
most adventurous, the most perfectly chivalrous, the handsomest man there
is—and yet a man without a name—we make a gift of this sword, and he
will be King. Know for a fact that anyone else who girds it on will have
cause for regret, for he will be slain despite his courage.' When we heard
this, dear friend, we left the sword alone, and it has not been looked upon
since, unless you were rash enough to do so, and the very thought troubles
me." {7207}

"Truly, my lady, I am not afraid, and not for anything anyone might say
would I fail to consider this sword as my own, and not for any harm that
might come of it would I fail to be of good cheer. And however much pain
I may have on account of this sword—if pain can be of any use—I am determined to find out who brought it to the spring." {7215}

When the Lady saw that she was getting nowhere by pleading with him,
she simply gave up. And whether his words pleased her or not, she acceded to his every wish. Then she commended him to God and left the
chamber; for his part, he made ready to retire and soon fell asleep, for his
bed was far from uncomfortable. {7224}

XIII

The Knight's Journey to the Gaste Chapele

The Knight slept and slumbered peacefully, and as soon as he saw the morning light he arose and got dressed. He fastened on the half-crimson sword over his hauberk and then the one he had ungirded at Cardueil. He left the third sword behind—the one with which King Arthur had dubbed him—for he did not want to be encumbered by three of them. Then, without a moment's delay, he mounted up and took leave of his mother, whom he left feeling very sad, disconsolate, and bereft of support, for she was in a desperate situation. And yet she did not want to hold him back since he could accomplish more by leaving than by staying there, and she realized that she had no choice at that moment but to grant him leave. {7243}

When the Knight had taken his leave of everyone assembled there, he asked his mother to make sure his sword was carefully guarded, and with that he departed. He was ferried across the lake and he rode into the forest right away, traveling all day long without finding either adventure or shelter, and night was falling fast. He drew to a halt because he heard a voice wailing in anguish. Then he started moving again, as he was determined to find out why the voice was grieving so, for it simply would not stop; indeed, it seemed to grow ever louder and more intense, so he made an effort to keep on going. The night was calm and clear, and he pressed on until he thought he was getting very close to the wailing voice. And then before his very eyes, sitting in a meadow beside a spring, he saw a lady voicing such grief that he felt great pity for her. He turned his horse in her direction, reached her quickly, and saw that a knight was lying in her lap clad in full armor. Beside her lay a squire stretched out prone on the ground, and neither one of the men spoke a word, or stirred, or gave any sign of life. {7275}

At once the lady cried out and said: "My lord, have mercy upon me! This knight and squire you see here are dead, and I have no way of burying them and no one to help me. Even if I were to die trying, I still could not manage to carry out the task he asked me to complete before he died." {7285}

"Please don't keep anything from me, not for any reason," said the Knight, "but tell me the whole story." {7287}

"Gladly," she said, "if you would agree to help me." {7288}

"Truly, I will do so, and I will assist you in any way I can." {7290}

"But first you must know the facts," she said. "I am the sister of Meliant of Meliadel. My name is Melie and I am the wife and sweetheart of this knight you see lying here so horribly maimed. Brien [. . .] him and his squire; and there was never such a knight as he was in all his native land. His name was Menelais, Lord of Chastel Paorous; of all the castles in Britain it is the one that sees the most adventures. He was a member of Brien's household, but I was a cousin of Bleheri's, and as soon as Bleheri was slain, Brien took possession of our land and did us every wrong imaginable; he even went so far as to make us captives, the villain, through his great treachery. {7310}

"But my lord got free and so did I; and then he managed to escape with me. Brien set out in pursuit of us before we had gotten very far. I was all alone in the company of these two men, and both of them were sleeping. Brien did not touch me or strike me, although I was wide awake, but he did not spare these two at all; he just slaughtered them as they slept and took off at once, breaking all the branches in his haste to get away. And the man who was caught in the throes of death cried out in agony and I collapsed in a faint, for I loved no creature in this world more than him. {7326}

"When I regained consciousness, I was holding his head in my lap. He told me he was dying, but if ever there had been any love between the two of us, I should see to it that he was buried in the Gaste Chapele, for the love of God. But I have no servant or maiden, nor anyone else who might help me. Two full days have already passed since he died, and I have not stirred from this place; I have been sitting here all alone, both day and night, and there is nothing I can do on my own. I haven't stopped crying since, for I couldn't control myself on account of my fright, and no man but you has passed this way. Now you know everything that has happened to me; I beg you for the love of God to give me your help." {7345}

"Gladly, my lady, here I am quite ready and willing to assist you. But I do not know which way to go, for I have never before been to the Gaste

Chapele, not one day in my life. If I knew how to get there, with a little help from you, we might bring this matter to a proper conclusion. There is nothing you could ask or require of me that I would not do." {7353}

"I am quite familiar with the road to the Gaste Chapele; indeed I know it better than any other lady or damsel does." {7356}

"Very well then. We will secure these lifeless bodies to the horses, and the two of us will go on foot." {7358}

And so they did, and as they were walking along together he asked her, most affectionately, how things were going for his sister and whether Brien had done her any shame. The lady told him that she had not been mistreated in any way, that nothing was being done to displease her, except that she did not want to marry Brien. And yet there was no doubt she was a prisoner, but being a mere child, she didn't worry about that; in fact, she didn't even give it a thought. Moreover, she had as her companions a great many maidens of high rank who gave her comfort every day. And while they were transporting the bodies in this way, and after they had traveled quite a long distance, the lady began to weep again, expressing such profound sorrow that it seemed she would rather die than live. And she cried: "Ah, what a wretched creature I am! I have fallen from such a high place, I have lost so much honor, and I will always be treated with contempt!" {7385}

When she began lamenting in this way, the knight was astonished and asked why she was expressing such great sorrow now, when she had kept her peace before. Then she started to cry again, saying: "Ah, noble sir, I cannot help my sobbing, for I remember Chastel Paorous, and I have to weep because we are passing close by it." {7395}

"Why is it called by that name?" {7396}

"Because no one makes his way past here by night without seeing or hearing something which will terrify him—but I am completely unafraid. And I do not say that for fear of passing near it but rather because I have lost the lordship of the castle, and I will never again have the man who used to govern it. Whenever I go there now, I will see my power greatly diminished. Upon my soul, never again will I meet anyone who treats me as a chatelaine or a lady, not one single day in all my life, not so long as the evil Brien remains alive, he who has seized and confiscated everything we own; may God give him shame and dishonor!" {7413}

And as the lady was saying these words, they heard a great commotion in the woods, so loud that one couldn't even have heard God thundering. The Knight, who had no desire to flee, kept moving on, showing no sign of apprehension; then they heard bears and lions roaring all round about, and thunder and lightning so loud it seemed like the very woods would be turned upside down and the trees uprooted; and yet they did their best to keep on going, advancing with determination. {7425}

Before long, they reached the chapel, which was ancient and imposing. At this the Knight was very happy and the lady too; and then they untied the bodies and carried them inside. The Knight of the Two Swords removed the armor from his hands and took off his helmet—his face was bathed in tears—and knelt down right at the head of the grave where his father lay buried. Then he said: "Dear father, how true it is, as people say, that you were the finest knight in the world—that you had greater beauty and far more courtesy than any other man then alive—may God have mercy upon your soul, you whose mortal remains lie interred in this place." {7444}

After he had spoken these words he stood up, and the lady—who was far from saddened by what she had heard—also made ready to work; although she was greatly moved, she uttered not a word. She unsheathed her husband's sword, and the two of them began to dig a grave; without saying a word they buried the knight in full armor, and they interred the squire outside the church, right in front of the door. Then the Knight quickly put his helmet back on, covered his hands, and returned to his horse; at that point he remembered the shackles which they said the maiden had placed on the altar when she took his father's sword. He turned around, went back inside, and found them sitting there; he took them, put them inside his hauberk, and then he turned to leave. And the lady also mounted and made ready to depart, and the two of them rode off into the forest. {7467}

When they had traveled for quite a while, neither saying a word to the other, they saw a great spreading tree standing in a meadow, and they headed toward it, for they hadn't paid much attention to the time. It was already midnight, and by now they were quite concerned about having stayed up so late, as they were weary and exhausted. They dismounted, removed their horses' bridles, and allowed them to graze freely. Then they gave some thought to themselves; they made beds of anything they could find, and they lay down to sleep as best they could. {7482}

The night was short and passed quickly. It was a very beautiful morning: the sun was already high in the sky, and the air was warm and still. The Knight awoke but the lady continued to slumber, for she was not accustomed to hardship. Without wasting any time, the Knight secured the horses and put on their bridles. The lady, who was still lying on her bed, had meantime awakened. She got up, troubled and apprehensive, not quite knowing what to say or do, for she knew that her situation would get worse if he left her; but she did not pursue or pressure him or make any demands on him. And he came over and asked her mount up so that they could find some safer haven. Both of them did so, and then they rode off toward the woods. {7503}

When they had traveled for a good long while—the hour of prime had already passed—the lady thought she would ask him for some information about himself. For when ladies or damsels are riding with an honest man, it is not proper if they fail to inquire about his person and his name. And so she said: "Dear lord, do not consider me impolite, but I would like to know who you are and what mission brings you here; for anyone who gets this far must pass by the Lac as Jumeles, and anyone who is so careless as to venture near that place will hear some very painful news indeed. For all who pass by are killed unless they are known to the residents of that castle, on account of the stranger who murdered Bleheri." {7523}

Then the Knight told her that he had spent a night there, that his mother was Bleheri's wife, and that he himself was Bleheri's son. When the lady heard this news, she was overjoyed. "Then I am not completely without hope," she said, "for I am in your company, dear cousin. And never a day in all my life have I been so happy as I am now. For in this land there were not even two people who knew the truth about you, or who had ever seen you. Everyone thought for sure that you were dead—although a few said that it couldn't be true because this land was supposed to be liberated by you and by the sword which was fastened to your father's side when he was buried." To this the Knight made no reply, but kept on riding, deep in thought. {7545}

# XIV

The Knight and Brien de la Gastine

The Knight looked on ahead and saw some tents pitched in an open field beside the road; and it seemed that the people there were expressing the greatest sorrow the world had ever known. At once he galloped toward the encampment, and as he approached it, the lady who was riding with him—and who knew what camp it was—said that if he took her advice, he would turn back right away, for there was no way he could possibly avoid harm; and on his return journey he would find himself in great peril. But nothing the lady said could make him lose his self-assurance; he did not even think of being afraid, for in his heart he considered it of no importance. {7563}

He rode until he reached the tents, dismounting at once in front of them, as did the lady. No one came forward to hold his horse, but after a while a lady ventured out, her head covered with a gold-trimmed kerchief. In a tearful voice she said to him: "You are most welcome here, dear lord, provided that you bear us no ill will, for we are in great sorrow and suffering as much shame as ladies ever could." {7575}

"I would certainly like to know," he said, "who has done you this evil." The lady led him inside and there he found as many as six other ladies, all in tears; he took a seat and had them all gather round about him. Then they began to tell him of their plight, explaining how Brien held them in his grasp and how he had killed their husbands—be they castellans or vavasors—and how he had them kept under guard by a company of knights, so that none of them could escape; and so they passed their days in great shame. {7589}

While he was listening to their story—the evil and misfortune of it all—he saw an armed knight approaching at great speed, accompanied by a lady who could barely keep up the pace. She made quite a pitiful companion, for she was riding a worn-out, good-for-nothing nag. And he goaded his steed on mercilessly, pricking it over and over again to make it race. And when the Knight heard this commotion, quite alarmed, he jumped up and quickly ran out of the tent; he mounted his horse right away, rode up to the other knight, and exclaimed: "What wrong has this lady said or done to you that you should escort her here so shabbily, and from whom do you hold such lordship and such power?" {7607}

"Now you really must hear my answer to your question," the man replied, "for clearly you need to be instructed." {7609}

"Indeed I do, sir knight, or else I think you'll regret your impudence!" {7611}

"May the man be damned who ever tells you anything!" {7612}

And the Knight replied: "I challenge you to battle then." {7613}

"That's the slightest scare I've ever had," he replied, "and you may be sure I'm telling you the truth now. I challenge you in return, for you don't frighten me one bit." {7617}

Then they took up their positions without delay and faced their horses off; they readied their shields and charged without losing a moment's time, as fast as their horses could carry them. With lances lowered, they struck each other so hard that both of their shields were pierced. The other knight's lance broke, for it could not penetrate the hauberk, but the Knight of the Two Swords struck his opponent and smashed the links of his mail; he sent the steel right through his body and shattered the saddlebow behind him with such force that both knight and charger fell down in a heap; and the rider fractured his collarbone. Taking his sword in hand, the Knight then came back and stood over him. And the man with whom he had no further need to fight begged him for mercy. {7637}

And the Knight announced that when the offense had been remedied just as he would prescribe it, and when his opponent became a prisoner in just the way he would set forth, then and only then would the man receive mercy. {7641}

"My lord," he said, "here I am, quite ready to promise you anything you ask, and I will never go back on my word, and you will never hear tell of me trying to do so." The Knight dismounted to accept the pledge, which the other man promptly gave him. {7647}

When that battle was concluded, the Knight looked over toward the forest and saw a sight that did not please him one bit: for there he noticed as many as six knights all clad in armor, heading for the tents. And when the six knights saw that he had defeated their companion, all six of them stopped and took counsel. They decided they would send out one of their number to fight him, and then another, and if those two men were defeated, the remaining four would go forth together and do battle with him, all four of them attacking him at once and taking him by force; and without further discussion, one of them came riding forward. {7665}

For his part, the Knight of the Swords mounted his horse and sized up the situation. His adversary spurred his steed and whipped it on, shouting over and over that he challenged the Knight to battle. The Knight of the Swords charged as fast as his horse could carry him, and when the two of them collided, he pinned the other man's shield against his arm, and his arm against his body, with such force that he pushed him right out of the saddle, knocking him to the ground; and in falling, the man broke his arm and his collarbone—for the ground was far from soft—and he was roundly trounced. {7681}

The Knight came back to stand above him as quickly as he could. He drew his sword, with which he had accomplished many a deed of prowess, but the other knight did not want to suffer any worse injuries than he already had. Since he could not get up, he begged for mercy, saying that the Knight could do with him whatever he pleased; and so he granted him mercy. {7689}

With that, the knight who had the second joust spurred his horse on. The Knight of the Two Swords saw him coming and charged against him at once; don't be surprised if he was eager to do him some harm! And the man who was driven by outrageous arrogance assailed the Knight, and he attacked him in return. And here is the outcome of the second joust: when they came together, the Knight of the Two Swords struck down his adversary, sending him and his horse to the ground in a heap, so that the second man broke his neck and was finished off. {7703}

With that, the Knight made ready to confront the rest of them, and he rode ahead, whipping his horse with the reins until he got a little closer to them. They faced their horses off at him, and he let them charge. He quickly dispatched the first one, and then he took on the others, dealing with the remaining three in such a way that they all ended up begging him for mercy. Then they returned to where the others lay, and all six of them promised that—with his consent and by his leave—they would go to the court of King Arthur—no matter how much trouble it caused them—and surrender to him on the Knight's behalf. And there they would announce that the Knight of the Two Swords offered this present to the King, despite the fact that members of the court had wronged him. All six of them agreed to this and departed, just as I have told you. {7725}

Midday was already approaching, and the Knight had not yet had any-thing to eat or drink. The ladies, who had witnessed this marvelous ex-ploit, came out to meet him, vying with one other to embrace him and inviting him to dine. He was greatly pleased by this suggestion and agreed to it without a moment's hesitation. One of the ladies spread a cloth on the ground, fetched the water for washing, and offered it to him, and then he sat down to eat. Before he rose from his meal, he had gotten to know each one of them personally and had heard news from them which troubled him greatly and caused his heart to tremble, but he gave no outward sign of concern. {7740}

He had eaten a leisurely meal and this pleased him very much, for he had gone without food for quite a while. And they had given him sour wine, black bread, and larded venison on bread they had saved from what the ladies of the neighborhood sent them, for that was all they had to eat. They gave him an abundance of such food, and he was greatly restored by it. And when he rose from his meal, he asked them what they wanted to do. They replied that they would like to go with him, if he didn't mind, for they would endure great abuse and shame by remaining there, and they would never be rescued by anyone, and so they preferred to take their chances with him. {7759}

When he heard these words, he reassured them, saying that he would be delighted to have their company, but there were only three horses for the entire group: so he suggested that the horses should carry their belong-ings and they would all proceed on foot. Everyone agreed to this and did just as he proposed; and so they set out on their way, heading into the forest. {7769}

As for the prisoners, they made ready to travel and set out on their jour-ney. After they had buried their dead companion, they rode on day after day, never stopping for rest until they reached Carahaix, where King Arthur was residing. It was right after Mass; the King had just eaten and was still sitting at the dais. Those who arrived were bearing three litters. They dis-mounted, placed the stretchers on the ground, and promptly went into the palace, where they found King Arthur. They went right up to greet him, introducing themselves and the wounded men. Then they declared: "De-spite the offense which has been committed against him at this court, the Knight of the Two Swords offers you this present. He has won six battles against the six of us, of that you may be sure." {7791}

When the King heard this, he was extremely pleased and replied: "May the man who takes such pains to send me a present like this have great good fortune. Truly I never had a knight who ever gave me such a fine gift. And if he has been wronged by any member of this court, I am greatly distressed, and the offense will certainly not go unpunished, if I can find out anything about it." At this the King grew silent and somber, for he did not know which of his knights he was threatening. Then he asked that the wounded men be brought in for him to look at, and he had them cared for just as if he himself had been one of their number. {7807}

At that moment, the Lady of Cardigan stepped up confidently and said to the King: "My lord, I have been living at your court for more than half a year now, and every day reports arrive here about this knight, and yet you seem quite unable to do anything to make him come back. Do you not think that this brings shame upon you and all your retinue, which is said to consist of so many worthy men? Truly, I will allow you no further delay or extension. Rather, I ask you to go in person and put forth some effort of your own so that he may be mine and I may be his. Why, I could wait here forever without seeing anything done to advance my cause." {7825}

"You are quite right, young lady, and I will secure your gift for you. I will never sleep, except in tents, until I have done everything in my power either to lose him forever or else to return him to the court. We will depart within three days." {7831}

Then he told Kay to get all his equipment and provisions ready, for he wanted to travel every day from then on, never sleeping in a town or city. And just as King Arthur commanded, so did Kay carry out his orders. Each man took responsibility for his own preparations, and everyone was delighted at the prospect of their journey. Within three days everyone was ready, and so they set out, the King, the Queen, and the maiden, who would not stop pressing her cause in earnest. They began to ride until they found themselves in the forest, one and all, and they were constantly on the alert to defend themselves or to attack; and they could hardly fail to do so, for from the very outset they had agreed to go out every day and seek adventures and return to their tents every night, so that they would not be sidetracked by anyone and held up on that account. So they moved on to a new location every day, and they lived in the forest for many a day and many a week. {7857}

As for the Knight who was guiding the ladies, he did not stray from his purpose; rather, he traveled with all his company like a man of utmost courtesy, to such a point that news spread throughout the land that a lone knight was escorting a good many ladies and that he was suffering great hardship and adversity in order to treat them with honor. Brien eventually heard tell of this knight, and he was furious because—through his prowess—this man had relieved him of these ladies he had dispossessed. He declared that they would rue the day they had escaped from where he held them in confinement. And the man who had taken them under his safe-conduct did not realize they would have a lot more to do with him before they saw another night go by. {7876}

Without saying any more about it, Brien armed himself and announced that he would not stop traveling until he found the Knight of the Two Swords, if he possibly could. No women had ever been so dearly purchased since God was born, so he declared. Then he set out, all equipped for battle, and began his quest. He did not pause for rest but earnestly pursued his solitary journey until early one morning he was nearing Chastel Paorous. As he was riding along, he looked ahead and saw a little wooded knoll. And beside it he saw a tent and some horses too. He did not tarry but headed straight for it, thinking that he would soon lay his hands on the man he was after; and so he approached the camp. {7897}

The Knight of the Two Swords and the ladies were already up making ready to travel, and he was outside the tent at the time, loading up their equipment. All at once he saw a fully armed knight coming their way all ready for battle, or so it seemed. He stopped what he was doing, took his horse by the reins, and mounted up. Taking his shield and lance in hand, he goaded his horse and raced out into the middle of the field, where he made a halt. {7911}

The man who was plotting this folly came galloping toward him and cried out: "Knight, to my way of thinking, you are not very smart to have come into my country and my land to shame me and make war against me. You are giving solace and comfort to these women for whom I bear a mortal hatred, and you have put yourself at their service! You have undertaken a foolhardy mission, and you will pay dearly for it!" {7923}

"You must take me for an idiot and a silly fool, sir knight, and I would very much like to know who you are." {7926}

"You'd like to know who I am, would you? I am Brien de la Gastine." {7927}

"Why, I've never been so pleased a day in my life. Are you not the man who abducted these ladies and relieved them of their husbands?" {7931}

"That's exactly who I am. And what business of yours is it?" {7932}

"Well then, since that's who you are, I challenge you to battle, without delay or postponement!" {7935}

"And I challenge you too, of that you may be sure; in fact, I came here for no other reason." {7937}

With these words they drew apart, took their distances, and set their lances on the fewters. They spurred their horses on, drew their emblazoned shields in front of their chests, and went charging at each other, lances held low. They struck each other so violently that the two shields hanging from their necks were pierced and damaged on impact and their lances went flying up in splinters. And it so happened when they met that their horses collided chest to chest, so that both of them fell to the ground in a heap, and they struggled back to their feet as best they could. The Knight of the Two Swords, who knew how to handle his weapons, removed the shield from his neck, brandished his naked sword, and went to take on Brien man to man. {7957}

He struck him so hard that he sent him reeling. Brien drew back, as he was quite terrified of the Knight, for he knew him to be extremely strong and powerful. He did not give Brien a chance to catch his breath but pursued him mercilessly, taking pains to do him harm. Brien defended himself as well as he could—he sliced up the Knight's shield and split it in half—but he couldn't manage to do anything else. The Knight of the Swords did not hold back but goaded him and made him back off; he pressed Brien so hard that no force in the world could have kept him from falling to the ground. He leapt on top of him, tore out the laces of his helmet, and knocked it off his head. Then he fractured and crushed his face with the handle of his sword, smashing and shattering his ventail, which was all stained and crimson with blood. And at that moment, the Knight of the Swords marveled at what was happening, wondering why such a badly injured knight wasn't begging for mercy. {7981}

But Brien held his tongue, for he was full of malice and he wasn't willing to say a word. The Knight of the Two Swords grew outraged and didn't think much of the man he had under his control; he thought that he could easily cut off his head if he wanted to, and still Brien was unwilling to beg for mercy. He said to him: "I don't think you gave Sir Gawain this much consideration, and you behaved like a simple felon toward Bleheri. You will be repaid for your misconduct shortly, because you are going to lose your head for it. Never again will you do battle with another man or commit another act of treachery. I am going to make you suffer eternal agony, so help me God!" {7998}

"That means nothing to me now," said Brien. "There is no reason for a vanquished knight to live on. Truly, I have lived long enough when I am forced to die in dishonor. I would not want to recover from this humiliation, for then I would live in shame for the rest of my days." {8005}

"And as for me, so help me God, I would be a very poor knight indeed if I let you escape. It is only fitting that you have your reward." Then he did not pause for a moment, but lopped off Brien's head, stood up, and went to get back on his horse. {8011}

It would be pointless to describe the joy the ladies showed; they ran up to meet the Knight with so much jubilation that they scarcely knew what to do. They embraced him and his horse so eagerly that, however he tried to hold them off, he could hardly manage to dismount. And as he walked back to the tent, they made a great fuss over him. First they took off his helmet, then brought him some water, and he washed his hands and his face. And they did for him whatever they thought might please him, as well they knew how, and then they dined on whatever food they had. {8026}

It was already past midday, and when they had eaten and relaxed long enough, they all agreed to go straight to Chastel Paorous, traveling just as they had been doing every day, and so they set off on their way. The Knight of the Two Swords took Brien's head, put it back inside the man's helmet, and said that he would send it to his mother as soon as he could, for nothing could possibly bring her greater joy. {8039}

They kept on going until they reached the castle, and neither adventures nor obstacles delayed their progress. Then they met a knight standing right at the entrance, a worthy gentleman, judging by his appearance, and quite handsome despite his advanced years. After exchanging greetings, the old man asked them where they had come from and who they were. The lady of the castle, who was one of their number, answered that he really ought to recognize her since he had seen her so often before. "'When the ball is lost, the game is over,'" the lady observed, "and, as the peasant says, 'when Samson died, his name died too, so that today no one knows who his offspring were.' People who once nurtured me and knew me well will turn their backs on me again and again! Sometimes even the bravest man may consider himself a fool." {8061}

When the old knight heard these words, he burst into tears, dismounted, and fell at her feet most humbly, beseeching her and begging her pardon. He said he simply hadn't recognized her and that she should do with him whatever she pleased. The lady did not have the time to straighten things out right then; instead she asked him to tell her quickly who was the bailiff of the place. {8071}

The old man replied that the warden of the castle was a knight who so mistreated the inhabitants that it was a wonder they didn't kill him a hundred times a day, they hated him so much; and all of them said they would like to flee the country. {8077}

"Dear friend, does this bailiff know that Brien is dead and slain?" {8079}

"Ah, my lady, no man on earth was ever so well protected as he is!" {8081}

"Is that a fact? Well then, take a look at this: here is his head, which has been severed from his body." {8083}

"Who did this to him?"

"The Knight of the Two Swords, whose fief this castle is." {8085}

When the old gentleman heard this, he felt so elated that he couldn't help but weep for joy, and he was unable to speak for the longest time. When he had wept for quite a while, he managed to say: "My lady, if you were so inclined, you could go inside. I know for certain that the bailiff will come and try to capture you and cast you into prison. But I am going to set up an armed guard of knights to come and take him prisoner, and then you can burn him at the stake, or hang him, or put him to death in any way you wish." {8099}

"What a splendid idea," she said. "You go on ahead then, and we will follow after." {8101}

They were not far from the castle, and the man entered in haste, full of confidence and greatly heartened by the news he had heard. He assembled some knights who were relatives of his, telling them: "Dear lords, if there is anyone here willing to help me, we can easily bring shame upon the man who holds us in such vile subjection. Look down there and you will see Milady at the gate of the castle, bringing us Brien's head; he was slain by the knight who is escorting her, and he seems to be a truly accomplished gentleman. Now let us all stay together, for she is coming here on foot." {8117}

When they heard this news, everyone was very pleased, and they agreed to everything he proposed. Before long they saw the ladies and the Knight approaching. Men and women came running quickly when they saw him, and all the common people hurried out to greet them, shouting "Welcome home, Milady!" {8125}

"And may you have good fortune too, my lords!" said the wise and prudent lady. {8127}

When he heard the commotion everyone was raising, the bailiff, who was hearing cases, asked why these people were causing such a stir; and they gave him an answer which did not please him a bit: the lady of the castle had just entered the town. Then he leapt to his feet, and so did his thugs, and they all rushed outside as fast as they could. The Knight, who was walking along with the lady, just stopped and stood there, not moving a muscle. Warily, the bailiff came running up to take him captive. The Knight of the Two Swords drew his weapon to defend himself and struck one of the henchmen who was accosting them, splitting him right down to the chest; then he skirmished and defended himself so well that no one could lay a hand on him. {8147}

The elderly knight who had had the other knights armed that day joined in the fight, and did so eagerly, taking the castellan's horse by the reins and telling him he wasn't going to be riding any farther; the common people crowded all around them to see how things would turn out. The castellan had no choice but to dismount. Then they all went off to the place where he usually heard cases, and the knights had all the people assemble in the courtroom; the castellan threatened them over and over again, saying that they would greatly regret having brought shame upon him. {8163}

The old knight stepped forward and ordered everyone to be still. They all calmed down right away and fell silent, and then he said: "My lords, you must know that vengeance has been taken on Brien for all this land. His head has been cut off and my lady, whom you see standing here before you, has brought it back to us. And if you don't believe me, here it is for all to see!" Then he had it taken out so that the truth would be more widely known; and he showed them all the head, and everyone recognized it as Brien's. They were so overcome with joy that everyone sought to torment the castellan; and it was a happy man indeed who could lay hands on him! Without bothering to call for a trial, everyone took hold of him and gave him what he deserved, him and all his henchmen. Their execution was soon arranged, and they dragged them out of the castle, down to where the gallows stood; right away, not wasting any time about it, they strung them all up together. {8186}

Then they all returned to the castle in great jubilation; everyone wanted to see their lady and their worthy knight. All the houses were readied right away, and everyone rejoiced and made merry. The Knight stayed a full three days in the town, and the lady did him proper homage. He had Brien's head sent off by messenger to his mother, and this gave her great joy. {8198}

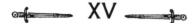 XV

The Knight of the Ladies

There they remained in great comfort, and the lady was restored to full possession of all her fortified castles and manor houses. And the Knight, who did not want to stay any longer, asked these women whose friend he was—the ones he had rescued in the forest—for permission to leave. But, just as women are so apt to do, they undertook to ask him for a gift. And he was armed and outfitted, his horse was brought to him, and he mounted up. Without wasting any time talking about it, the ladies involved all came and knelt before him—the chatelaine was one of them—and they asked him to grant them a boon, if it weren't too much trouble, one that would bring him neither shame nor harm. It upset him to see them on their knees, so he had them get up, promising that they could ask him for anything they wanted and he would grant them everything. {8223}

Once he had offered them this assurance, the chatelaine exclaimed: "You have just agreed unconditionally to take us to King Arthur's court, and to do nothing else along the way except escort us under your protection." {8229}

When he heard these words, he declared: "It troubles me greatly that you are requiring me to return to the King's court, but I will do so, and I will not fail to keep my promise to you, to the best of my ability. But you must agree to act in my best interests, once I have presented you—whether the King is at the court or not—so that I may get back here as quickly as I can, while you stay there; and you must never tell anyone who I am, no matter who may ask." {8243}

"We will follow your orders in every respect," they said, "and we thank you most sincerely." {8245}

They didn't take very long getting ready, and the lady mounted her horse, as did eight others ladies, by my count. The Knight of the Two Swords mounted up as well, and when they were all in their saddles, they rode out of Chastel Paorous. The courageous knight set out with the ladies, unaccompanied by lads or squires, not delaying their departure for a moment, and they rode through the forest all day long. They had had nothing to eat, and it was almost the hour of compline when they spotted the spire of a distant church, and not a single house stood outside the churchyard walls. They headed for it in great haste, reached the main gate, and found it closed. The Knight of the Swords began pounding on it and calling out at the top of his lungs, but no man or woman inside would answer. And so he started to hammer on it once again, as forcefully as he could, and this time it wasn't long before a woman of advanced years came to the door, a wise and prudent lady, so it seemed, and she was wearing a nun's habit. {8271}

When she saw the ladies and the Knight, she asked: "Would it please you to take shelter here? Do come in, and you will find lodgings all ready and waiting, for the sake of Christian charity." {8275}

"That suits us perfectly," everyone replied, "and we thank you for your kind invitation, for night is falling fast, and we would never find another place to sleep." {8279}

Then the lady opened the gate and they all went inside. Some ladies escorted them to their lodgings, and then the Knight dismounted, intending to help the ladies later. But there was not a servant, stable boy, or a man to be found in the entire house, apart from the Knight himself. And so he set about looking after their horses, attending to all their needs quite capably and removing their saddles and bridles. The lodgings had been very well furnished, and the ladies all helped the Knight to remove his armor. Then they dressed him in whatever clothes they could find, putting one of their mantles on over his doublet, for they had nothing else for him to wear. He was tall and handsome, and the mantle was entirely appropriate, for the iron of his armor had soiled his clothing rather badly. {8300}

The tables were set, and the ladies who kept the lodgings went about serving the meal. They brought their guests fish, which they had in abundance, and gave them the kind of ale that the convent members drank every day. Under that roof lived a rather young lady—the keeper of the lodgings—who kept gazing intently at the Knight's face. Suddenly she began to cry so violently that she had to sit down and compose herself. When the Knight noticed she was weeping he was deeply moved, and one of the nuns went over to ask her why she was in tears. She replied: "Truly, if I were to die at this very moment, I would never have been so happy in all my life. For when I saw this man I was reminded once again of the person whose death caused me great distress; for here I see this man who so closely resembles my brother Bleheri—the son of my mother and my father—whom Brien killed, that evil felon! Truly this man looks so much like my brother that no man or woman who didn't know Bleheri was dead would have a moment's doubt about it. And that is why I could not help but weep for pity's sake and because of the love I have always felt for him." {8331}

When the Knight heard the lady speaking in such terms, he was quite unable to control himself, and he too had to weep. He quickly got up from the table, and the ladies, who could hardly help but notice his tears, also began to weep for his sake. And he went over to comfort the lady, whom he asked to sit down beside him, and he said: "My lady, I am just as distressed about your plight as you are, if not more so, and there is no man alive who has seen as much affliction as I. And since it happens that I know who you are, you should know who I am too, for I do not think that you have yet asked or been informed. To tell the truth, my father's name was Bleheri, and I am the son of his wife. And I want you to know that I killed Brien a few days ago; and I am known as the Knight of the Two Swords." {8353}

And before he could even finish telling her this news, she hugged him with such joy that she couldn't speak for the longest time, nor could he. At length, when their embrace was ended, the lady cried: "My dear sweet nephew! My life has never been more sad and painful than since I learned of your father's death; and I had heard nothing for certain about you. For you had been disinherited and your mother had been exiled, and she was not receiving counsel from any man alive because Brien, in his treachery, had all of her men killed. In addition to that, he held your sister in such contempt—she whom he was supposed to marry—that he had her returned to this convent. And she was supposed to take the veil in time, like a woman who doesn't expect to have aid or assistance from any man in the world." {8377}

"Is my sister here then?" {8378}

"Yes, she is."

"And will I be able to see her?" {8379}

"Yes, indeed." And at once she went to fetch her niece, returning without delay. And the two of them could not help but weep for pity's sake, and that is hardly surprising for no one there was left untouched by compassion. And the other ladies were all so stricken with tears on account of their sorrows and regrets that they simply couldn't bear it. He began to comfort and console his sister, telling her not to think of pain and sorrow, or of anything at all that might cause her distress; rather she should live in joy and peace, fearing nothing on this earth. {8395}

When he had comforted his sister, she grew cheerful, and for good reason because now she had her brother with her, whom she had never seen
before. And by the time each of them had managed to console the other—
and that was not a bother for them—it was well past midnight and time to
retire. Within the hostel, soft beds were made ready and the mattresses
stuffed quite full of straw—but not with fresh new straw—and each mattress was covered with two smooth, finely loomed sheets which the ladies
of the place had provided. These ladies went to great trouble to offer them
blankets, and they had many kinds of lovely pillows brought to them. When
the beds were made and arranged to their liking, they lay down to sleep
just as they should, each one in his or her own bed. The young maiden
slept in a bed next to her brother's—not for any wicked delight—simply to
converse and ask him questions, for that was the only way she could sat-
isfy her curiosity. {8422}

The night was short, so those who wanted to stayed up while the others
slumbered, and the morning dawned bright and clear. The brother and
sister had slept a little but not very much. As soon as he saw the light of
day, the Knight was first to rise, and when the others saw him getting up,
they all rose too and got dressed quickly, not wasting any time about it.
And the keeper of the lodgings came in with the ladies because it troubled
her that everyone had gotten up so early, but by then it was too late to do
much about it. The Knight said that he would very much like to speak to
the abbess and the people of the convent, so right away the abbess was
informed of their presence. The members of the order had already heard
Mass, and they sounded the chapter-house bell and summoned the Knight.
He went along and had all the ladies accompany him, and the abbess had
him sit down at her side. He took off his helmet and said to her: "Lady, I
thank you, as do these ladies with me, for the honor you have shown my
sister; she is extremely grateful for it, far more than I can tell you at this
moment. But if ever any difficulty should arise, anything with which I might
help you in any way—anything that a single knight might be able to accomplish—you should know that I am entirely at your service. And I hope
it will not trouble you if I take my sister away from this place. I do not
want to make a nun of her just now. She has sufficient land—if anyone can
win her—to make an excellent marriage." {8463}

"My lord, you may certainly take her with you," said the abbess, "though
we are sad to lose her. You almost took too long getting here, and then you
would never have gotten her back without causing her great shame. All
the arrangements have been completed to make her a nun—either today
or tomorrow—for so we had been instructed. But since you have acted in

such a timely manner, do take your sister with you. We are delighted that she should have such an honor, and your arrival was certainly opportune." {8477}

This conversation did not last very long; they commended each other to God, and everyone wept at the leave-taking, for they were all quite concerned about the young maiden. The abbess acted graciously by freeing the maiden, who was a beautiful creature and most nobly attired. With that they departed, taking cordial leave of one another, and they entered the forest, riding until the hour of nones without meeting anyone. They kept pressing on, and as they were riding, the Knight looked ahead and saw another knight in the distance. Although he had neither companion nor squire with him, he seemed to be a very fine knight, but he was riding along in a state of great discomfort. The Knight quickened his pace and hurried toward the man, and as he approached he could see that he had no lance and he appeared to be wounded. His shield was badly damaged from recent combat and his horse was drenched in sweat, for this man had suffered great injury and not so very long ago. He was gripping the pommel of his saddle and trembling as he rode along, all hunched over his horse. And it seemed that his journey was very long for him and that it was causing him great pain. And when the Knight saw this man in such a sorry state, he caught up with him and greeted him. And when the other knight heard him speak, he stopped at once, raised his head with considerable difficulty, and replied: "Welcome, dear lord, both to you and to these ladies. Would you be kind enough to direct me to the tents where the King is staying." {8517}

"By my faith, that comes as quite a surprise," he said. "I thought you would be able to tell me the way to the court, and here you are asking me for directions! Where have you come from, and who has so mistreated your horse and damaged your shield with so many recent blows?" {8524}

"I will tell you what you want to know, but never will I gain any honor from recounting this tale. I am a knight from Wales, and I set out seeking adventures throughout these deep forests, and indeed I found some very harsh encounters. This very day I met a knight who quickly defeated me in battle and made me swear to become his prisoner. And I have not stopped riding since this morning when it happened, for I had to agree that I would seek out the King's tents in the forest and surrender to him on that knight's behalf." {8539}

"And what was his name?" {8540}

"He told me it was Gaheriet and that he was seeking adventures too, just like I was. But I do not know the way to the King's tents, and I have absolutely no idea where I'm headed." {8545}

"What? Are you telling me that the King is traveling through this very forest?" {8547}

"Yes indeed, he is out looking for the Knight of the Two Swords. He has assembled all his men and every one of them is in the forest; they travel by day, and at night they all return to their tents." {8553}

"Sir knight, let us ride on together, for I too am looking for the King." {8555}

"Gladly, but what land are you from, my lord, and what is your name?" {8557}

When the Knight of the Two Swords heard this, he was annoyed and thought to himself that the wounded knight would not learn his name that day. And so he replied: "I am the Knight of the Ladies, and I have come in search of the King." The other man was unable to ask any more questions, as exhaustion prevented him from doing so. The sun was getting rather low in the sky, and they had no idea where they might find lodgings for the night. At that moment, they came upon a shepherd belonging to a vavasor who lived nearby, and the Knight of the Ladies approached him and said: "Tell me, young man, if there is any fortified place or town or manor house close by, where we might sleep tonight." {8571}

"Yes indeed, there is a vavasor who gladly offers hospitality to all knights—a very worthy and wealthy gentleman he is—and he lives on that estate straight ahead surrounded by that picket fence." {8577}

"My friend," he said, "may God watch over such lodgings." And with that he left the man, and he and all his company headed off in that direction. And as they rode along, he could hear people inside the enclosure. Then he knew that the shepherd had told him the truth, and so they went inside. There they found the lord and some people at the head of the courtyard, sitting on the steps of a wooden staircase in front of the house, which was big and beautiful. As they drew near, the vavasor got up and came forward to meet them, greeting them all as one, and they returned his greetings. "My good people, it is high time for you to dismount; here you will find lodgings all ready and waiting, the very finest I could possibly offer you." {8597}

And when they saw that the lord was such a worthy gentleman, they were quite delighted; they thanked him for his kindness and dismounted. Many men took charge of their horses and provided them with everything they required. The lord and his people took pains to provide for his guests and make them comfortable, and they put the wounded knight to bed, for he badly needed rest. Everyone did his very best to get the dinner ready quickly, and they resolved to spend the rest of the day in conversation. Before long all the food was ready and the tables were set. The meal was delightful and impeccably prepared, for they had meat pies, which pleased them greatly, and then stuffed suckling pig and tiny roasted birds in pastry; they were very well treated indeed. When everyone was satisfied, the tables were cleared and they washed up; then they sat around for a long while talking about anything they liked. And the vavasor was the first one to mention going to bed, for he knew how much they needed rest, because they were exhausted from their travels. And the servants on duty waited no longer to make up the beds; then everyone lay down and fell asleep. {8630}

And when the light of day appeared, the Knight of the Two Swords did not lie in bed for long; instead he got up and got dressed and outfitted, for that was his responsibility. When the ladies saw that he was up, they got up too, and some of them went to help the other knight arm himself; he had been in such agony the day before that he still had great difficulty allowing anyone to help him on with his armor. Then they went out to mount their horses, which were all ready and waiting in the middle of the courtyard, and there they found the vavasor, who was already up. He was dressed in his shirt and had thrown a surcoat over top of it—the kind they wear in Rennes—and he was begging them as earnestly as he could to stay at least until breakfast could be prepared for them. But despite his best efforts, he could not persuade them to accept his offer. {8653}

He mounted his palfrey and rode along with them as their escort, and once they were on their way and had ridden a little while, the Knight of the Two Swords said: "Dear host, could you please tell us anything you may know about King Arthur's whereabouts?" {8661}

"My lord, he is somewhere in the middle of the woods, and he changes his camp's location every day; sometimes he goes hunting to amuse and entertain himself, and sometimes he goes out in full armor seeking adventures. And he has brought his knights along with him for company, all of whom go out in pursuit of chivalry every day, each one by himself, and I am told that they are looking for the Knight of the Two Swords. They have met with many adventures, but they cannot find that man no matter how hard they try; and they are deeply committed to their task. They have undertaken their mission with such resolve that they will never leave the forest until they find him, if they can, not even if every one of them were to die trying. But I don't know exactly where they are, nor do I know of anyone who could tell you." {8683}

"I am troubled to hear that, kind sir! But please feel free to turn around now and go home! Great thanks for the good cheer you gave us at your lodgings. You deserve to be well rewarded for the honor, and may God grant us the power to repay you the favor." {8689}

Then, as they took their leave of one another, the vavasor commended all of them to God. The sky was clear and the day was growing warm, and they rode on until they reached the forest, traveling until the hour of prime had passed. Then they came upon a field which seemed to stretch out for at least half a league, and it appeared to be no wider than a good bowshot. They made their way down its length, and as they advanced a little way, they found a very attractive little spring and a beautiful stream flowing over clear gravel. Around the spring they noticed a great many horses, stamping impatiently at the ground, a lot of broken shields, and a good deal of blood drenching the earth. {8710}

When the Knight of the Swords saw all this, he stopped and thought for sure that this blood must be that of knights who had been there and done battle not long before. And as he was reflecting on this, he looked ahead and spotted a very tall and handsome knight, obviously quite capable of defending his person and armed as if ready to protect himself; he was deep in thought. Not waiting for a moment, the Knight of the Two Swords rode ahead briskly—yet as quietly as he could—and approached the man. And the knight who was riding along so engrossed in thought drew closer and caught sight of him. As soon as he noticed him, he spurred his horse to full speed, skillfully bending his head forward and ensconcing himself in the saddle. For his part, the Knight was ready because it looked like the other man intended to do him harm. And as they were approaching one another, the Knight of the Ladies cried out to the other man first and said: "Sir Knight, please tell me who you are." {8735}

"I belong to King Arthur, who is so greatly renowned." {8737}

"And what is your name?" {8738}

"I am Girflet, the son of Do de Cardueil, and I am seeking adventures. And now I want you to tell me your name." {8741}

"That seems reasonable enough to me," he replied. "I am the Knight of the Ladies." {8743}

"The Knight of the Ladies? To tell the truth, I've never been in any place where I ever heard any good spoken about such a knight. Knights of your kind are worthless; they have the hearts and souls of women." {8747}

"I am the Knight of the Ladies, make no mistake about it. And if you were so inclined, you could very soon find out what kind of man I am." {8750}

"I ask for nothing better," Girflet replied, and at once they took their distances and faced their horses off against each another. They drew their shields in front of their chests and positioned their lances on the fewters. Then they charged one against the other and jousted, securing their lances under their arms. Girflet's lance broke into splinters when they collided. The Knight raced as fast as his horse could carry him and struck Girflet a forceful blow, straight and true, hitting him high on the leather panel of his shield and smashing him so hard that his horse completely lost its footing. Girflet left his saddle and hit the ground so hard that he almost broke his shoulder. He was completely outdone in this battle, and the Knight thought to himself that he would not take the fight any further; so he came back, stood over Girflet, and said: "I will not lay a hand on you or do you any more harm, Sir Knight. In that way, I will pay great honor to your lord, King Arthur, and to you as well." {8775}

He left him there—that much I can tell you—he fought no more and tarried no longer; meanwhile Girflet managed to struggle back into the saddle, for he was seriously injured, and he headed back to the tents as best he could, by the shortest route. {8781}

The Knight of the Ladies resumed his journey, but he did not know which way to go. He was very anxious and preoccupied about finding lodgings for the ladies, though if he had been by himself he would not have been nearly so concerned. Yet if he had only had some food for the ladies he would have considered himself quite fortunate. The sun was setting, twilight was approaching, and he was pondering the situation when he thought he heard the sound of a horn far off in the distance. It seemed to him that it was sounding to announce the capture of some game and for no other reason. He headed off in that direction and directed his course straight toward the sound, leading his company confidently on until night began to fall. It started to grow dark, and the underbrush was tearing all the ladies' clothing, for they were following the Knight at great speed, not knowing the way. {8803}

Then they saw the brightness of a fire, and they were greatly heartened. They kept on riding in that direction, approaching the light, where they found a fire and some huntsmen out hunting deer; and they had just caught one, as plump and mature as you could possibly imagine. The Knight of the Ladies greeted them, and as soon as the huntsmen saw the company, they ran forward to meet them, making a great display of good cheer and fussing over every last one of them as if each were in charge. They said they hoped the company wouldn't object to dismounting there, for they would never find lodgings, not even if they traveled all night long and all next day. {8819}

This invitation greatly pleased the Knight, and he had his ladies dismount at once. The huntsmen came and took the horses, doing everything for them they possibly could. When they had taken care of the horses, they cut up their venison into pieces and prepared a great many spits for roasting. And another group looked after the dainty morsels. Meanwhile, the Knight took pains to construct some leafy bowers. When the food was all ready, everyone sat down to eat. There were no tablecloths, and they did not ask for bread or wine, although they had some flagons of beer—I don't know exactly how many—and seven large dainties. They did not ask for anything else, and yet they had not a taste of salt in any of their dishes. And that is how they fared that night, not expecting to sleep on soft couches or plumped up beds; instead, I do believe, the ladies and the Knight lay down on mounds of moss and tiny twigs until the day grew fair and bright; and none of them bothered to undress or take off their clothes. {8844}

In the morning before sunrise the Knight got up before anyone else because he was eager to move on; the ladies arose without delay and made ready to depart, and the huntsmen outfitted their horses for them and they mounted up. The Knight of the Ladies asked where they might find the King, and they said they didn't know, for he changed his camp's location every day; at that time a week had passed since they had last heard word of him. Then the Knight and the ladies said their farewells, left their shelters, and went seeking their course, entering a vast forest. As long as this open woods lasted they traveled haphazardly, until finally they came upon a broad, well-traveled road which they did not spurn; rather they were quite relieved to find it. They had already journeyed until around the hour of tierce when they saw a squire mounted on a very handsome horse, riding about for pleasure; he had a boy with him on foot, holding two greyhounds on a leash. Right away the Knight realized that he could not have come from very far away, so he quickened his pace, headed for the squire, and said to him: "Tell me, young man—may God protect you—if you know where I might find the King?" {8877}

"My lord," he replied, "I could easily take you there if you wished, if only you would wait here for me until I return. For my lady absolutely insisted that I hurry home because she wants to hear news of Girflet, who was wounded yesterday." {8885}

"Great thanks to you! Now do your best to hurry back, and I will wait for you here, along with all this company." The young man did not tarry but set out at once, urging his packhorse to a quick trot so as to carry out his errand promptly. And as soon as he had done so, he returned to those who were waiting for him in the woods. They were overjoyed when they saw him coming back, and they all set out on their way together. The Knight of the Ladies, who knew that he had injured Girflet, went up to the young man and asked him: "How is that knight doing? Is he badly injured?" {8901}

"He will be perfectly all right by tomorrow, and quite able to take up arms whenever he pleases, should there be the slightest need to do so." {8905}

"My boy, are the King's tents very far away?" {8906}

"No, my lord, you will soon be there, but the King has gone hunting in the woods, along with all his companions, and I believe that the only people remaining at the tents are the Queen and her maidens, of which there are a great many lovely ones. I don't know how many knights she has with her— all bold and valiant men—but they are camped quite close by in a meadow." {8915}

The Knight of the Ladies did not ask the squire any more questions and grew quite pensive. Meanwhile it happened that they entered the meadow, and none of them slowed their pace or drew back on the reins until they reached the tents; then they went to dismount right in front of the King's tent. The young man who was acting as their guide told them to follow him, for the Queen had gone into the woods that day to enjoy the shade. And so they followed the squire, and not far away they found a most attractive spot: there was a meadow shaded by some trees and a spring in the very middle of it, and there was no more sun in the meadow than you would find in a deep cellar whose door faced northwest. There was neither chair nor couch of straw or sheaves, but green grass was growing all about, fresh and clean, and there were seats nicely arranged all around the spring, as if Nature had devoted all her arts to the task. {8942}

The Queen was relaxing there, very finely attired in summer clothes. She was wearing a simple and most becoming dress fashioned from purple cloth and lined with green sendal. She was wrapped in a surcoat all made of the same material, and on her head she had put the whitest kerchief you could ever imagine; and in her hands she held a romance, which she was reading aloud to the knights and maidens. The man who brought the news of Girflet fell to his knees and announced: "My lady, Girflet sends you word through me that he will soon be well again. Before long he will be able to take up his arms without doing himself any harm, but he doesn't want to get up just yet, for the doctors have forbidden it." {8961}

And when he had delivered his message, he got up and withdrew. The Queen was extremely happy to hear this news, and so were all the knights and maidens in her presence. But the one who most rejoiced on hearing this news—the one who was more pleased and delighted than any of the others—was the Lady of Cardigan, for whom this quest had been undertaken. And it brought great suffering to many a knight, for Girflet was no coward; both in word and deed he was far more anxious than all the other knights to bring the mission to a successful conclusion. {8976}

And so the Lady was pleased and delighted at this news; not only was she joyful, she was also tall and elegant, young, lively, and talented. She was endowed with such remarkable beauty that neither Polyxena nor Helen—on account of whose beauty Troy was reduced to ashes—could possibly be compared with her. And joy so enhanced her exquisite beauty that the Knight of the Ladies could do nothing but marvel at her loveliness. Without delay, he removed his helmet and came forward; at once he knelt before the Queen and declared: "My lady, may God who created you protect both you and your companions, and give you counsel and assistance in all your thoughts today! I am your faithful knight forever. From far away I have brought you these ladies who have been dispossessed, and that is both a great wrong and a great evil. Nevertheless, the man who committed this heinous crime has been slain; never again, in all their lives, will they have to worry about him doing them any more harm. {9004}

"To ensure and guarantee their safety, I have brought them to you, for I have no doubt that you will do everything in your power to show them honor [. . .] who are here with you right now. May it please God, they will pay them honor, and I beg them to do so, both them and this lady to whom Cardigan belongs; she is a lady who understands—and has not forgotten—what it is like to lose all the honor she is entitled to. And above all, I implore you to care for the maiden who is my sister; I have no other, and she has no brother except for me. And I want you to know that I am not asking to see the King at this time." {9021}

As he was speaking, he grew so flustered that words began to fail him; he began to stammer and lost his color. And the Queen took note of this as she gazed upon him with obvious pleasure, for she saw in him a very handsome man; but she did not realize—as she should have—that he was a foreign knight. The maiden gazed upon him just as eagerly and was quite smitten by him. Her heart told her that she just couldn't help but love this man, so she said: "Tell me truly, without hiding a thing, Sir Knight, what your name is, for by learning it, I will consider myself greatly honored." {9037}

"At the moment, my name is the Knight of the Ladies," he replied, "and now I would like to ask you for a gift in return, one for which I would be extremely grateful, if only I could have it." {9041}

"I will gladly do whatever you wish, my dear sweet friend." {9043}

"Thank you, my sweet lady! Then I earnestly pray you and request that you ask me no further questions of this kind." {9046}

"I find that most distressing," she replied. "Now I really must insist that you await the King's return." {9048}

"Absolutely not," he retorted, "and I commend you to God." {9049}

Then he went to mount up, returning shortly on his horse, so sorely stricken with love that he almost begged the maiden for mercy. He commended the Queen to God, and then he said to the damsel: "May God grant that you hear such news as sets your heart more at ease; and may God also grant the kind of gift that would please the man who has been cast into pain and suffering on your account." And having said this, the Knight made haste to leave as quickly as he could, but he departed in great distress. {9062}

Tormented by desire, the Knight—with whom Love shared its vast store of woes—left that place lamenting his wretched life and regretting that he had behaved so badly toward the woman who held his heart captive and had it under siege. He rode on deeply engrossed in thought and said to himself that he would keep on searching until he found someone who could give him some good information about the sword he had fastened to his side—if indeed anyone knew anything more about it—the sword which was stained with blood and indelibly tinged halfway up the blade. And from then on—if ever he wanted to engage in battle, or endeavor to assist ladies, or be of service to them—he thought it vital to try to increase his worth and to become more courteous and accomplished. He swore an oath and made a vow to Love that he would devote all his efforts to achieving this goal. And as he was thinking about this, he sought to put some distance between himself and the tents. {9087}

Meanwhile the King and all his companions returned from the hunt in high spirits and good cheer, dismounting at their tents. The prisoner whom Gaheriet had defeated was waiting there; he went up to the King and surrendered himself as a captive, and the King was overjoyed at this. The Queen set out for the King's tent, taking with her the ladies whom the Knight had left in her care. When they saw the King, all of them were overjoyed; they stepped forward and fell down at his feet. {9102}

The King had them stand up, and the Queen, who was never slow to act, at once began to speak on their behalf, saying: "A knight offered you this present today, a gentleman by all appearances, and then he went away, and there was nothing I could do to prevent him from leaving. He said his name was the Knight of the Ladies, and it suited him perfectly, for I have never seen a man show so much honor to ladies. If he had stayed here, I think you would have learned a great deal from him, but he wasn't the least bit inclined to await your return. And yet he prayed earnestly that God might bring you such news as would give the Lady of Cardigan cause to rejoice. By Saint Alban, as well as I can judge a man, he knew the knight you are seeking, or else he had some reliable information about him." {9125}

On hearing this, the King was extremely troubled, and it disturbed him that the man had already left and that he had not been able to speak to him. Then he asked the ladies who the man was, but they could tell him nothing for they had promised the Knight that very day not to say a word about his identity. But they let it out that one of their number had made no such agreement with him, one to whom he was very close, for he was her brother by blood. {9137}

Then the King went right over to her and said: "Young lady, if you please, tell me what you know about your brother." {9140}

"Gladly, my lord! His name is the Knight of the Two Swords, of that you may be sure." {9143}

On hearing this, the King grew angry and marveled that the Knight had departed just like that. Nonetheless, he embraced the maiden affectionately and inquired about her plight, and she told him every detail. Then he learned the truth about how the Knight of the Two Swords had recovered Chastel Paorous not long before. And he heard all about the war and the dealings between Brien and Bleheri, all about how Brien had tricked Bleheri, and about how Sir Gawain had killed Bleheri. This news upset the King and made him apprehensive, for he knew perfectly well that as soon as the Knight of the Swords and his nephew met—wherever and whenever that might be—the outcome would be disastrous, for they would surely kill each other. The very thought of this plunged him into a deep melancholy, but he did not know quite what to do about it. {9165}

Supper had been prepared and tables set throughout the camp, and the Queen took the ladies and escorted them back to her tent, devoting all her efforts and attention to honoring the maiden. And the Lady of Cardigan, who wanted to have the maiden's brother as her husband, showed her greater honor than all the others did; but it seemed quite unlikely that she would ever have him as her lord, and even if she did, he might well abandon her, as he had done just a little while before. And so she often sighed plaintively, murmuring to herself. The news spread quickly through the household, and everyone was quite astonished to hear it. {9181}

And when the members of the court had finished eating, they sat around discussing the news amongst themselves and with the King. They earnestly resolved to set out and pursue the Knight next morning at the hour of prime, never resting until they found him. And then the King urged them all to work together as friends, because it was crucial not to waste any time, for he greatly feared that the Knight and his nephew might come across each other in some place where they would set to fighting. {9192}

When morning came, they got all their equipment ready and entered the forest, advancing steadily and changing their location every day, for in that way they thought they would accomplish their mission more quickly. {9197}

Now let us return to the Knight, who was riding off in great haste, as you might expect of a man who did not want to meet the members of the court if he could help it, and who did not want any of them to find him either. It was well past the hour of compline and he still did not know where he would sleep or where he was heading; that didn't bother him, however, and he didn't give much thought to it. It was starting to get dark, and he had not yet had anything to eat or drink; he sat up when he saw in the distance the glimmer of a fire. He headed for it, although he did not know where he was going or just what path to follow, I can tell you that. He had to leave the main road and go through the dense underbrush of the woods, which broke off as he advanced, causing great pain and injury to the Knight and his horse; but he had to endure it, for he didn't know what else to do. {9220}

He kept on riding at a good speed until he approached the fire, drawing ever closer; and there he found four charcoal makers digging their trenches in the woods. They had built a fire and were eating their bread, and when they saw the Knight, they took fright and ran off in all directions, as if they were scared out of their wits. That bothered the Knight, and he quickly went after them, calling out to them and assuring them that they had nothing to fear. {9235}

Before long, two of them ventured up to him and said: "Have mercy, my lord, for not long ago, some people passed through this place and caused us such a fright that they almost scared the life out of us." {9240}

"Who were they?" {9241}

"We don't know for sure, but they were so devastated by grief and lamenting with such sorrow that we thought they were out of their minds." {9245}

"And these people who displayed such enormous grief, were they armed or what were they like?" {9247}

"Not at all, there were only ladies, but a great many of them. And in the midst of the company there was a lone knight lying on a litter—he looked like quite a rich and noble gentleman—and he was being transported by two small white palfreys. As he went along, full of sorrow and anguish and moaning so intensely, it seemed as if he would die before long, and that was a great pity. Such companies have been coming through here almost every night, and they have filled us with so much fear that we have neither sense nor wisdom left and our hearts are all trembling with terror." {9261}

"And do you know where are they gathering, or where are they heading?" {9263}

"Yes, dear lord; they are headed for the Fontaine des Merveilles, where they hold their vigils by night; and often they assemble there by day as well, in splendid tents, for it is quite a delightful place, and the surrounding meadows are fair and wide." {9270}

"And where may I find this fountain?"

"It is rather far away; you could certainly think of going there if you wanted to, but you would not be able to reach your destination today, and there is no place around here where you could sleep tonight." {9277}

"I have no great desire for shelter," he said, "but I would gladly go to the fountain and find those people if I could. But since I cannot do so right away, I will stay here in your company, and I am most grateful to you for everything you have told me." {9283}

"We would be pleased to have you stay, but you may be sure we don't have a bed for you to sleep in, or anything for you to eat but bread and water." {9286}

"That is quite sufficient, and don't even think about a bed for me; I will sleep well enough on the bracken." {9289}

And so it was arranged, and he dismounted there at once. The other two men came out of hiding when they felt confident enough, and before long they brought him some bread and wild berries, which he ate, drinking great drafts of water with his meal. They found plenty of ferns and moss thereabouts and gathered it to make a bed for him. And without further ado he went and lay down on the couch, which was quite soft and comfortable, and there he slept the whole night through. {9302}

In the morning when the sun came up, the Knight arose and made ready to depart. He mounted his horse, commended his hosts to God, and asked them for directions. Then he set out on the road that he didn't expect to leave until he found both the ladies and the fountain. But he did not know what pain and suffering lay ahead, or what road he was following—and indeed trouble was waiting for him right around the corner. He did not know if he would have to travel far, or if he would face any challenges or encounter any adventures worth telling about. {9317}

 XVI

The Battle for Tygan Castle

The Knight's mother, to whom he had earlier sent Brien's head, was absolutely delighted. Indeed she was so overjoyed that she could not resist summoning all her people from far and near, and no one dared refuse to comply with her wishes. Before long, all those who held any land from her came to do her bidding and her pleasure; and she took possession of her castles once again, as she was entitled to do, and refortified them. And it was urgent that she do so, for Brien's son Galien was seeking to gain control of all the castles that Brien had held during his lifetime. And he had summoned and convoked all the knights of his land to serve his evil purpose, and there was a great war. And Galien's men did everything they possibly could and used every imaginable scheme to cause her harm, burning down towns and plundering them. And so in due course it happened that Galien defeated the Lady's people one day and put them to flight, forcing them to take refuge inside Tygan Castle, where the Lady was residing. And along with them, he laid siege to her with such force that she thought there was no way to escape without being captured; for there were people in great numbers at Tygan, and the castle was so heavily besieged, and they were hemmed in so tightly that not a soul could manage to get out. {9349}

Sir Gawain—who had been seeking the Knight of the Two Swords for so long through forests and through foreign lands, and who had been the victor in so many battles—did not know what to do next or how to find out where the Knight really was. And so he was at his wits' end, because he had searched in so many places without finding anyone who could give him any news, or anyone who had seen him, or anyone who could tell him anything at all, so he began to grow disheartened. He couldn't remember ever having undertaken a mission which he did not complete successfully.

So he thought he would turn around and go back the same way he had come, all the way back to the fork in the road where he thought he had lost track of the Knight. He set out in great haste, as you might expect of a man upset at having wasted so much time to no avail. And he retraced his steps, never changing his course until he reached the fork in the road, where he took the other branch, entering it at a gallop and with a renewed sense of optimism. {9377}

That day he had ridden until around noon and was getting quite discouraged when he thought he heard some people coming along behind him, and he turned around and saw that they were leading a convoy of packhorses and chargers. He wondered what this could mean and where they were going, so he stopped to ask them where they were from and where they were heading with all these supplies. {9387}

And they answered that they were going to Tygan Castle to bring them relief and try to enter the fortress if they could. {9390}

"And who has it under siege?" {9391}

"Galien and his men are encamped all round about, so that no one can get in or out, except by stealth." {9395}

"And whom has he besieged within those walls?" {9396}

"The Lady of the Lac as Jumeles." {9397}

And when Gawain heard this news, he was very pleased; and as they were talking, those who were bringing up the rear approached, some fifty knights and their squires along with mounted soldiers. And as they arrived, he greeted them at once: "My lords, a hearty welcome to you one and all! If it pleased you to have my company, I would gladly go to the rescue of the Lady you are seeking to assist. And for the sake of courtesy— if you please—I request that you not try to find out my name as long as this war may last, and not before the Lady has all her land restored, to her total satisfaction. If God is willing to grant us His protection, you will have nothing to lose by accepting my assistance." {9417}

"Dear lord," they replied as one, "we will be glad to have your support. Now let's make haste and move along!" {9419}

With that they quickly departed and journeyed on day after day until they met a good fifty people fleeing from Sandic, which they had abandoned. And they asked them who they were, where they were from, where they were going, and what news they had of the war. They answered as soon as they could—terrified as they were—that Galien had so plundered the towns that there was nothing left inside them, for he was taking everything and carrying it off and razing all the castles to the ground—even the fairest and most beautiful of them—so that not a soul dared remain be-

hind. "And there is something even harder to accept: he has so badly damaged Tygan Castle, which he has been besieging for so long, that it won't
last another three days unless help arrives soon, for he has already taken
the outer defenses; and if he captures the castle itself, the whole country
will fall into his hands and lie totally defenseless." {9443}

"And how is the battle going? Are there no troops inside?" {9445}

"Yes, plenty of them, but they can do nothing for they have no lords
among them, and not one man is willing to venture outside, not for anything in the world. Like it or not, we greatly fear that Galien will capture
the Lady before long; and that is why we have abandoned the castle we are
from, for we are in exactly the same situation without any hope of protection." {9455}

"My lords, please go no further but come with us instead, for we can
tell you right now what kind of outcome you will have. You have nothing
to lose by accepting our assistance, for we will help you as loyal friends."
{9461}

They readily agreed to what the knights proposed, and together they all
went back until they neared Tygan Castle. They recognized the tents and
pavilions of the army which was besieging the castle, for between the two
camps there was very little space; and the battlefield was an impressive
but appalling sight. Then Sir Gawain advised the men to arm themselves
right away and to send word to the army of their impending arrival, and
everyone agreed to his proposal. {9473}

Each man armed himself as quickly as he could, so that very little time
was lost, and then they mounted their horses. And they organized their
people carefully, for they had two hundred soldiers on horseback and just
as many squires; so they put twenty knights in one battalion along with a
hundred other men, both soldiers and squires, all bold and seasoned warriors, and in the other battalion there were another twenty knights and the
same number of soldiers. And as it happened, the ten men from Sandic
had two hundred others with them as well. When the townspeople looked
around and saw what was happening, they decided to go back to Sandic
and arrange things so that they could look after the troops; for it might
turn out that they would have to receive the attacking forces there, and
they thought they should let their people know about this, so they departed.
{9493}

And it had been decided that the ten armed men from Sandic would
have a go at the enemy forces at once and try to do them some damage,
attacking them from the rear. The troops were divided up in such a way
that these men had Sir Gawain among their number; and they went

galloping off at full speed, riding right into the enemy camp, screaming defiance at them; and they slaughtered and massacred their foes, for they found them completely unarmed. And the alarm spread throughout the enemy camp, and they equipped themselves as quickly as they could. Sir Gawain, who knew a great deal about the art of war, skillfully forced them to back off so as to give heart to the others. {9508}

The enemy troops—cruel, wicked, and brutal men—took the offensive, striving to harass and attack the eleven companions and attempting to make them retreat. And their squadrons, which were trailing along behind them, allowed them to strike out on their own. Realizing this, Sir Gawain took pains to skirmish in earnest, and the combat was so fierce that the first knights put those of the opposing army to rout; and then the well-arrayed battalions began to advance. The other side regrouped its forces and drew back toward the castle, for the sun was beginning to set. The attackers pursued them mercilessly, pressing them very hard, for nothing could divert them from their purpose. Sir Gawain returned to the battle for he did not want to leave the field without a kill, and he rallied all the other men as well. He charged at the enemy, toppling knights and horses, taking ground from them by sheer force; and anyone who wanted to do so captured plenty of horses and knights. {9535}

The battle and the skirmish began all over again in earnest. At that moment, thirty knights who had been guarding Sandic, and who were fresh and well rested, came to their assistance; and they were a great help, for those in the enemy camp were in no way afraid of being attacked. And the seneschal who was leading the enemy forces headed straight for Sir Gawain, charging at him at full tilt. Sir Gawain did the same, and they struck each other so hard that the seneschal's lance shattered on impact and Sir Gawain sent him flying over his horse's hindquarters. Then great numbers of men from all over the place came to the seneschal's rescue, but the thirty fresh recruits succeeded in holding them off, with considerable difficulty. And, despite all their attempts at rescue, Sir Gawain managed to lead his opponent off the battlefield and into safekeeping. And then he charged at the enemy once again and did it with such skill that everyone was astonished to see how much strength one man could have, until at length nightfall forced an end to the hostilities, though both sides were reluctant to stop fighting. {9563}

Then the enemy withdrew, and the other side sought shelter inside Sandic, taking the seneschal with them along with a good many other knights, soldiers, horses, and squires. They were very joyful there because they had launched their campaign so successfully on the very first day;

and so they took the time to celebrate inside the castle, and they had no fear or dread of any creature on earth. {9574}

Great was the tumult and great the noise of celebration throughout the castle, and the inhabitants were overjoyed with the remarkable assistance they had received. And the next morning at daybreak, all the knights assembled in the palace and discussed what to do next, that is, whether they would go out and do battle or remain inside; and each man offered his opinion according to his view of the situation. {9585}

Then Sir Gawain, who had both common sense and courage, spoke up: "It would not be fitting, my lords, for us simply to lie low in here. Rather, let us torment the enemy every day so that they can never get a moment's rest. We have nothing to fear since we have shelter close at hand to which we may quickly withdraw, and we have not yet lost even one of our number. If you agree, let us so arrange it that half of us stay inside while the other half go out each day to torment the enemy, so that they are in constant fear by day and night. And let everyone do his best to break through to Tygan Castle by any possible means, so as to give heart to those who are trapped inside. And once the people of Sandic hear that our men are inside Tygan, then let them come forth every day and keep up the pressure of battle; and let those within the walls of Tygan venture forth and attack the enemy and endeavor to harass them from behind. In this way our troops will cause the enemy distress and damage—perhaps even destroy their confidence altogether—for they have no fortress and they will be in jeopardy from both sides." {9615}

This strategy and wise counsel pleased all the knights greatly, and they gladly agreed to do everything Gawain proposed; so they asked him to take charge of the plan and act as their leader. This strategy was well received because Sir Gawain had given them sound advice; and he was delighted because nothing could have pleased him more than when they put him in charge of the operation. So he took forty of the men whom he knew to have the greatest wisdom and experience and had them armed right away. They left Sandic Castle quietly and in secret, completely hidden from view by a valley, and they divided themselves into two parties. When the time came, the courteous Sir Gawain assigned them to their groups, and twenty of them headed right off in the direction where they had seen lookouts on patrol. Meanwhile, Sir Gawain and his twenty men waited patiently in the valley. It turned out that the other party put all the lookouts to rout, so that the opposing army saw them. Then the enemy troops armed themselves and came out from behind their barricades, each one doing his very best to chase their adversaries back to Sandic. {9645}

And when Sir Gawain and his men saw the enemy forces doing this, it pleased them and suited their purpose perfectly, as they were able to take up a position behind them, so that they had their enemies on the one hand and Tygan on the other. And they managed to get close to a little lift bridge near a postern gate. And as the struggle between the pursuers and the pursued was proceeding with great fury, it so happened that there was a nephew of the Lady's in Gawain's party. This knight knew everyone inside who held power and they all knew him very well, for he was the man who had gone to seek help and he was the seneschal of the Lady's land. He had them open the gate of Tygan and send out a great many knights, all of them anxious to prove their worth. {9666}

Seeing this, Sir Gawain wasted no time but turned around and went to attack the pursuing army. His companions followed after him, and the men from the castle came out and charged so aggressively at the enemy's rear guard that not one of them paid any heed to his fellows; instead they all took flight and scattered in disarray across the battlefield. When they saw this offensive taking place, the enemy forces did a complete turnabout. Sir Gawain gladly guided them back toward the postern gate, and those who were frightened came spurring along behind the others, following Gawain and his men so closely that they thought they were just about to capture them. {9683}

Seething with rage, Galien overtook all the others in his haste to attack, for he recognized Sir Gawain by his arms, having seen him capture his seneschal by his own hand the day before. And as Galien was pursuing him, Sir Gawain looked back and saw him coming; at once he turned his horse around and charged at Galien—right there in front of the entire army—jousting and knocking him right out of the saddle. And knights came rushing to his rescue from all sides, and the melee of knights and horses was so incredible that Sir Gawain could scarcely extricate himself from it, despite all the confusion. {9701}

The enemy looked after their lord, and Sir Gawain led away his opponent's charger, a prize which had cost him dear, and the enemy troops were quite infuriated about that; both sides recognized his valor on that occasion. When they saw that the time was right, and that they could not endure any more fighting despite all those who were backing them up, Gawain and his troops withdrew into Tygan and handed the prisoners over to the Lady, in the palace whose floors were all of stone. She accepted them with gratitude, thanking her men over and over again. Her nephew, who had witnessed Sir Gawain's courage and prowess and the enormous pain he had endured during those first two days, said to her: "My lady, neither my support nor my strength would be of much use to you if this knight wanted to harm you as much as he wants to help you. The day before yesterday, he accompanied us of his own free will; he was coming to your assistance, he said, and that is clear for all to see. But we know nothing about him, not even his name, for we promised that no one would ask him a thing as long as this war might last. He said that he would not stir from here until you had gotten all your possessions back; you must honor him for that, more than any other man on earth. He has already captured Galien's seneschal for you, and today he would have captured Galien too if he had not been so quickly surrounded and attacked by all the enemy forces. As a matter of fact, things did not go at all well for them, for he captured several of their noblest men. Now, dear aunt, I would like you to take pains to show him honor. Do absolutely everything he may ask for and don't act haughty about it." {9747}

"My sincere thanks, dear lord," she said, "and may God yet grant me the strength to reward him for his service." {9751}

With that Gawain undertook to disarm himself at once, and they dressed him for the occasion. And when he was suitably attired, everyone said that they had never before seen such a handsome man, and they showed him great honor. And then the rejoicing and celebration of the inhabitants was so tremendous that the whole town resounded with it. Every man and woman showed their jubilation, and they caroled throughout the castle in throngs, something which was hardly pleasing to the enemy troops outside, who were almost dying of humiliation. {9764}

The people inside Tygan were joyful, but the men in the besieging army were furious and so badly shaken that they kept absolutely still all night long, making not the slightest noise, so that everyone in the castle thought they had all departed. {9771}

In the morning when it was light, Galien had it proclaimed throughout the army that every man should arm himself and launch an immediate attack on the ramparts. And those inside had the gates opened, so as to expose the enemy forces to greater danger, and had their people prepare for battle once again, posting soldiers on the walls. Then the great assault began in earnest, for those outside attacked quite fiercely; but those inside defended themselves extremely well. As the first of the attackers grew weary, they were replaced by fresh troops; but before long they would get another taste of steel, because the knights inside were well armed and highly esteemed, you may be sure of that, a good three hundred of them. And together they had selected Sir Gawain as their leader; and they could not have chosen a wiser or a better man. And the Lady had her people tell him so, and she even gave him personal assurance of her confidence in him. {9796}

And he took great pains to array the troops: the three hundred knights were arranged in three battalions, and they assigned two hundred worthy mounted soldiers to each one, and it looked quite impressive, for all of the men were accomplished and carefully chosen, both squires and soldiers. Sir Gawain rode out ahead of the troops with his ventail closed, and they had arrayed the men extremely well, and they received their opponents expertly as soon as they saw them coming. Sir Gawain went at them so fiercely that he managed to break through their ranks before anyone else. And they found Sir Gawain so fierce and aggressive that it was nothing short of amazing how no one dared wait around for his blows to fall. The attackers strove to defend themselves vigorously though they were far more numerous, for there were at least two of them for every one of Gawain's men. {9818}

The troops from the castle were just recovering from the initial encounter when, all at once, the second battalion came riding alongside; the men were greatly encouraged by this, took heart, and dealt the enemy a crushing blow. Then the battle began in earnest, and the skirmish was intense. Sir Gawain quickly joined forces with the fresh troops and fought through the entire conflict as long as it lasted. He struck and he killed and he wrought such havoc that the entire battlefield was strewn with the lifeless victims of his sword. {9831}

Galien readied his battalion and let them fly, forcing all of Gawain's front line to retreat and break ranks. Then all of a sudden the third battalion rode out from the castle, raising an incredible clamor; they were all young and aggressive and eager to prove their worth, and they all struggled to outdo one another, but there were far too many of them. When Sir Gawain saw them coming out so bravely, both he and his men took heart again and he set to work more energetically than before. Everyone was awed at how a single knight could have so much stamina; it seemed that he had the strength of four hundred men, so often was his presence felt here and there and everywhere. And when the troops from the castle had held out successfully for quite a long while, along came as many as fifty knights in serried ranks from Sandic. And they had a great many squires and soldiers with them, a good two hundred men on horseback, all beautifully arrayed in a single battalion. And once again, as soon as the King's nephew saw them, he joined forces with them and undertook to lead them, to their great satisfaction. And all at once they clashed with the opposing forces, raising a deafening noise, and the strife was just as fierce as each man could possibly endure. {9867}

Sir Gawain advanced, and Galien, whom he had been seeking for so long, had drawn to one side to cool off; and he had laced up his helmet again and was about to return to the fray. And Gawain, who had accomplished so many exploits that day, went to joust with him. The two of them collided with their lances—stout and strong—both of them shattering on impact; then they took each other on with swords. With that the fighting broke out anew and the press of battle overwhelmed the pair, so that they had to break off their encounter despite their eagerness to continue, and yet they kept on getting back at each other all day long. And as the sun was setting, they made a truce until the next day, sent their men back to camp, and parted company. {9889}

And as they were disengaging, Galien, who had been so badly battered and who did not know who the other knight was—and he was enraged and humiliated at this, for he was a proud and combative man—went after Sir Gawain and told him that tomorrow, if he dared, he would have a man-to-man battle without fail; then he extended his hand and proposed that the entire conflict hinge on the outcome of their encounter. {9901}

When Sir Gawain heard this proposal, he too held out his hand to his opponent, and Galien accepted his pledge, as did Gawain from him. And Gawain was far from upset or concerned about this, and he thanked him for his offer in a loud, clear voice. With that, the matter was settled, and everyone went back inside the castle, where they relaxed in total peace and security. They had both gains and losses on that day, and the people inside were amazed at the fact that the troops were returning with such a truce. Some went back to their lodgings and others went to the palace. And when they were ready, the tables were set and they sat down to dinner, and neither Sir Gawain nor any of the men was at all worried or concerned. But when the seneschal gave his aunt news of the battle, saying that a fight would be undertaken without fail the next morning—and that pledges had been exchanged—the Lady was quite upset and apprehensive; and the seneschal recounted the whole story and told her who had taken up the challenge. {9927}

And the Lady said: "May God be on the side of justice, dear nephew, and may He counsel the man who seeks to assist me in this way." {9930}

The news traveled everywhere that Sir Gawain was to fight in the morning; the castle was alive with talk of it, and everyone in the army knew all about it, and that is how they spent the whole night long until the break of day. Sir Gawain made careful preparations to defend himself, and the seneschal ordered all the men to arm themselves, and so they did. {9941}

When everyone was outfitted, Sir Gawain asked them to be patient for a moment, until he could speak to the Lady and to them; and so they all gathered in readiness. Gawain had not yet laced on his helmet, and the Lady was standing in front of the palace. He went to see her, along with all the others, and declared: "My lady, however this battle may turn out, if it pleased you and all these knights assembled here, I would like to ask you for a favor, if you would be so kind: I would ask you to pray for me, and pardon me if I have done you any wrong." {9957}

"I will certainly do so, and God will too. Just as surely I have justice on my side—for I have never committed any offense against Galien—may God be with you today and truly I will have nothing to fear." {9963}

"Indeed, my lady, I do believe you, and may God grant me the strength to defend your cause." And so he left without saying another word. And he had not made this request because of any fear he might have felt but rather in the hope that when he returned, she would pardon him his sinful heart and forgive him for having killed her husband. With that, the seneschal rode out accompanied by the knights—all nicely arrayed in serried ranks—and sent word to Galien that their knight was asking to do battle with him; and Galien was happy to hear this. Galien was also well prepared for combat, as were his troops right down to the very last man. And the two sides exchanged oaths that they would not intervene for any reason and that they would submit to the victor's will without evading their responsibility. {9984}

Before long they had cleared the field and drawn themselves up in ranks. The two knights faced their horses off, one against the other, and charged with as much force as they could muster from their strong and robust steeds. And as soon as they collided, their lances shattered, so they drew their swords; and they took the leather thongs of the shields hanging from their necks and wrapped them round their hands, the better to protect themselves from injury; and then they moved on to sword play and to mighty blows, for both of them knew how to handle a sword. They did not spare each other in the least, for each was strong and self-assured, but they did not do each other any harm except to batter one another's shields. {10001}

After he had drawn back a little way, Sir Gawain let his horse fly; as fast as the steed could travel it struck Galien with the full force of its chest, causing him to lose his balance. Then, with some trouble, Sir Gawain forced Galien backward and yanked at him so hard that he fell right out of the saddle. And when his opponent was unhorsed, Sir Gawain dismounted and went at him, but Galien defended himself, for there was still plenty of fight left in him. At length, Galien grew weary, for Sir Gawain was very aggressive and goaded him mercilessly, to the point that he took ground from him by force and struck him down; then he tore off his helmet and cut off his head, for Galien did not bother to beg for mercy. And the enemy forces saw everything perfectly, but none of them broke ranks or made a move because of the promise they had made. And although they were greatly shaken, they asked for mercy and pardon, saying that they would become captives on any terms he might see fit to dictate. {10027}

"My lords," he replied, "you will do whatever the Lady decides, in every detail. But since you are begging me to intervene on your behalf, I am quite prepared to do anything I can to assist you." {10033}

And without saying another word all of Galien's men dismounted as one and marched off to the castle, but before leaving the field they all removed their swords. Gawain's men followed along behind them, after having taken whatever they could find inside the tents. And as they entered the castle, Sir Gawain quickly rode out ahead of the troops, and he had his ventail down. The Lady had come down from the palace and went to receive him. When the two of them met, the Lady hugged and kissed him; she was happier and more relieved than anyone could ever imagine. Then she declared: "My dear, sweet lord, my heartfelt thanks for such a great favor, for you have rescued and delivered me from oppression." {10055}

"My lady," he said, "I am most gratified by your thanks, and I ask only that you not allow your prisoners to suffer any harm. And please understand that I am offering you this advice in your own best interests, for it would be a disgrace if any harm befell them after they had surrendered voluntarily. Nevertheless, have them securely confined and held under armed guard until you have recovered all of your land and you are completely safe and free from danger." {10067}

"Yes indeed, that is exactly what I want, kind sir, and everything will be done just as you suggest. But I beg you not to leave this place, dear lord, not until I have everything under my control, for I am quite convinced that I would lose all that I possess if you were not here with me." {10075}

"My lady, since you insist, I am quite willing to stay a while." {10076}

And so he remained, and no one failed to serve him in that castle, and they were happy to do so. All of the prisoners promised her seneschal that they would serve him in every possible way, and they sojourned there in peace and comfort, finding nothing to displease them. {10084}

The whole story came to be known throughout the land about how Galien's life had been ended by a mercenary. And the castellans and any people who held castles they had taken from the Lady during this war began to get worried. And there were some who came to court seeking mercy, and there were others—cruel and contemptuous men—who planned to hold out against her. But Sir Gawain managed to bring everything to a satisfactory conclusion. He put an end to the war, and before long the land was at complete peace everywhere, thanks to his wisdom and diplomacy, for he was an expert in such matters. The Lady loved him and held him in high esteem, as did all her people, and there was absolutely nothing he could ask of them, bad or good, that they would not gladly do for him. Furthermore, he was always so trustworthy in matters of courtesy and good conduct that they never found a thing in him which might redound to his discredit. Still, it troubled them greatly that he had been keeping his name secret for so long, until the time came when Sir Gawain decided to take his leave, for he realized there was nothing more he could do there. {10114}

One day he appeared before the Lady and announced: "My lady, I must depart, and I ask you for your leave, for it seems to me that you have your affairs in reasonably good order, and I have business elsewhere for which I bear a heavy responsibility. I beg you for your permission to go." {10122}

When she heard this request, which displeased her greatly, she was most saddened and replied: "Dear lord, you must want to make our lives wretched, since you wish to leave us so soon. If prayer can be of any avail, I beg you to stay with me a little longer, by your grace." {10131}

These were not the words he wanted to hear, and he replied that it was out of the question and she should not even consider keeping him there, for he had been wrong to stay as long as he had. The Lady wept when she saw that her pleas were having no effect, and both she and her people grew extremely sad. And she was much troubled that she hardly knew the man who had done so much for her, and she thought that she might have acted somewhat improperly and that he might be offended because she had not asked him his name or the name of his country. {10145}

So she gave some thought to what kind of reward he ought to have, for even if she gave him one she still didn't think she would be adequately compensating such a worthy man, such an accomplished knight, for everything he had restored to her possession. Still, she had to offer him something pleasing and appropriate, for otherwise she would be shamed everywhere people might hear tell of it. So she said to him: "My dear sweet lord, although it does not suit you to stay here any longer, please do not think that I am happy—nor are any of my people—to lose such a worthy gentleman, and one of such wise counsel as you. And so I freely offer all my land to you; take of it whatever you may wish, for you have surely earned it. And for the love of God I beg you, please do not take offense if I have failed to ask you who you are or what your name is. My people and all my barons advised me not to do so until I had all my affairs in order, for you had made that request of all of them. Now I pray you, tell me both your name and that of your land, so that we will better understand who has brought this war and conflict to an end." {10177}

It was upsetting to Sir Gawain when he heard her ask him for his name, yet he did not lose his composure. Instead he replied: "My lady, I am truly happy that you want to know my name, and that you are grateful to me for having all your land back. Thanks be to God, I should by rights be happier than any other man alive, for I had done you such a great wrong that I did not expect to find any way to make amends. I did not come here hoping to get a reward from you—of that you may be sure—but only to secure your favor if I could and nothing more. For I have no desire to hold your land; I leave it all to you. But so that no one will think I am hiding my name out of cowardice, I will conceal it no longer; but please understand that I am not revealing it so as to boast about my worth. I am Gawain, the nephew of King Arthur, have no doubt about it." {10201}

And when the Lady heard what he said, she was thunderstruck; her heart almost stopped beating and she nearly collapsed in a faint. She managed to remain standing only with great difficulty because of all her people she saw gathered there. Yet she knew that her husband had forgiven Gawain for his death, and she remembered that some time earlier, before he had done battle with Galien, she had told Gawain that she pardoned him with a sincere heart for every wrong he had ever done her and that all her knights did the same. Before long she regained her composure, although she was sad to lose him, I can tell you, because she understood that had it not been for him the defense of her people would have been very poor indeed and she would never have gotten her land back. And so she handled the situation as well as she could, saying: "My lord, since you must leave, and since that is your will, it is only right that you should have whatever reward you might care to ask for, and it will never be refused you. I sincerely apologize to you, here in the presence of these assembled knights, for all my anger and bitterness, for we have heard it said that my lord also pardoned you before he departed from this life, and he made that fact known to all of us." {10233}

And then Sir Gawain knelt down and thanked the Lady and the knights gathered there, and the Lady had him rise, whereupon Sir Gawain asked that his armor be brought in and he had himself outfitted. He mounted his horse, as did the Lady, and all the others mounted theirs, for she said she would escort him on his way, taking the opportunity to survey her land once again. And then they all mounted up and rode out in a lengthy procession, and they traveled a long way together. {10247}

XVII

The Fontaine des Merveilles

One day, the Knight of the Two Swords, who was tormented by love of his sweetheart—he who had accomplished so many deeds of chivalry since he had last seen her—was riding along searching for the Fontaine des Merveilles, which he had been seeking for so long without success. He saw a courier running along at great speed, so he quickened his pace and caught up with him. Then he asked him to wait a moment and explain where he was heading, where he had come from, and what he was looking for. {10261}

The young man stopped in his tracks and said: "My lord, I belong to the Lady of the Lac as Jumeles, and I am seeking help and assistance, for Galien wants to take all her land away from her, and he has already seized most of it. And he has besieged her inside Tygan Castle with such a mighty force that she will soon have to hand over the castle, or else surrender her person, and that is a desperate state of affairs." {10272}

"My boy," he said, "may God come to her rescue! And may He be with you too!" {10273}

Then the Knight abandoned his first quest without a moment's hesitation, and set out in earnest because he wanted to go and save the Lady if he could. And he had traveled a good four days when he encountered some knights from Tygan, men who had left his mother and her people there not long before. He greeted them at once and asked them where they were heading and where they had come from. And they told him everything that had happened, from beginning to end: all about the great love and immense generosity Sir Gawain had shown his mother and all about how he had brought her war to an end and restored everything that belonged to her. {10291}

And when the Knight had heard the whole story, he grew very pensive and wondered how this could be, and how Gawain could possibly have brought this about, when before he had done his mother so much wrong and treated her so villainously. For he was the man she hated more than anyone else alive, and justifiably so. He simply could not believe that the story was true, so he asked which way Gawain's company was heading and whether he could catch up with them that day. {10303}

"Yes, you could," they replied, "for they are not far off, if you would only hurry up a little." {10305}

And he didn't want to waste any time, so he commended them to God and set out after Gawain and his party like a man determined to learn the truth if he possibly could. And he spurred his horse on so eagerly that it was not long before he caught sight of them. When Sir Gawain saw him coming, he drew to a halt at once, for he recognized the Knight by his shield. And he pulled off the road, sure that he would soon have a fight on his hands. He waited there very quietly, so that no one even noticed he had fallen behind. Meanwhile the Knight of the Two Swords approached, and as he drew near he recognized Sir Gawain. {10323}

At once he let his horse fly at full gallop, crying out to him in an angry voice and shouting that he challenged him to battle. And although Gawain was much troubled at this, he was not slow to react but made ready to joust with him. The two of them went at each other as fast as their horses could carry them, and when they crashed together, the impact smashed their shields and shattered their lances. Then they began to fight in such earnest with their swords that those who were riding on ahead heard the noise of clashing steel. And when they looked back, they saw the battle and turned their horses around at once. The Lady was extremely anxious to know who these two men could be, and her knights told her that one of them was Sir Gawain and the other was her son. Then they pulled on their reins and raced back to the field of battle as quickly as they could. The combatants would have been badly injured had the others not arrived in time, for I don't think they would have had much left but the bosses and straps of their shields. In any case, they were doing each other great harm and injury; and when they saw the Lady coming, they backed off a little bit. {10353}

As fast as her horse could carry her, she raced to her son and embraced him tearfully, imploring him not to fight any longer. For he would be acting wrongly and doing her a great disservice if the man who had ended her war and restored her land to her—the man who had done her the greatest honor in the world, the man who had put his life at risk of death—should suffer any harm or villainy on her account while he was under her safe-conduct. Furthermore, everyone knew that her husband had pardoned Gawain for his death on the day he died, and her son and all his knights knew it too. "And so, dear son, I beg you to pardon him as well, and I want the two of you to remain loyal friends from this day on." {10373}

Her face bathed in tears, she dismounted and fell down at her son's feet, and when the others saw her do this they all fell to their knees as well. When the Knight saw what was happening, it seemed to him that he ought to do as they wanted. His mother's words had fully persuaded him and won him over, and since he couldn't stand it any longer, he dismounted and told her he would be glad to do absolutely anything she wanted, whatever it might be. Never in her entire life had she asked him for anything, and because she was so pleased with the favor he had granted her, the Lady reconciled the two men; and they kissed one another and returned to their places. And the Lady took both men with her, and she and all her knights were delighted at the resolution of this conflict. {10395}

That night they took shelter in a castle of hers, and the two of them had all the time they wanted, talking together and telling each other about their plans, and they were served at their pleasure. And the Lady learned that her daughter was one of the maids-in-waiting of the Queen of Britain, and that increased her joy no end. She was delighted and greatly heartened that the companionship between these two men had been restored. And her regret was great and grievous that they had hated each other before. {10409}

As soon as they saw the morning light, the two men got up and donned their armor. They asked the Lady for permission to leave, explaining that they had to go off on their travels. She could not stop them from going, so she granted them leave, but she was quite upset about it. She mounted her horse, like the courteous lady she was, and so did her people, and she escorted the two knights for quite a long distance; and when they had found their way, they commended the Lady to God. They did not ask for directions but simply embarked on their adventure, entering the forest in great haste. The two men exchanged a pledge of loyal companionship until the end of their days, and each of them was extremely pleased about that. {10425}

They had ridden a long way, talking about anything they liked, when Sir Gawain—who had a way with words—declared: "I would beg you, dear companion, if I didn't think it would trouble you too much, to do me the favor of returning to the court. For I have made a solemn vow never to set foot there again unless you are in my company. It has been a long time since I last saw the King and the Queen because I have been out searching for you; and if the love between us is genuine, please grant me what I ask of you." {10439}

"Many thanks, my lord," he said, "but I couldn't possibly agree to

return to the court until I have been to the fountain where so many marvels occur, and not before I have learned the whole truth about this crimson sword. And as soon as I have seen that place, I will indeed return to
the court, that I promise you." {10447}

"Truly," Sir Gawain replied, "I could ask for nothing more, and if it does
not trouble you, please allow me to go with you on this quest, and let the
covenant between us be such that should we have occasion to do battle,
the man who requests it first shall have the honor." {10455}

"By all means, that is perfectly acceptable to me." {10456}

"And I thank you most sincerely for your kindness." With that they set
off, as they had decided on their course of action. And they traveled for
many a day without finding any adventure, or anything else worth telling
about. But one day they had been on the road all day long until around the
hour of compline, and neither one of them had any idea where they might
find shelter for the night; it began to grow very dark, but they kept on
riding all the same, though they had absolutely no idea where they were
headed. And the night was growing quiet and still and black as pitch, and
they heard not the slightest sound. Still they rode on resolutely until around
midnight, when all of a sudden they heard a tremendous tumult in the
forest, so close to them that it made their horses shudder, and they had
great difficulty getting them to go on. {10478}

And then the moon began to shine quite brightly, and they entered a
meadow where they saw animals gathering in such vast numbers, so it
seemed, that in all of Christendom there couldn't have been so many, or of
so many different kinds. They were all going to refresh themselves at a
fountain in that meadow, escorted by a tiny dwarf. He was dressed in clothes
of silk, both coat and cape, all adorned with precious stones and settings
worth at least five hundred marks, and they weren't exactly scarce. Rather,
there was such a profusion of them that the whole field was illuminated by
their radiance for a good bowshot's length all around. He had a staff of
balsam, a whip and a satchel made of silk, and he wore a glittering circlet
on his head. On it a ruby was shining so bright and clear that he guided his
animals by it every night, so that it was never any problem for him whether
the night was cloudy or clear. According to the story—which would never
wittingly tell a lie—he was leading a great dog on a silken leash, and the
animal was taller than he was by a good large palm's breadth. {10507}

When the two knights saw the herdsman so fair, so splendid, and so
nobly attired, they headed in his direction at once, riding down the length
of the meadow; and he shouted at them to get out of his pasture. They kept
on riding at a good speed, whereupon the herdsman gathered all his ani-

mals together like so many lambs and vanished so fast that they lost sight and sound of him in an instant. It came as a great surprise to the knights to lose him so suddenly, so they drew aside to talk. And the Knight of the Two Swords explained that the charcoal maker he had met in the woods had told him all about this and that marvels happened near the fountain every night. {10528}

They waited there patiently, and before long they heard the sound of a great many horns, and along with that they heard dogs barking at the sight of a deer bounding across the field before them. And I can assure you that the deer was not alone; indeed, there was a great crowd of huntsmen and dogs close behind it, and it raced all the way across the field, and they were going after it in hot pursuit; and just as it had happened earlier with the herdsman, they suddenly vanished without a trace. {10541}

The knights did not have to wait very long before they heard the sound of horses whinnying and causing a marvelous noise to resound throughout the woods as they drew near; suddenly a great many squires and young lads on foot entered the meadow, where they set up tents and pavilions, and the squires shouted orders at their boys in loud voices, telling them to make fires. But the two knights didn't stir because of anything they saw, and it wasn't long before they heard people approaching, lamenting so noisily that it sounded like they wanted to die right there and then. And then it dawned on the Knight of the Two Swords that this was the grief he had heard tell of, the sorrow for the knight who had been so gravely injured. And he was happy and much relieved at this, for now—if he were able—he would find out what it all meant; so he didn't move a muscle but kept on waiting patiently. {10564}

And then ladies began to appear in the field, bringing with them a litter and grieving aloud; and along came the knight, moaning constantly, and it was a pity to hear him, for he was grievously wounded. They reached the pavilions and dismounted all at once; then they carried the knight into a tent, but they did not stop at that, for they prepared him a magnificent bed in which they placed him very gently, as nothing else could be done for him. Then the squires made ready to roast the meat. {10579}

Sir Gawain asked his companion what he thought they should do; and the Knight replied that they ought to go over to the pavilions, if he agreed, for it would be an act of great courtesy to inquire who these ladies were and where they had come from. {10585}

"That's a good idea!" replied Gawain, and the pair headed for the tents. The huntsmen I told you about earlier came riding back at a gallop, for they had caught the deer. At once they unloaded their prize near the fire, which was blazing brightly. The two knights were somewhat hesitant, but they ventured forth anyway, going straight to the tent where the knight lay suffering. {10597}

They both dismounted and walked ahead quietly. A lady who saw them came over to greet them saying: "My lords, nothing but good can come from your arrival; now, God willing, what we have been seeking for so long may come to pass. Although we do not yet know for certain just what it may be, if you were willing to stay here now, we are sure that nothing could help us more than your arrival; and we will not lack for pain and suffering until it happens, [. . .] that which we have been seeking for so long." {10613}

Sir Gawain then asked her what she meant by that, and she replied: "My dear sweet lord! For the love of God, I implore you—both of you— please stay here for a while and you will learn all about our plight, for we expect to have great need of your aid and assistance." {10622}

"We will gladly stay the night, my lady." {10623}

"Our sincere thanks, my lord! We couldn't be happier to hear that." {10625}

With that the ladies got up and went to kneel before the knights. They disarmed, dressed, and outfitted the two of them and marveled among themselves at how handsome both men were. Then Sir Gawain had the lady to whom he had first spoken sit down beside him, saying: "Now tell us, my lady, how will it benefit you if we stay?" {10637}

"I will tell you gladly, for I have great faith in God that we will be much better off for your presence." Then tears began to fall most sweetly from her eyes, and all the other ladies who were sitting round about began to cry as well. Nonetheless they controlled their feelings a little bit because the knights were there, and with great difficulty the lady began to explain: "My lords, this wounded knight who lies inside set out from court one day, quite eager to search throughout these vast forests—as gentlemen often do—for the adventures which lie within them. And one day he had traveled a long way—as you might expect of a man unwilling to rest from seeking what he knew would bring him honor—and night was falling fast, so he directed his steps toward this spring, where he found a knight who went at once to greet him. The man was armed and seemed to be a worthy gentleman, for he was on horseback and quite tall. And the newcomer, who was eager for battle, asked the other man to state his business and let him know if he wanted to fight. 'Indeed I do,' the other knight replied, 'for I did not come to meet you for any other reason; but you would be more foolish than I to undertake this battle; and if you would sooner drop the matter, then I for my part would be glad to forget about it too.' {10673}

"The challenger replied: 'I am not the least bit afraid of you; so do the very best you can.' {10675}

"'I will indeed, for that is only right; and you had better look out for yourself too!' {10677}

"Then they jousted, and it so happened that the two of them broke their lances, and with their swords they entered the second stage of combat, very bitter and very fierce, and the battle went on so long and the sword-play was so brutal that the foreign knight badly maimed the man who is now lying inside the tent, for he gave him a wound he will never recover from. And when the stranger realized that his opponent was injured, he drew back and said: 'My lord, if you please, things are going rather badly for you now, for you are wounded. And you may be sure that you will not recover from that wound until the man without a name strikes you once again with this sword. Furthermore, it must penetrate halfway up the blade, and on the steel shaft his name is engraved in enameled gold; and the blood will keep it covered until the man I have told you about you wounds you for a second time. {10701}

"'I am a creature of the spirit world, and because I was once a knight of the good King Arthur of Britain, I beg you to leave our fight as it stands, for if you were to be struck another blow with this sword right now, you would surely die. I am leaving now, but you may be sure that the man who can heal you is the most courteous and the handsomest knight who ever lived, the man with more virtues than any other. And he will come to this place when the time is right, but first he must endure many hardships. Now I must go; I have lingered too long and can stay no longer; but rest assured that I will leave the sword with you. Have it taken to a place where you hear tell that knights pass by frequently. I leave it to you with this promise, that any knight or squire who girds it on—whoever he may be— will be slain by that very sword unless he is the man who truly deserves to have it. Now ponder this matter carefully, as well you should.' {10725}

"Then the spirit-knight departed without another word, and his opponent was left behind so badly wounded that he could scarcely manage to make his way to shelter. And so, in great agony, he did his best to reach this place, where he found us encamped. And because we knew him, he told us the whole story, and we fastened a message to the scabbard of the sword, and it was taken at once to a place where they said that knights often pass by in search of adventures. And we have traveled far and wide, but we have yet to hear any news that would give us cause to rejoice. And so we wait by this spring every night, and we have suffered so much pain and sorrow that no one would ever believe it. My lords, it would be a great courtesy if you told us your names, for you might well have brought us our deliverance if, perchance, either one of you had the crimson sword." {10750}

Then first of all she asked Sir Gawain to tell her his name, if he would. "Certainly, my lady, I have no desire to conceal it; I am called Gawain, but you will not have any assistance from me, and I am very sorry to have to say that." {10756}

"And we are sorry to hear it, my dear sweet lord," she said. "And what is your name, dear lord, you who have been sitting beside Gawain listening to us so intently?" {10761}

"I am called the Knight of the Two Swords." {10762}

"That is a nickname, dear lord; tell us what your real name is." {10764}

"Truly, I do not know what it is, although I have heard myself called the Knight of the Ladies." {10766}

"My lord, perhaps you might like to tell us your true name, the one you received from your godfather." {10769}

"So help me God, from my earliest years, when I was a young lad at the court, I was always called the 'Handsome Young Man,' and I do not know for sure if I have any other name." {10774}

"No, dear lord? But do you know anything about that sword I was talking about?" {10775}

"I do indeed; I brought it here a short while ago." {10777}

When he heard these words, the wounded knight let out such an incredible moan that it was truly pitiful to hear. And right away all the women fell to their hands and knees and begged him—might it not displease him—to free the knight from the great torment in which he lay, for in so doing he would be performing an act of charity. {10785}

Then the Knight of the Swords replied that he would gladly do whatever he thought might bring deliverance to the wounded knight. Without waiting a moment longer, he went to fetch the sword, and before the eyes of all those present he unsheathed it; and never was such great joy ever displayed on account of a sword. The lady went on ahead and gave the wounded man news of what she had just seen. And when he heard this, he was overjoyed. He forced himself up as well as he could, until he managed to assume a sitting position. The two knights then walked toward the tent, and the ladies followed after them. And when they got a little closer, Sir Gawain recognized the man; he did not hesitate to go before all the others to hug and kiss him—even though the stench caused him great distress, for the man smelled so truly horrible that no one could get close to him—and he lamented over him and sobbed so uncontrollably that the ladies following him found it truly pathetic, and the Knight of the Two Swords wept too. And when these tears had passed, the Knight asked him, as a worthy and valiant gentleman should, whether the ladies had told him the truth. {10817}

"Yes, my lord, so help me God, and you are a most welcome sight! Unless I am wounded once again, there is no way I will ever recover." {10821}

"Since I must strike you, I will do so; but please do not bear me any ill will because of it." {10823}

"Even if you were to kill me by doing so, I would pardon you for it in advance." {10825}

And he lifted the sword and struck the man very gently, of that I can assure you. And all at once the poison drained from the wound and turned white, and suddenly the sword lost its crimson stain and became fair and clean and shimmering bright, and the knight no longer felt any pain which might give him cause to complain. Nor did it please him to lie there a moment longer; instead, he bandaged his wound and got up with the rest of the company, for he felt no more pain or suffering. So everyone rejoiced as one that night, and they all feasted and enjoyed themselves immensely, for all three men were companions of King Arthur's household. And to tell the truth, the knight was Gaus, son of the King of Norval, and one of the best men—when in good health—who ever rode a horse or bore a lance or shield in those days. {10846}

Sir Gawain was delighted that the knight had been restored to health. After they had eaten, everyone reported everything they knew about this event, and they certainly needed to talk about it. And Gaus had a lady go and fetch the sword, telling everyone that before the knight who had first wounded him departed, he told him there was a name engraved on the blade in enameled gold and that would be the name of the man who would strike him the second time. "And for that reason I am asking for the sword to be brought in," he said, "because from now on it is only right that you should know your name." The Knight was happy to hear this, and the sword was carried in right away, and engraved on either side of the blade they saw the name Meriadeuc. At once, the Knight of the Swords exclaimed that that had been his grandfather's name. And they talked about this for a long time, and about other matters too; and then they went to bed, for they were quite exhausted and in great need of rest. {10871}

In the morning they awoke, and Sir Gawain was among first to get up, as was his custom, along with the Knight of the Swords; the ladies were up as well and so was Gaus, and they all mounted their horses. Gaus considered it a great pleasure to be able to travel once again, for he was completely free from pain; this delighted him immensely and did him a world of good. The others rode slowly on his account, for they had decided that Gaus would go and stay at the court, putting himself in the care of a doctor there. And he would certainly inform the court that Sir Gawain and the Knight would be coming back shortly, for everyone wanted him to return. And that is exactly what he did, escorting the ladies who had suffered such great pain on his account. {10891}

# XVIII

Le Roux of Val Perilleus

The two companions rode off into the deepest part of the woods, and they promised each other not to return to the court, if they could help it, until each one of them had found adventure, whatever it might be, unless some difficulty cropped up to divert them from this quest. Everything was settled to their mutual satisfaction, and they agreed to go back to the court right afterward, not seeking further respite or delay. {10903}

But things were going rather differently than they expected for the members of King Arthur's court. News was traveling throughout the land that King Arthur had gone into the forest of Sandic with his armed knights looking for the Knight of the Two Swords. And this news reached so many distant places that some people heard it who nursed a deep-seated hatred toward King Arthur and his companions, for there are many evil and jealous men in the world. {10917}

And Le Roux of Val Perilleus had assembled a great many armed men. He was a relative of King Arthur's, and he and his followers were always eager to do everything they could to bully others and cause trouble, for his land was so secure and well defended that he did not fear war by siege or attack by mounted troops. So he got his men ready and they rode into the forest, where he captured every one of the King's knights he encountered as they were traveling about, each man on his own. He had taken as many as two hundred of them, all men of great worth, and had them sent off to prison, for a single knight cannot hold out for long against two thousand. {10937}

Le Roux had played this trick for such a long time that he had seriously reduced the size of King Arthur's company. And the King was greatly astonished at the decrease in his people's numbers but was unable to find out what was going on. Le Roux, whose goal was to betray King Arthur and cause him shame, thought that he could very easily slip into the King's land without his ever knowing a thing about it until after he had taken as much of it as he wanted. And when he had strengthened his position in this way, the King would never be able to recover his land. {10951}

So with that goal in mind Le Roux set out from the forest with all his people, vast companies and countless troops—for he had brought a tremendous number of men along with him—and headed straight for the place where he thought the King's defenses would be the weakest. In that way he expected to take the rest of the land more quickly, through intimidation. And he advanced so rapidly by force of arms that he soon entered the land of Cardigan, waging a brutal war and laying waste to the whole region—for he didn't meet with any opposition. He took two castles and laid siege to Disnadaron, and then he went around burning everything in sight; for people who think they are perfectly secure seldom give much thought to defending themselves. And often he drove them to the wall, attacking his foes and doing them great harm, like a man who didn't think he could possibly fail and who didn't seem to be afraid of anything. {10973}

And news was sent at once to the King, and he was told in every detail just what shame and villainy was being done to him. That caused him great distress, and he thought it only right to go and defend his land and his fiefs; for a man who loses land has good reason to be outraged. {10980}

King Arthur was very sorrowful because he had lost a great many of his men and because he had heard news which displeased him greatly. He had letters and dispatches written and distributed to couriers ordering all those who could bear arms to make ready as soon as they saw the letters and to come at once to Cardueil prepared for battle, for they were urgently needed. {10992}

The messengers departed as quickly as they could, each one setting out for his appointed destination. And all the King's men came as one to assemble at Cardueil. One day, just before sunset, it happened that Le Roux breached the walls of Disnadaron, which he had under siege, and he and all his men managed to get inside by force; they seized the towers and keeps and threw all the residents into prison, as they were unable to defend themselves. For Le Roux's army knew neither fear nor caution, and they promptly refortified the walls and repaired the castle, which was fair and well situated. And there were such vast quantities of food inside that they didn't think they would ever be dislodged as long as they lived; and before long they began planning how to lay siege to Cardigan. {11015}

And King Arthur, who had sent so many messengers to every corner of his kingdom, and who had assembled so many shields and helmets in such a short time, left Cardueil with a good two thousand knights to go and recapture Disnadaron, because staying at Cardueil no longer gave him any pleasure. And they began to ride, day in and day out, until at length they reached Disnadaron, where they set up camp right in front of the fortress. The troops outside blanketed the fields for a good half league all around, and the troops inside were amazed to see how many men had arrived; and they were so taken aback that they didn't even think of asking for a truce. {11033}

The sun began to set, much to the chagrin of Arthur's troops, who immediately launched two or three assaults on the ramparts. Then right away the noble King had it proclaimed throughout the army that they would take up arms again next morning, as soon as they saw the light of day; and the men inside the castle were very frightened and apprehensive about what might happen to them. Guard duty was arranged within the attacking army, and there was great rejoicing that night. But no matter who was joyful or boisterous, those inside the castle were extremely upset, and not one of them made the slightest noise, for no one could see any way out. {11049}

But Le Roux, who had stirred up all the trouble in the first place, decided to save his own skin if he possibly could, leaving his men inside the castle to do their best to negotiate a suitable truce, if they could. And so it goes with those who serve the devil; but in the end they are always put to shame. {11057}

Le Roux got up long before daybreak, armed himself, and made ready to escape. He went riding around the town as if he were out on patrol; then he approached a gatekeeper and had him open the door, saying that he would be gone for a short while and that the man should await his return, for he was going out to harass the night watch and he would be right back. So on the one hand he slipped away from his own army, and on the other he wasn't noticed by his enemies; he stole away quiet as a thief until he was out of sight of the army and the fortress of Disnadaron; then he pulled at the reins and fled down the side of a valley until he reached the forest. {11075}

Then he felt a little safer, and all night long he did his best to keep to the thickest part of the woods. But once the sun came up, he didn't budge all day. The day was bright and clear, and the army made ready to attack. The people inside could certainly have used a good leader, and they went looking everywhere for Le Roux, but he was very far away by then. They found their situation hopeless, so they took counsel and decided to surrender the castle, for they might wait a very long time indeed before anyone came to their rescue; and they could not have chosen a wiser course of action. {11091}

And King Arthur, who was furious and greatly incensed because Le Roux had dared to take up arms against him so disloyally, had the impending assault announced throughout the army, and everyone made ready for battle. The men inside the castle, who had already made a sensible decision, came marching out totally unarmed as soon as they saw the opportunity. They went up to King Arthur to surrender their persons safe and sound, if he were willing to accept. Their seneschal presented himself to the King first, then all the others did the same, begging for mercy and pardon. {11107}

"My lords," said the King, "since you have surrendered as you have, in a matter which is of great concern to me, it is not right that any harm should come to you; but your surrender must be acceptable to the Queen of Cardigan since you have transgressed against her and since you were captured in her land; and if she pardons you out of consideration for me, I will be most grateful to her. Since you have surrendered of your own free will, there is nothing for me to do but show mercy. But where is the man responsible for this act of treason, I ask you? Whatever may happen, I will soon hear a death sentence pronounced [. . .] without delay." {11122}

And they all replied as one: "The fact is that he fled under cover of darkness, all alone, so no one was aware of it, and there is not one of us who doesn't consider himself a perfect fool for having served him." {11127}

"And do you know where my men are, those whom he has taken captive?" {11128}

"Yes, indeed we do, but you couldn't possibly get them back!" {11129}

"And why is that?" {11130}

"Because the way into his land is barely wide enough for a single cart to pass. And there is no one who could ever escape from there, for mountains enclose it on all sides. And in the middle of his land there is a dungeon tower so impregnable that Le Roux fears no siege; and that is where he holds them captive, your knights and other men as well. {11139}

Arthur was troubled to hear this, for he knew perfectly well it was the truth. Le Roux's land was so well situated that force and power were no threat to it, and he didn't think he would ever get his knights back. King Arthur's fear was great, but above all he was deeply concerned for Sir Gawain's safety; and so he called on Sir Yvain and Girflet, whom he saw before him, and said: "My lords, because I am in a difficult situation, and since this fine castle has been surrendered to us, we must not bungle our mission now; rather let us work to bring about peace and reconciliation. You must take a message to the Queen; and the two of you will deliver it to her on my behalf, advising her to forget her enmity toward these people, so that by covenant they agree to offer themselves to her as prisoners, until such time as they do whatever she wants to compensate her for all her losses. And from this day on, they promise not to invade—by stealth or by war—either her land or her jurisdiction, and this I beg and request of her." {11167}

With that, the two went off and delivered their message, as you would expect of bold and prudent men, and the Queen was in perfect agreement. In this way they brought about peace and harmony, and they returned to the castle very pleased with the outcome. All the men who had been prisoners were released and set free, and they took their ease and enjoyed themselves within the fortress. {11176}

The King remained inside that day, angry at the fact that Le Roux—the villain who had taken his knights in such a cunning way—had escaped from him. And that night they were quite a melancholy company because the King was greatly concerned about his nephew's welfare. Nonetheless, he had to put on a brave face for the sake of his knights, and the Queen went around reassuring the men, for she saw how important it was to do so. And no one had to tell her what to do; she just made light of the whole situation. {11190}

King Arthur remained at Disnadaron for a good week, and neither he nor his barons left that place; those who were occupying the two castles came to Disnadaron, for they saw no hope of deliverance, and they made up for all the misdeeds they had committed against the Queen; and they gave her assurances that they would make whatever amends she might see fit to ask of them. One day after dinner the King was sitting at the dais with the Queen and all those who had been present at the meal. He was very pensive, and as he gazed down the hall he saw some ladies coming in on horseback, and there was a lone knight with them, and they all dismounted. As soon as the people saw the knight arrive, they recognized him and crowded all around him, each one doing his best to get close and greet him joyfully. And the King wondered what the reason was for this great display of joy; and they informed him that the knight was Gaus, son of the King of Norval. {11217}

King Arthur came down from the dais at once, for he was quite delighted at his return [. . .], and the Queen went with him. He embraced Gaus and made a great fuss over him, saying: "Welcome back, my lord! You have been gone for a long time indeed, and it has been ages since you were last at court." {11225}

"Quite true, my lord, and never have you heard tell of such a great adventure as that which befell me, or of one so perilous and sinister." {11228}

At once he came forward to recount his misadventure, leaving out no detail. And he told of the great kindness the Knight of the Swords had shown him when he struck him a second time with the sword. And he said that it would not be very long before both men would be seen at the court—Sir Gawain and the Knight—for the two of them were currently traveling together. And then he added: "These ladies have seen him too." {11239}

"How long has it been since they left you?" {11240}

"Less than a week." {11241}

And when the King heard that, he was overcome with joy, as was the Queen, who loved the Knight with a pure heart and noble love untouched by base desires; indeed, no knight had ever seen her cry unless she was weeping with compassion. And all those within were so joyful that no man could possibly describe it. The King summoned every physician and doctor in the court in the presence of all those assembled and personally ordered them to attend to Gaus at once and devote their skills and efforts to caring for him; and so they did. Gaus was taken away to a bedchamber, and the doctors worked so expertly that within a week there was not the slightest trace left of his wound. And often he sat at the dinner table assuring the King of the two knights' impending return, and he confirmed this news to the Queen of Cardigan—she who never stopped thinking about having that man of such remarkable prowess and wisdom as her own—for there was no one in the world she loved more. {11267}

One day she urged King Arthur to return to Cardigan to stay and wait for the knights to return there directly. He could not do otherwise—for she held him to his word—so he made ready to leave, as did every other member of the court. And they set out one morning and traveled for three days until they reached Cardigan, and their stay there pleased them greatly. The town was attractively situated and it was quite a fine place, for everything they needed could be found there; so they stayed a good long while. {11281}

And after they had taken leave of Gaus, the two companions traveled for a long time; and they had chosen a route leading through the deepest part of the forest, as you might expect of men eager to confront adventure. And they traveled in great haste, like men forever impatient to discover something new just a little further down the road. And it was late afternoon and neither one of them had yet had anything to eat or drink. At that moment they saw a convoy of packhorses moving along ahead of them, and some knights as well. They caught up with them quickly and asked where they were from and where they were heading. And the men stopped and said that they had come from the army of the mighty King Arthur, through whom the cause of honor was maintained and defended, he who had assembled a great army before Disnadaron at that time and had recaptured it. {11303}

"And how did that come about? What was the reason for it?" {11305}

And one of the knights told him from start to finish how Le Roux had dared to transgress against the King: how he had captured King Arthur's knights, how he had assembled his own knights to wage war, how he dared to betray the King and take his castles, how he had managed to escape from Disnadaron by stealth, how things had gone for the men who were left in the castle after Le Roux had abandoned them, and how they had heard no further news of him. {11319}

After the knights had finished telling them this story, the two companions were greatly saddened by the fact that their fellows had been lost through such treachery. They were shocked and dismayed and didn't know quite what to say. The Knight of the Swords grew angry with himself and declared that it was his fault that King Arthur had all this strife. For the King—might he have good fortune—had set out through the forests and across the lands in search of him, and because of that the scoundrel had caused him damage and destruction. The Knight said that he would never be happy in all his life so long as his companions were in distress or in captivity, and he was entirely right to feel that way. However the search for the captives might go, and however the matter might turn out, he would never again return to the court as long as one single knight was missing. And Sir Gawain, who was also angry and distressed, exclaimed: "Dear lord, at the very least allow me to go with you as your companion." {11345}

"Your offer causes me great distress," replied the Knight. "No one but I should suffer pain from this task, for through my pride and ignorance I have brought shame upon the finest king that ever lived; and there is no one who could ever prevent me from making amends for it." {11351}

Then, saying no more, they took their leave of the knights and departed. They did not seek out any fortress in which to take shelter for the night; instead they intended to ride on without stopping, for they were angry and determined. The night was growing very dark, and the forest was quite menacing, but they did not wait around for pain or harm or distress to beset them; and that is how they traveled all night long, not wasting any time. The moon rose just at daybreak and the dawn grew bright and clear, and they thought they heard a horse whinnying far off in the distance. Both of them drew to a halt at once and listened; and as the two were stopped there and it was growing light, they saw a knight come riding toward them in great haste. And it looked as if he was very much concerned for his safety, for he was spurring his horse on mercilessly. {11375}

And before the Knight of the Swords had gotten a good look at him, he approached Gawain and said: "My lord, in keeping with our agreement, I ask you for this battle, if you think it appropriate." {11379}

"I grant it to you gladly," Sir Gawain replied. {11381}

And the knight, who was riding as fast as he possibly could, approached the pair at great speed. The Knight of the Two Swords spurred his horse toward the man, racing across the sprawling meadow. And he asked him where he was going in such haste. {11387}

"What business of yours is it where I'm going, be it near or far?" he retorted. "You won't find out a thing about it." {11389}

"Oh yes I will, and you would do well to tell me what I want to know, or else I could send you to a place where you would have plenty of company, so you would do well to give me an answer." {11393}

"I have no need of company and I can't stop here and talk to you, so let me proceed, for I am on an urgent mission." {11395}

"What kind of mission?" {11396}

"What concern of yours is that?" {11397}

"I want to know, so help me God, since you are making such a big problem out of it. It's been a long time since I've met a knight who is so stingy with his words." The other knight, who would rather have been in Lincoln Town, kept on edging toward the woods. {11403}

"What's the matter with you?" said the Knight. "Do you think I'm joking?" {11404}

The other man said not a word, for his predicament did not please him one bit; instead he took off as fast as he could, and the Knight of the Swords went after him, shouting that he challenged him to battle. {11409}

Hearing the challenge, the other man grew alarmed and did not know what to do, for the Knight was following him in such hot pursuit that he could not possibly escape. Yet he would rather have died than disclose the purpose of his mission; for he would have been completely mad to say a word about it. "In adventure there is many a battle to be fought," he thought as he decided to take up the challenge. If the Knight defeated him, people would talk about it forever; and yet it might turn out that he would somehow defeat the Knight. But because there were two of them there, he asked if he needed to be on guard against [. . .], because they appeared to be companions. {11427}

"Don't be concerned about anyone but me," replied the Knight of the Two Swords. {11429}

With that they pulled at their reins and directed their horses toward one another. The other knight was bold and fierce and sure of himself; the meadow was fair and wide, and the sun was not too hot. And the knights charged eagerly, spurring their steeds with lances lowered—strong ones too, and they hefted them expertly—and they drew their shields forward and struck each other so hard that the shafts of their lances could not withstand the force. Their collision was so fierce and the impact of their horses so violent that they were all thrown to the ground in a heap, knights and horses alike, and there they lay in complete disarray. {11446}

They struggled to their feet as quickly as they could, drew their swords, as indeed they had to, and got down to the skirmish. Neither one held anything back, and they did each other as much harm as they possibly could, so that there was nothing left of either man's shield worth so much as a saddlebow; and yet they kept on striking one another, each seeking to take ground from the other. The Knight of the Swords was anxious to bring his battle to an end and was pressing and goading his adversary mercilessly. The other man couldn't even catch his breath, and he hadn't enough strength left to defend himself; his sword blows had absolutely no effect. Despite his best efforts, he backed off so much that he stumbled and fell, whereupon the Knight leapt on top of him, tore off his helmet, and made ready to cut off his head. {11465}

The man did not want to die just yet, so he cried out: "Do not harm me, knight! If you promised to spare my life, and if my person were not put at risk in prison, this matter might still turn out for the best." {11471}

"And how could that possibly be?" {11472}

"When I have a promise of personal security from you, I will tell you how, and I will do absolutely anything you want." {11475}

"Truly? Then you will have what you wish." {11476}

"Provided that I have your solemn assurance." {11477}

The Knight gave him his word without hesitation, then he got off of his body. Then the man, who was badly wounded, struggled painfully to his feet. Sir Gawain drew close to hear whatever he might want to say. "Dear lord," he said, "since things have turned out this way, know that I am Le Roux of Val Perilleus, and I was fleeing all alone just now, as you could see. And you did well to capture me as you did, for if I were back in my own land I would not fear the King or all his might, and he would never be able to recover his knights, whom I have taken captive. However wrongly I have acted, I surrender myself to you, who have promised me safety of life and limb." {11495}

"I don't want you to surrender to me," the Knight replied. "Instead, it is right that you go to Cardigan as a prisoner of the Queen. And do not fear that you will suffer further harm from this encounter, except that you will have to wear around your ankles a set of shackles that I have here." {11503}

"Sir knight, have mercy! You couldn't possibly expect me to go to the court fettered in such a way!" {11507}

"I most certainly could! And before I take my leave of you, be sure of this: I must have some credible token that I can show your people—so help me God, our one true Lord—so that I will be able to get back the men you hold captive." {11514}

Le Roux then answered him: "Willingly, since that's the way things are; you will have my signet ring as your token, which you must show to my seneschal. You will have no cause to fear that anyone there might do you harm once he has recognized this ring. But, dear lord, how will the Queen know who has sent me to her?" {11523}

"Tell her that I am the Knight of the Two Swords." {11525}

And when they had settled their business, the Knight gave him his shackles and told him to go all the way to his destination, then put the fetters on, and acquit himself of his task just as he was required to do. And they did not prolong this discussion; instead they simply parted company. {11533}

Le Roux went off to the court all by himself, and the two companions departed together, rejoicing over the token they had with which to recover the captive knights. And they set out eagerly on their way and traveled for a long while, not losing any time. {11540}

Le Roux set out on his way too, like a man who had not forgotten to keep his covenant faithfully, and he was determined to put in good long days so that he would get to Cardigan quickly, find the Queen, and surrender to her. And because he had chosen his route so well and traveled with such determination, it was not long before he reached Cardigan. There it was midmorning and the King had already heard Mass in the great church, along with the Queen and the knights, of which there were a great many at court. And it was a good four days before Ascension, and knights were gathering there according to their custom. And the King was sitting at the dais just the way he liked to do, with the Queen and a few others, and there were a good many tables in the great hall and plenty of people present. The Lady of Cardigan was at the table where the King was sitting, and just as the first course was about to be served, Le Roux walked in looking quite handsome and elegant, tall and well dressed; indeed he looked like a true gentleman. And just as they were going to serve the first course, the King noticed him and made those who were bringing in the food pause and wait. Everyone stopped when they saw Le Roux, and with that the dinner service came to a standstill. {11575}

Le Roux dismounted, took out the shackles from his shirt, and as quickly as he could he stepped right into them, not pausing for a moment. The knights assembled there looked on in sheer amazement at the sight of these chains, exchanging comments on what they had just seen. And when he had fastened the shackles on, Le Roux stood up and hobbled forward, but before he reached the dais he paused, beckoned to two young lords, and asked them which lady was the Queen who governed Cardigan. They pointed her out, and as soon as he saw who she was he went forward, fell to his knees, and began saying what he was obliged to say. {11595}

"My lady," he declared, "a few days ago I happened to fight with a knight in single combat, and he well and truly defeated me by force of arms. Then he compelled me to promise that I would put these shackles on when I reached the court and that I would present myself to you as a captive. He was not interested in getting any other kind of ransom from me, and I was greatly humiliated by that. And know that he has taken it upon himself to extinguish all hatreds, misdeeds, and transgressions, and he has put an end to all hostilities. He told me that he was the Knight of the Two Swords, and from him I have come to you as your prisoner, wearing shackles. And I ask you to intercede on his behalf—if you have the slightest bit of loyal love for him in your heart—and ask the King to pardon me for every offense I have ever committed against him." {11617}

"Yes indeed, I will gladly do whatever he asks of me, in any way possible. I am greatly indebted to him for his present, and may God grant me the power to reward him for it in return." {11621}

Without hesitating, she got up from the dais, went over to the King, and fell at his feet—she was not interested in postponing the matter—and requested that he pardon the captive, without requiring amends, for any offense he might have committed. The King did not forget the many fine presents the Knight of the Swords had sent him, so he pardoned Le Roux for all his misdeeds right there and then, declaring: "Dear lord, it seems to me only reasonable that, from this moment on, we should know the facts about your name and your land." {11635}

"My lord," he said, "I would have been far happier if you had asked me something else, for I would never have revealed that information if you had not just granted me your pardon. And so that you may know the truth, know that I am Le Roux of Val Perilleus, who has caused you and your people so much hardship and adversity." {11643}

"Then you are a relative of mine?" said the King. {11645}

"Indeed I am."

"So how is it then that I have never seen you anywhere and that I have never come across you before, not one single day in my life?" {11647}

"My lord, I was never in great distress or urgent need." {11649}

"Dear lord, what about my knights, where are they now?" {11650}

"To tell the truth, I took them captive, but for every offense I have committed, I will make amends in such a way that you will find everything to your complete satisfaction; your knights will soon return, with a minimum of delay. The matter has already been settled, and the Knight of the Swords is on his way there now. Sir Gawain is in his company, and they have a token to ensure their success; don't be at all concerned about that." {11661}

"Then," said the King, "consider yourself a truly welcome guest, a hundred thousand times over! From now on it is only right that you be free of your chains." {11665}

Right away knights ran up and removed the shackles. They looked at them in amazement and brought them over for the King to examine. "My lord," said the Queen, "these are the very chains which I left in the chapel when I took the knight's fine sword, the one which no one could loosen from my side, except for the man who wears it now." {11675}

"I do well and truly believe you," King Arthur replied. And then he commanded Le Roux to remove his armor, and he ordered clothes of silk to be brought in for him; and so it was done, and Le Roux sat down to dinner. {11680}

The court, which had been so sad and melancholy just a little while before, was now overcome with joy and happiness. Meanwhile, the two companions who had set out for Val Perilleus reached their destination without incident and negotiated the entrance passage successfully, for no one prevented them from getting through. And it was extremely dangerous and exceptionally challenging, and barely wide enough for a single cart to pass, and it was such a rugged trail that it would have exhausted the most vigorous man, even if he were mounted on a sure-footed horse. It was bounded by a steep cliff on the one hand and by the Sea of Norway on the other, and it was an extremely perilous passage. And they pressed on for a full day before they finally managed to get through; then they journeyed forth until they saw the great tower where the knights of King Arthur's court—whom Le Roux had imprisoned—were being held captive. {11702}

[. . .] right away, for they had stayed in that prison far too long, they were quite sure of that. The seneschal and some other knights mounted up immediately to escort them, and they all set out on their way; he accompanied them until it was well past midday. Then the seneschal turned back, promising them safe-conduct until they managed to traverse the narrow passageway once again. And after that they put in good, long days until they approached Cardigan, where throngs of people of many different kinds were gathered, milling through the city. {11719}

XIX

Return to the Court

Ascension Day dawned bright and clear, and the two who had set out on their journey were eager to reach their destination. And the King had gone to hear Mass, as had the Queen, along with all the knights, ladies, and maidens, in great gladness and rejoicing. Then news arrived that Sir Gawain was on his way back to the court, accompanied by the Knight of the Two Swords, and that the two of them were bringing back the two hundred missing knights. The news spread throughout the town, and the King and the nobles were overjoyed; and not a soul failed to make ready to ride out, for the King had commanded it. He mounted up as quickly as he could, as did the Queen and everyone else, and they all went forth to meet the two knights, who were returning with their entourage. {11741}

As soon as they saw the King approaching, they removed their helmets and unlaced their ventails, like the courteous and cultivated men they were. Then the two of them dismounted in readiness to meet the King, who also stepped down, as did the Queen, and at once all the others dismounted too. Sir Gawain ran forward to greet the King, then they embraced each other joyfully, and the Queen just could not stop hugging and kissing the man she had desired to see for so long. And as soon as he was able, the King left Gawain and went over to kiss and embrace the Knight of the Two Swords, saying: "My lord, you have been wrong to delay your return so long. And yet if you had stayed at court, you would not have sent me so many fine gifts, or so often, and may God grant that I find a proper way to reward you for them." {11765}

Waiting no longer, the Queen came up, accompanied by the maiden who had so long awaited his return. And they thanked him for his presents, which understandably pleased them and for which they were most grateful. {11771}

"My lady," he said, "it was my duty to do so, and yet I do not spurn your thanks." {11773}

And waiting no longer, the beautiful young maiden—the daughter of the castellan of Chastel du Port, who was joyful and excited at seeing her sweetheart, Gawain—went right up to him and greeted him most affectionately. He recognized her at once and embraced her gently; then he said to her, "My dear sweetheart, now do you believe what I told you?" {11783}

"Yes, my lord, I do indeed," she replied, "and I thank God and praise Him. And I thank you greatly for the honor which the King and my lady have shown me on your account. May God, our great King, reward them for it! Dear lord, since you have the gift of my love, please be faithful to me wherever you may go; for I will be truly loyal to you all the days of my life." {11794}

And he replied: "My dear sweetheart, do not be concerned about that, for never will I separate my heart from yours and never will I deceive you." {11798}

Then he embraced her very gently, and he could not resist kissing her on the eyes, despite the people gathered there, and the knights enjoyed a hearty laugh over that. {11802}

And no matter who felt sad or angry about this, I can assure you that the beautiful maiden—the Knight's sister—had great joy in her heart because of her brother's return. She kissed him over and over again and thanked him sweetly for the honor and the noble love she had found in both the King and Queen since the day he left her. And she also expressed her gratitude for the kind treatment she had received from the Queen of Cardigan—that lady of noble bearing—who honored her greatly on his account. And in turn he embraced her joyfully and showed her brotherly love, as you might expect of a man who is neither false nor deceitful. And the Lady of Chastel Paorous was quite overjoyed, you may be sure, and the other maidens of her company all considered him to be their lord. {11822}

Without waiting any longer, the liberated knights went up to the King to express their gratitude for the Knight of the Two Swords, who had endured such hardships on their behalf and delivered them from captivity. And the King, who was very sensible, wise, courteous, and genteel, replied: "May God grant that such a friend remain faithful to me forever and desire to remain at my court." {11831}

With that he went to mount his horse, and all the others did the same. The King and the Knight rode along together, talking freely. And when the King found the right moment, he asked the Knight, for the sake of courtesy, to join his fellowship and to be one of his close friends. And he whose prowess was unsurpassed agreed to that proposal without a moment's hesitation. This so pleased and gratified the King, and his joy was so complete, that he just could not stop offering his thanks to God. He declared that now he had absolutely everything his heart could possibly desire, and he could not think of anything else on earth he might ask God to grant him from that day on. {11849}

They went on talking until they reached Cardigan, and everyone accompanied the King until they got to the palace. He dismounted and promptly ordered the tables to be set, and so it was done. And Sir Gawain went off to his lodgings, and the Knight of the Swords went with him. They took off their armor and they washed their faces and bathed their bodies where the armor had soiled them, and they dressed in fine clothes. Then, waiting no longer, they mounted up and returned to the court. Everyone watched the two of them in wonderment, declaring that never had they seen two such handsome knights, for they were tall, well built, and good looking. They were attired in red samite, both coat and mantle, with lining made of ermine trimmed with zibeline that flowed like jet-black water. And each of them wore hose made of a black silk, nicely tailored and trimmed with crimson; and they wore chaplets of silk and gold on their heads, and their locks were blond and wavy. They rode fine, imposing, long-haired palfreys with good-sized bells of precious gold on the chest straps and the bridles. And the bows of their saddles were adorned with gold leaf and ivory, very finely crafted and superbly engraved. They came in so nobly arrayed that everyone stared at them in amazement, and the King commanded that the water be poured. And the hall was great and wide and overflowing with tables; and Kay, the seneschal, took pains to oversee the table service, as was his duty, along with Bedevere, the constable, and Lucan, the wine steward; and there were plenty of pages to help out. They were graciously served and the knights, ladies, and maidens all dined together, exchanging many fair and pleasant words, talking freely with one another, and taking all the time they needed. {11904}

The court was joyous and full of good cheer, and the ladies, maidens, and knights were far more interested in good fellowship than eating. The chamberlains cleared the tables, but no one got up from the tables because they all wanted to go on talking together; and they took note of the Lady of Cardigan, who had been waiting for almost a year. She wanted to have the Knight as her husband, and as she was accustomed to doing, she reminded the King of their covenant, saying that it would be inappropriate to keep her waiting any longer now. And he couldn't make any more excuses, for the Knight had indeed returned to the court, so she insisted that he fulfill the terms of his covenant. {11923}

And King Arthur, who was a very wise man, replied: "My beauty, you are right, you have waited for him long enough. I will do the very best I can to make him yours, if I do not find him too stubborn or headstrong. I will devote all my might and prayers to the task, sparing no effort." {11930}

And then he got up and called into counsel the men who were sitting with him at the dais. And the Queen was there and King Lot, and then there was King Urien and King Arés and Girflet's father, the Count. The King withdrew to a chamber with the men and stretched out on a couch, as did the others, and then he said: "My lords, you are quite aware of the covenant I have with the Lady of this city, and you know the trouble we have gone through to seek and find this worthy gentleman. And, with your advice and counsel, I would like to have him do my bidding and take the Queen as his wife, for there would be great honor in it for him, and the entire business would then be successfully concluded." {11950}

"You have spoken wisely," they said, "and we can think of no reason why it should not be so." {11952}

"Go and get him, then," he told the Count, "and bring my nephew Gawain in with him." {11955}

And the Count left the room and went to summon the two knights; and they went with him quite willingly, for they already had a fairly good idea of what was going on. They entered the chamber where the kings were gathered and sat down together with them. King Arthur was neither silent nor pensive; rather he spoke out and said: "Almost a year has passed, my friend, since I and all those present at the court of Cardueil saw you ungird the sword—the truth is not in question—where all my knights had failed utterly. And everyone there heard the Queen ask me to promise that the man who succeeded in removing the sword from her side would have her as his wife. She was right to make such a request, since everyone knew perfectly well that if she could have such a man, she would have as her lord the finest and handsomest man in this world. I granted her the boon, and I have often postponed its fulfillment because I could not manage to get you back here; and now I am making the request of you so that I may not be criticized for going back on my word. The honor and the land involved is immense, and, undeniably, the young lady is so brave and so beautiful that she lacks absolutely nothing—neither breeding nor possessions—and she is a Queen and the rightful heiress of land. And so I wish to beseech and request—as do all these noble men here assembled—that you do as I ask, for in so doing your honor will be assured." {11991}

These words were most welcome to the Knight, since his heart was favorably disposed toward the lady in any case. And he said he knew that the King had granted her that boon, and he would never do anything contrary to the King's will; moreover, this was the first request he had ever made of him. And King Arthur thanked him sincerely for his answer, as did all the company he had gathered there with him. And the King, who was quite pleased with the outcome, left the chamber, and all the others filed out after him. The young lady who was holding the King to his covenant came back to see him. And without hesitation the King declared so that everyone could hear: "Maiden, I hereby grant you possession of the gift I made to you at Cardueil." {12009}

With that he took the Knight and joined his hands with hers, and she was overjoyed at having brought her affairs to such a successful conclusion. She asked the Knight if what the King had done was agreeable to him. And he replied that he was delighted and had no reason whatever to be displeased. Then the King had them pledge their troth and exchange their vows. And right away they set a date for the wedding and the coronation, the day that everyone was waiting for—the approaching Feast of Pentecost—and everyone happily agreed to that. {12024}

Enjoying themselves as you have heard, they spent that day in great festivity, [. . .] but he and Sir Gawain had become acquainted long before. And then around the hour of prime a rumor spread throughout the court that he was Brien. Then he acquired as many enemies as he had friends before; but the worthy Sir Gawain intervened, prevailing upon him and all the other guests to make peace, so that afterward they were all obliged to get along with one another. And when they found out all about Brien at the court, he quickly lost the name of "Handsome Prisoner," you may be sure of that. {12038}

At the end of the day, when night had fallen, the respected Sir Gawain had his fill of pleasure, because he went to lie with his sweetheart for whom he had yearned so long—and she was by no means displeased with him. Indeed, she let him do everything he wanted, for she was entirely his and he was hers. They kissed each other on the lips and on the eyes, and they gave each other all the shared delight they possibly could, for they had wanted to do this for a long time. The beauty allowed him to go so far that night that she lost the name of virgin: she didn't put up any resistance, or try to run away from him, or start to cry when he had his way with her. That night they did not sleep a wink but set their minds to joy and pleasure, sharing the details of their lives with each other. And he asked her: "Sweetheart, tell me the truth, why was it that you wouldn't believe me before?" {12062}

And laughingly she replied: "Please, my lord, by Almighty God, how could I possibly have believed you? I had no reason to, so help me God!

Tell me now, and don't take offense, how I could ever have believed that you would let me go on account of my tears or because of anything I might say, when you had me pinned beneath your body? So help me God, I didn't think that Sir Gawain would ever be so weak or unworthy that a woman could escape from him simply by crying or protesting, especially one he had under his complete control, as you had me on that occasion." {12078}

And when Sir Gawain heard her say these words, which were most pleasing to his ears, all his bitterness quickly vanished. Instead he began to laugh a lot, embracing, hugging, and kissing her. That night they played it free and easy, until the morning finally came and they arose. And that is how they took their pleasure: every night, whenever they pleased, they would go and lie together. And so, in this joyful manner, they awaited the coronation. {12090}

Great were the festivities at the court, and those who heard of this coronation were filled with joy. And messengers were sent out everywhere the King exercised authority to announce to all those who owed him homage or held fiefs from him that they should assemble on the Feast of Pentecost at the court of Cardigan. And there was not a soul who failed to make ready to attend the coronation in a spirit of joy and gladness; everyone did so willingly. There were so many kings, counts, knights, ladies, and maidens in attendance that never had the King seen so many at any court he had held in all his life. And no one would have thought that so many people could come from so many different places. King Lot of Orcany was there, King Urien too, and King Ris, who was so powerful, so highly esteemed, such a bold and valiant knight. King Arés, King Yder, and King Estrangaré, who held the fortress of Pelle, were also in attendance. King Anguisel the redoubtable and King Bademagu were there as well, and the mighty King of Galoee, who brought a great entourage along with him, and King Amangon, who held the land from which no man returns, and King Caradoc of Vannes. All these men came to the court—they were eleven in number—and many dukes and counts were present as well. {12126}

I should not keep silent or overlook the worthy Knight's mother, the Lady of Lac as Jumeles, who by fair and pleasant roads journeyed to the court, where she was warmly welcomed and most graciously received, for she was the very first person to be invited. On seeing her again, her son displayed great joy, and she responded with the same enthusiasm, for they loved each other most dearly. King Arthur showed her great honor, and the Queen did at least twice as much. The Lady felt great joy for her daughter's sake and for her son's intended wife as well; she could not decide which one of them she loved more or which one she found more compassionate or of nobler character. Each of the young ladies was so devoted to her service, and so earnestly concerned for her welfare, that it seemed as if she had carried both of them in her womb; and they were greatly praised for their devotion. {12148}

So many noble people had come to the court that it would be folly to try and name them all. The town was so crowded that half of the visitors could not find lodgings inside; there were so many people of one kind and another that some of them had to seek shelter outside the walls. The feast day arrived and throughout the city people got up and made ready, each one for himself and in his own way. There is no need to describe the richness and nobility of the kings' vestments, for that would soon become tedious; but if ever precious garments were worn at a feast, you could have seen them there in all their luxury and vast abundance. {12167}

The kings were all on horseback, and the Lady who was going to be crowned was wearing a dress of black samite so splendid that no man had ever seen its like or one so finely tailored. It was trimmed with gold and silk of many colors, and so resplendent that it looked as if it had never been dyed, for its hues were just as vivid as the flowers you see in trees and meadows. And her mantle was covered with scenes depicting how Merlin had transformed Uther's appearance and voice so that he resembled Count Gorlois. And it showed how Igerne had believed that he was her husband, and how the noble Arthur was conceived at Tintagel, and how she later suffered grief because of the news which reached her that night— for those who managed to escape from the battle thought that her lord had been slain—and how the barons of Britain concluded an agreement that she should marry Uther, and how he planned to crown her as his queen. And on the mantle were portrayed both the acts of prowess and the military exploits which Arthur had accomplished up to that time. {12197}

And she had wavy blond hair, bound up with a golden cord, and her forehead was wide and smooth and free of lines; her innocent blue-gray eyes gave her even greater charm, and she had fine dark arching eyebrows; her nose was long, straight, and attractive, and her throat and neck were as white as new-fallen snow on the branch, smooth and slender, as they ought to be; her mouth was small, with full red lips, and her complexion had a marvelously healthy glow, unblemished by the slightest flaw, just like a dew-covered rose blossoming on a bright May morning. Her body was very finely proportioned, her waist was slim, her thighs shapely, and her curving hips were padded just right. Her breasts were nicely filled out, and it was a delight to see them so firm and pointy, pressing hard against her dress; they suited her just perfectly. And to top it all off, on her head she wore a chaplet adorned with gold and rubies, and she was seated on a long-haired white palfrey whose saddle cover was of red samite. The bridle was rich and beautiful, as befitted a person of her standing. {12229}

King Arthur and King Ris came to escort her, and they set off briskly for the great church. And the Knight of the Two Swords followed after them, keeping up the pace. The great broad avenues were overflowing with knights and all sorts of other people who managed to move ahead only with great difficulty, so tremendous were the throngs. And everyone gazed in wonderment at Sir Gawain and the Knight, for both of them were attired in blue samite embroidered with golden birds; and on their heads they wore chaplets trimmed with gold and precious stones, and they were tall and strong and good-looking [. . .], and so very attractive that no one in the entire crowd had ever seen or heard tell of two men so incredibly handsome. And there was little to choose between the two of them, except that the one who was to be crowned was the younger of the pair. The two men rode along side by side, and there were so many minstrels making music that the whole city resounded with merriment, of that I can assure you. {12257}

The Archbishop of Canterbury was in readiness at the church; he had them exchange their wedding vows right away, and then he sang the Mass. And after that he crowned and anointed them, and everyone said that never before had they seen two such beautiful people united in wedlock. There is no need to describe the gaiety which everyone displayed, for every corner of the town resounded with the singing of joyful songs and the noise of jousting; the din was so loud that you couldn't have heard God thundering. And Kay went on ahead with Lucan to make ready for the banquet. {12273}

When they all reached the crowded palace, the tables had already been set, and the pages handed out basins and towels and poured the water. The King did not lose any time taking his seat, nor did the Queen, nor any of the kings. And I can tell you this: there were eleven of them present, and King Arthur was the twelfth, and the newly crowned king was the thirteenth. And all thirteen of them sat at the dais wearing their crowns, and what a fine sight they were to see! And only dukes, counts, knights, ladies, and maidens were permitted to sit within the great hall. The banquet was in readiness, and all the guests were served at the same time; and they stayed at the tables for hours because the meal was very long and elaborate. And there were at least thirteen thousand dinner guests in the hall. And from each household there was no one present but knights, ladies, and maidens, and they were all delighted to be there. And everyone felt free to discuss anything and say whatever they liked, and no one hurried them along. {12298}

Everyone sat and dined at their leisure, and when the time came the servants cleared the tables. There were some who got up and left the hall, going off to entertain themselves, for everyone had their minds on that. And so they passed the night, caroling throughout the city until the break of day. And as for whether the new King and Queen spent that night in bliss—those two whose hearts true love had joined as one—you need have absolutely no doubt about that! {12310}

The King rose early and went to church, and the others did the same. And when they had heard Mass, King Arthur took the new King as his vassal and immediately asked him—if he could find a bit of love for him in his heart—never to stray from the court but to stay by his side. And he promised he would do absolutely anything King Arthur wanted. Everyone returned from the church full of joy and good cheer, and then they breakfasted together. They did not leave the city for a week, for that was how long the coronation festivities lasted, and the King bestowed so many presents that everyone was quite amazed. They all took delight in each other's company, and the stay at Cardigan pleased them immensely; but the court drew to a close after a week, and they all took their leave and went away. {12331}

And though the others had departed, King Meriadeuc stayed behind with his wife and a great many others who were members of King Arthur's court, and they had a marvelous time and went on enjoying themselves until the longing to travel took hold of them. And so, without further ado, they made preparations to depart and assembled at the court [. . .]. {12339}

King Meriadeuc always remained part of King Arthur's court and a member of his household, and sometimes he went back to his wife's court. She bore him children, and the two of them lived long lives, and the Lady's name was Lore. {12345}

The man who must arrange to bring his tale to a close will end it now, adding nothing and leaving nothing out. He has told it just the way the original story goes, and never—to the best of his knowledge—did he discover any new information which he ought to report as true. {12352}

Here ends the story of the Knight of the Two Swords. {12353}

Appendix I. Glossary

accolade/*colee:* the final act of the dubbing ceremony, when the officiant strikes the candidate on the shoulder with the flat of a sword.

bailiff/*baillius, baillieus:* minor court official or person responsible for the administration of justice; once, in this text, a usurper in charge of a castle.

ban/*ban:* an edict or proclamation; in the feudal system, a summoning of the sovereign's vassals.

baron/*baron:* any feudal vassal holding his lands under direct grant from an overlord or king.

blood brother/*frere germain:* brother-german, brother by blood, or brother born of the same parents as the speaker, as distinguished from a stepbrother or a half-brother; possibly a brother legitimately entitled to inherit the family estate.

boon/*don:* a gift, but not of a physical sort; the gift often involves a promise to perform a certain action; in romances, the promise is often given without the giver's knowing precisely what the boon may be.

boor, boorish/*villain(e):* a low-born or ill-bred person and his or her conduct; also translated as "churl," "churlish," and "ill-mannered."

boss/*blouke, blouque:* convex projection in the center of a shield, intended to deflect direct blows; the strongest point of the shield.

bracken/*feuchiere:* fern-like plant or underbrush; MF *fougère.*

breeches/*braies:* loose-fitting knee-length trousers for men.

carol/*calorer* (metathesized form of *caroler*): to dance and sing in a circle; in romances, caroling is often associated with the joy following deliverance from captivity or affliction.

castle/*castel, castiel:* sometimes synonymous with modern "castle," this word may also denote an entire city and everything within its walls.

chaplet/*capel, capiaus:* garland of flowers worn around the forehead, sometimes adorned with costly materials or precious gems.

charger/*destrier:* trained warhorse.

chivalry/*chevalerie:* the institution of knighthood; the abilities and qualities expected of a knight; the opportunities to prove one's worth, as in
querre chevalerie, "seek chivalry" (2756).

churl, churlish/*vilain(e), villain(e):* a low-born or ill-bred person and his or
her conduct; also translated as "boor," "boorish," and "ill mannered."

compline/*(eure de) complie:* the last "hour" of the day, whose time varied
with the seasons.

cornel fruit/*cornilles:* also called cornel berries or cornel cherries; edible
red fruit of the dogwood or cornel tree.

courteous and courtesy/*courtois(e)* and *courtoisie:* polite, well bred, consid-
erate, respectful, displaying manners and conduct proper to the noble
class; occasionally translated as "gracious."

covenant/*couvenant, convenant:* formal agreement or binding verbal promise, sometimes sealed by the exchange of pledges, gifts, or boons.

dainties, dainty morsels/*dainties:* delicacies, delicious tidbits, especially
deer's testicles; may also designate other organ meats such as the heart,
liver, kidneys, or sweetbreads.

dais/*dais, dois:* a table on a platform or dais; usually the head table or the
place of honor at a banquet, as in *maistre dois.*

doublet/*porpoint:* close-fitting vest or jacket.

drawstring/*tassel, atace:* the cords or ribbons of a mantle, which may end
in a decorative tassel.

dress/*bliaut:* lady's court dress, usually costly and ornate.

dub/*adouber:* to confirm a new knight in an official ceremony, which in-
cluded the granting of arms; cf. "accolade."

ermine/*(h)ermine:* precious white winter fur of the ermine weasel, used to
fashion expensive coats and mantles; often these are trimmed with jet-
black zibeline or sable.

fewter/*fautre:* felt-lined holster attached to the saddle, used to support the
lance when charging an opponent.

fief/*fié, fief:* the lands held by a vassal from his overlord; under the feudal
system, one did not own land but held it at the will of one's lord, who
might require that it be forfeited.

flagons/*bouchiaus:* corked bottles or flasks.

gentleman/*preudon, preudomme:* man of quality, honor, worth, and wisdom,
usually but not always a knight.

greatcoat, surcoat/*sercot:* warm but loose-fitting overcoat.

greaves/*unes cauces, cauches:* set of leg armor (3476).

hauberk/*hauberc:* shirt of mail extending down to the knees.

hour/*eure:* between sunrise and sunset there are twelve canonical "hours," points in time rather than periods of duration; the precise time of each varied according to the season. In Old French, the "hours" typically singled out for mention are called *matin(s), prime, tierce, seste, none(s), vespre(s),* and *complie.*

league/*liue, lieue:* measure of distance, roughly speaking three miles, but varying with the country (e.g., *lieues d'Irlande*) and the historical period.

liege man/*liges hon, son hon:* vassal who has pledged loyal service and faithful allegiance to his feudal overlord.

nones/*(eure de) nonne:* the ninth "hour" after sunrise, whose exact time varied with the seasons.

palfrey/*palefroi, palesfroi:* riding horse or saddle horse, especially a gentle mount suitable for a lady.

petit-gris/*vair:* fur of different colors or of mixed color, used as trim on costly garments; possibly the bluish-gray fur of the northern squirrel.

pommel/*puing:* decorated handle or knob on the hilt of a sword or at the front of a saddle.

postern gate/*postis, posterne:* any door or gate in a fortified wall, other than the main entrance.

prime/*(eure de) prime:* the first "hour" after sunrise, whose exact time varied with the seasons.

recluse/*hermite:* religious hermit; person who has withdrawn to a solitary place and leads a life of religious seclusion.

samite/*samit:* precious silk fabric, sometimes interwoven with gold thread.

scabbard/*feurre:* protective sheath or holster for a sword; Modern French *fourreau.*

scarlet/*esca(r)late vermeille:* material of superior quality, produced in a variety of colors; hence the qualifying adjective, as in "crimson scarlet" (169) and "vermilion scarlet" (4265).

sendal/*cendal/cendé:* precious silken fabric, produced in various colors.

seneschal/*senescal, senescaus:* senior court official responsible for the administration of justice, governance of the royal household, and the conduct of important ceremonial events.

shackles/*pastures:* pair of leg irons or fetters, originally used to hobble horses or other animals at pasture.

shield straps/*guinches, coroies:* leather straps used to suspend the shield from the neck so that both hands remained free.

shift/*chemise:* long-sleeved undergarment, worn by either sex.

squire/*escuier, eskuier:* mounted personal servant who carries a knight's shield (*escu*) and weapons, or acts as his guide and escort; generally speaking the squire is a young man who aspires to knighthood.

surcoat/*sercot:* loose cloak, worn over armor.

sword belts/*renges, rengeure:* the belted harness used to secure a heavy sword to a knight's side.

tierce/*(eure de) tierce, tierche:* the third "hour" after sunrise, whose exact time varied with the seasons.

trefoil emblem/*trifoire:* probably the fleur-de-lis.

vassal/*vassal, vassaus:* feudal subordinate, often a knight allowed to hold land in return for homage, fealty, and military service; the term usually occurs with the respectful sense of "courageous knight"; however, it may also carry scornful overtones if one knight applies it to another of greater worth or higher rank (4643).

vavasor/*vavasor:* vassal or tenant of a feudal lord; a country gentleman lower in rank than a baron.

ventail/*ventaille:* defensive armor for the lower part of the face.

vespers/*vespres:* evening religious service, evening prayers; one "hour" before sunset.

worthy man or worthy gentleman/*preudon, preudom(me):* term used to describe an accomplished knight, a man of good reputation, or at least one who appears to be.

zibeline/*sebelin* and *sable:* precious fur of the sable, dense and jet black, often used as trim on costly coats and mantles made of white ermine.

Appendix II. Textual Notes

Places where there is an obvious lacuna in the text are marked with [. . .]. For the most part it seems that only a single verse is missing, due to the scribe's inattention. Given that romance poets tend to give lengthy descriptions of scenes such as the reconciliation between Gawain and Brien des Iles (following line 12026) and the rescue of Le Roux's captives (following line 11703), it is possible that dozens or even hundreds of lines have been omitted.

303: The manuscript is illegible at this point. We follow Foerster's suggestion and read *vallés* "young men."

429–30: We have punctuated these lines differently from Foerster, ending the dwarf's speech after the words: *A ma dame.*

562: With Ivey, we accept Tobler's emendation ("Li chevaliers as deus espees." *Zeitschrift für romanische Philologie* 2 [1878], pp. 142-52), *a la parestrousse*, where Foerster reads: *a la par descousse.*

595: Foerster punctuates this exclamation as if it were a question.

1000: Here the manuscript reads *prinst arriere;* Foerster's emendation, *prist a rire*, is certainly correct and suggests either that the scribe had not read further in the romance or that he was not prepared for the sudden shift in power between King Ris and the Lady of Cardigan.

1363: We follow Foerster's textual note, reading *sa merci* for MS *sans merci.*

1543: MS *quan k'est mestier;* Tobler emends to *quan k'a mestier.* The MS reading may actually stand for *quan k'ait mestier*, "anything he *may* need."

1896: we follow Foerster's textual note, reading *quint* for MS *quins.*

2206: a familiar Old French proverb; cf. Joseph de Morawski, Proverbs français antérieurs au XVᵉ siècle (Paris: E. Champion, 1925), #283.

3035: *Mais ce fu parmi le uuit bu;* literally, "but it went through the empty belly, gut, or abdomen." This phrase presents a semantic challenge; we have glossed it according to the broader context: "but the blow missed the vital organs."

3117: We accept Mussafia's emendation (Li Chevaliers as deus espees," *Zeitschrift für österreichische Gymnasien* 27 [1877], pp. 197-231), preferring *mantelet* to MS *mautalent;* cf. also 3273.

4147 (and 4159, 7634, 7679): *canole* ought to mean "neck," but a knight with a broken neck would not be able to do the things that knights in this poem do after breaking this bone. In Old French, the complete expression is *canole du cou,* literally "stem, stalk, or tube of the neck." Some translate this as "trachea" or "windpipe," a rendition clearly unsuited to our text. Given the co-occurrence of *brisier* and *la canole,* we have settled on "collarbone." Cf. Middle English *cannel-bone* ("neck-bone," "clavicle").

4451: MS *viex* must represent *vils;* read *vix?*

5822: MS *Menré* seems to be a scribal error for *Mené;* cf. Modern French *malmené.*

6206: MS *de porpiece* could be a misreading of *de porpens,* "thoughtfully, carefully, considerately," given the occurrence of *grant piece* in the preceding line.

7753: *quel le feront;* an apparent error for *que il feront,* literally, "what they would do."

9854: Here, we take *Cil du castel* to be the scribe's accidental repetition of words from the preceding line. Guided by the context, we supply the bridging phrase: "to reinforce the troops."

11418: a familiar Old French proverb; cf. Morawski #630.